Two Kinds of Rationality

Alan Benjamin

To Alan,
With thanks for
the expert assistance
Terry Evens

Contradictions of Modernity

Edited by Craig Calhoun
University of North Carolina at Chapel Hill

The modern era has been uniquely productive of theory. Some theory claimed uniformity despite human differences or unilinear progress in the face of catastrophic changes. Other theory was informed more deeply by the complexities of history and recognition of cultural specificity. This series seeks to further the latter approach by publishing books that explore the problems of theorizing the modern in its manifold and sometimes contradictory forms and that examine the specific locations of theory within the modern.

Volume 3   T. M. S. Evens, *Two Kinds of Rationality: Kibbutz Democracy and Generational Conflict*

Volume 2   Micheline R. Ishay, *Internationalism and Its Betrayal*

Volume 1   Johan Heilbron, *The Rise of Social Theory*

Two Kinds of Rationality

Kibbutz Democracy and
Generational Conflict

T. M. S. Evens

Contradictions of Modernity, Volume 3

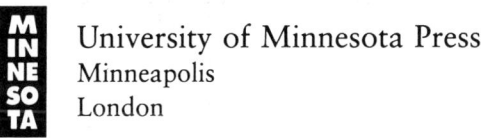
University of Minnesota Press
Minneapolis
London

Copyright © 1995 by the Regents of the University of Minnesota

All rights reserved. No part of this publication may be reproduced, stored in a retrieval system, or transmitted, in any form or by any means, electronic, mechanical, photocopying, recording, or otherwise, without the prior written permission of the publisher.

Published by the University of Minnesota Press
111 Third Avenue South, Suite 290, Minneapolis, MN 55401-2520
Printed in the United States of America on acid-free paper

Library of Congress Cataloging-in-Publication Data

Evens, T. M. S.
   Two kinds of rationality : Kibbutz democracy and generational conflict / T. M. S Evens.
      p.   cm. — (Contradictions of Modernity ; v. 3)
   Includes bibliographical references (p.   ) and index.
   ISBN 0-8166-2642-1 (hc). — ISBN 0-8166-2643-X (pbk.)
   1. Kibbutzim—Case studies. 2. Democracy—Israel—Case studies.
3. Conflict of generations—Israel—Case studies.   I. Title.
II. Title: 2 kinds of rationality.   III. Series.
HX742.2.A3E94   1995
307.77'6–dc20   94–41350

The University of Minnesota is an equal-opportunity educator and employer.

To Ida and Jules
for the gifts of humor and heart

Contents

Acknowledgments	ix
Prologue	xiii
1. Dualism and Anthropology	1
2. The Kibbutz	17
3. Democratic Procedure and Secret Ballot	30
4. Conflict between the Generations versus Social Differentiation: The Empirical Picture	51
5. Conflict between the Generations as a Normative Expectation	75
6. Conflict between the Generations as a Metaphor	86
7. Conflict between the Generations as a Primordial Choice: The Paradigm of Genesis	118
8. Primordial Choice and "The Universal": Kibbutz Familism and the Sexual Division of Labor	148

9. The Historical Link between Genesis and
   Timem's Story: Rousseau as Biblical Redactor   163

10. Two Kinds of Rationality   192

Conclusion   218
Notes   225
Bibliography   238
Index   247

Acknowledgments

This book is based on field research that was fully supported by the Bernstein Israeli Research Trust of the University of Manchester, England, in the 1960s. The Bernstein project was anthropological, concerned to describe and analyze the nature of the absorption of immigrants in Israel. I remain grateful to that project and its sponsors for the professional opportunity that was afforded me. In addition, I received, in 1977, a small grant from the National Institute of Mental Health, which helped to support an early piece of the writing of this book.

I am deeply indebted to the members of Kibbutz Timem for allowing me to do long-term, invasive anthropological research on their community. No doubt, the presence of an anthropologist and his wife created some difficult decisions for Timem's administration. It seems to me that the community was remarkably cooperative with its social anthropologist. I was given an inestimable amount of time and assistance from the members. Moreover, as individuals they always received my wife and me in the spirit of friendship, and with a great deal of warmth. In particular, there were certain members without whose support and assistance I could not have accomplished the fieldwork at all. As "Kibbutz Timem" is a pseudonym, it seems best to keep these members — friends for life — anonymous. But they know who they are. I returned to visit Timem for a few days in the summer of 1979. Seeing our friends and acquaintances there, I could not help but be reminded of just how warm and receptive the kibbutz had been to us, and of what a wonderfully decent community these social pioneers have created and sustained. Indeed, my wife and I felt so at home there that, taking advantage of a hospitality for which we will always remain grateful, we made Timem the place of our firstborn.

The two teachers who were most important to me, Max Gluckman and M. G. Smith, are now gone. Both were critically instrumental in my thinking and in my choice of what to think about. Gluckman's powerful person and patriarchal concern left an enormous impression on me. It was from him that I first strongly sensed the meaning of social anthropology as a vocation, and when he died in 1975 I felt as if I had lost the sole anthropological audience that mattered to me. Mike Smith, with whom I had studied before going to Manchester, continued to offer me his invaluable professional support and advice until his death in January 1993. For better or for worse, it was the extraordinary quality of his massive intelligence that moved me, at a critical time in my graduate career, when I had grown terminally weary of yams and clans, to keep at it and become a professional social anthropologist.

To Don Handelman, who was my fellow student at Manchester, I owe the stimulation and support that come with good friendship and intellectual companionship over the years. Bruce Kapferer is also a friend from my Manchester days, and I learned much from our exchanges and his exceptional intellectual vitality.

If one waits long enough to finish a scholarly project, one is placed in the advantageous position of being able to benefit from the help and reflections of those of one's students who have gone on to a professional career of their own, scholarly or otherwise. Lee Schlesinger, Craig Calhoun, and Steven Klein all fall in this category. Schlesinger and Calhoun, who studied with me only briefly, have provided enormous intellectual stimulation and penetrating criticism through the years. Schlesinger is about the most intellectually difficult person I have ever come across. No scholar should have to do without such a person. Though painfully little in it got by his critical acumen, he never failed to take my work seriously, even as I doubted its value myself. I also took advantage of reading his. I do not think there is anyone with whom I have exchanged as much intellectually. Calhoun has also been a source of intellectual strength and warm friendship, and as the editor of the series in which this book is published, he has tirelessly read and reread the manuscript.

His superbly astute critical suggestions have moved me substantially toward making this a better book. As to Klein, his powerful mind and unorthodox thought and scholarship have been a strong influence on me in recent years. I think of him as an intellectual "bad guy," so bad that, after obtaining two Ph.D.'s, one in philosophy and one in anthropology, he still found that there is no real place for him in the especially compromised halls of the academy. From the first day he came to see me, I felt a profound kinship with the way he tends to think about things, so much so that, though I lack his genius, there were times when I could not tell our general ideas apart. He is also the sort of friend one wants when the going gets tough.

Jane Bachnik has been my intellectual companion and departmental comrade in arms. We have taught together and fought together. Her dedication to excellence, quest for new ideas, and willingness to take anthropological chances have been of enormous importance to me and my work. Nancy Scheper-Hughes, who was for too short a time my colleague at the University of North Carolina, has moved me by example. Her outspoken, critical understanding of anthropology as an implicitly ethical undertaking, though I cannot hope to emulate her ethnographic and humanistic gift, has made inspirational sense to me in thinking about what the discipline ought to be.

To Ronnie Frankenberg I owe an insight that has played a major role in my thinking about the kibbutz. For it was he who, many years ago, after kindly reading parts of my Ph.D. dissertation, got me to see beyond the Marxian aspect of the kibbutz to the community's strongly Rousseauian character. My good friend Jeffry Obler, a teacher of Rousseau, kindly applied a critical eye to chapter 9, leading me to refine further my interpretation of the French master. Gila Budescu and Sandi Morgen, as my students, read very early drafts of this book and provided comments. To the first-named, who was born and bred in a kibbutz, I also owe thanks for checking and correcting my translations from the Hebrew and for giving me confidence in my interpretive sense of the kibbutz. Lisa Aldred read, with a gentle, prodding editorial hand, a much more recent draft. To Alan Benjamin, a one-time kibbutz member himself, I owe the uniform Hebrew transliteration. Rob Lawrence and Victor Braitberg, charitable conscripts both, constructed the index. Patricia Galloway benevolently lent her imposing intellectual and editorial skills to a reading of the conclusion, at a point in time when I myself had lost, through too much familiarity, any power to appraise the work. Virginia Dominguez and Jonathan Boyarin reviewed the manuscript for the University of Minnesota Press. Their thoughtful, constructive criticisms, as regards details, argument, and organization, have done much to guide me in revising the work. From Boyarin I received a host of useful questions and references; from Dominguez an understanding of my theoretical intentions so sharp as to renew my confidence.

In the spring of 1978, I gave part of an early draft, in three consecutive sessions, to the Anthropology Department Seminar at the University of Chicago. I am grateful to Marshall Sahlins for the invitation to Hyde Park, and to David Schneider for his early encouragement in relation to this publication. The interpretation of Genesis, in chapter 7, benefited from a reading and discussion by members of my university's Program in Social Theory and Cross-Cultural Studies. Most recently, in 1991, a section of this work was presented in Delhi to the Centre for the Study of Developing Societies, and a much larger portion, over a series of six lectures, to the Department of Anthropology at Calcutta University. I wish to take this opportunity to thank Dr. Manibrata Bhattacharya, who received me with such kindness at Calcutta University, and also the Fulbright Scholar Program in India for giving me the opportunity to present some of this work to scholarly audiences there.

To Susan and to our sons, Aden, Noah, and Gabriel, I owe the kind of personal support that one's family alone is likely to provide in an undertaking as odd as writing, over many years, books that will entertain no one and the value of which depends on the judgment of persons who have chosen to do the same. Naturally, for a book so long in the making as this one, I am indebted to far more people and works than I can remember, even though I sincerely care to.

Prologue

This book has been too long in the making, at least by any reasonably prudential standards. It began in the early 1970s as an article-length, extended case study centering on an attempt to introduce secret balloting into the direct democracy of Timem, an Israeli kibbutz I researched in the mid-1960s. As I proceeded, however, the case study took on a life of its own, obliging me to grapple more generally with the closely associated questions of change and of the conflict between the generations in the kibbutz. The former question took me into an analysis of growth and social differentiation, whereas the latter question moved me to construe the idea of the generations as a kind of ideology, and, then, in turn, to confront the grand matter of the relation between ideology or idea and behavior. Combined with the limits of my ability, this intellectual confrontation, that is, the struggle to understand how the *idea* of the generations moved Timem's members, constitutes the principal excuse for the slow rate of my progress.

Of course, the inquiry of social anthropology centers on the issue of the relation between idea (norm, value, belief, ideology, and so on) and behavior (conduct, action, fact, and so on), and has produced in this connection a rich and exciting intellectual tradition. This consideration notwithstanding, the discipline did not, as far as I could tell, equip me with an approach that could *satisfactorily* cope with the ethnographic problem presented by my data. I found that in order to come to terms with that problem, it was necessary to take up directly certain other questions, questions the answers to which anthropologists were more accustomed to presume than to think through. I have in mind such questions as How is it possible for the mind to interact with the body? What is the nature of human agency? and What is the nature of reason? Because of its focus on other cultures, and the apparent irrationality of these, anthropology could not so easily avoid addressing the last question (though even in this case, the discipline has tended to run shy). But, given the empiricist foundations of anthropology, these questions have largely been regarded by anthropologists as so abstract as to be fit to ponder only by philosophical types, or, indeed, as too abstract to take notice of at all. Nevertheless, my ethnographic problem seemed to me to leave no choice but to confront these questions, and others like them, head on.

Naturally, I did appeal to philosophy (among other disciplines) for help, and was duly inspired. I was especially attracted to the existential phenomenology of Maurice Merleau-Ponty, whose sustained assault on the doctrine of mind–body dualism remains profoundly edifying — even though, if there is anything in a name, his philosophy has been superseded by the various post-isms that currently hold the intellectual world in thrall (and sometimes in smug and dogmatic stupor). While I take poststructuralism and deconstructionism seriously, and fancy I have learned much from them, it is sobering to think that when you deconstruct poststructuralism, you end up with, funnily enough, postdeconstructionism.

In this connection, I have most recently been drawn to the work of Emmanuel Levinas, whose philosophy is surely as *re*constructionist as it is deconstructionist. Levinas's argument that the questioning of all foundations is, far from a matter of free play or nihilism, itself "founded" in an unavoidable responsibility to otherness, furnished me with a way of making anthropological sense of the nondualism I gravitated to in the work of Merleau-Ponty. The way is, as will emerge below, ethics: human conduct is the conduct of choice, and as such it cannot help constituting "mind" and "body" as it runs a course, endlessly, right between them.

At any rate, as I was trained in social anthropology rather than philosophy, and in a staunchly empiricist school of anthropology at that, my philosophical reflections were hardly philosophically systematic and were always referred to and informed by the relevance of empirical anthropology. In this connection, I left off work on the kibbutz, turning instead to the ethnography of a people more typical of anthropological inquiry, a people made anthropologically classic in the works of E. E. Evans-Pritchard — the Nuer.

I found contemplation of the philosophical matters at issue easier going in relation to the empirical puzzles presented by Evans-Pritchard's ethnography. I now think that the chief reason why the Nuer materials proved so inviting is not because the Nuer were simpler subjects of study (they are not), making it easier to learn *about* them, but because their perspective on the world made it easier to learn *from* them. That is to say, through my intensive efforts to rethink their ethnography, as it was already recorded in the literature, I received instruction from them that helped to promote a solution to my pressing theoretical questions, especially the ontological question of the nature of the relation between mind and body.

In thinking through the questions at issue, I have tacked back and forth, in a mode of constant comparison, between the kibbutz and the Nuer. As a result, in respect of these questions, I am unable to separate fundamentally my studies of the Nuer from those of the kibbutz. Indeed, at some point in time I hope to continue the present study, broadly considered, by bringing together as a book the corpus of my Nuer studies.

But the main point here is that, in my own deliberate way, I was enabled to return to my study of Kibbutz Timem. However, as the study moved toward completion, it gradually lost its singular definition as an ethnography of the kibbutz. Instead, the case study came to serve as the empirical midwife of a broader study: the investigation of the behavior–consciousness question, an answer to which seemed presupposed by the endeavor to tackle the highly empirical questions raised by my field data. In effect, the original emphasis of the inquiry was reversed, marking the ethnography as an occasion for the theoretical investigation. The empirical questions, questions concerning social differentiation and generational conflict in Timem, moved me fatefully to an understanding of the constitutional primacy of ethics in human society, even as my ontological reflections facilitated my inquiry into the specific ethnographic puzzles. In result, the present book is integrally tied, as both source and extraction, to a companion volume I expect to publish shortly hereafter under the title *Anti-dualism or Anthropology as Ethics*. The latter, to which this prologue is also preliminary, develops more single-mindedly the ethical ideas of reason and human agency projected below.

To underscore the importance of the ontological question to social anthropology, I should note here that the issue constitutes the first question of Durkheim's sociology. For all his concern to show the inadequacy of the philosophical endeavor to understand society, Durkheim's intellectual enterprise was keyed at all times to the question of the ontological status of "things" social. Each and every one of his books may be fruitfully construed as an attempt to answer this question (the proposition that social facts are indeed "things" was only one of his answers). However, despite his positively crucial insight that social life is essentially a moral process and his truly extraordinary efforts to describe what this means in the concrete, he never did find a satisfactory answer. I would like to think that the present work helps to answer this presuppositional question.

Anthropological and social thought have advanced considerably since I began this study, taking on, in one critical way or another, some of the same theoretical issues that challenged me. As I see it, the novelty of the present study rests most critically with the ontological explicitness of the approach. Unlike, for example, another anthropological theory that has been informed by postmodern thought and reflexive concerns — the valuable "experimental ethnography" school — the approach I advocate here is not primarily methodological, but ontological and existential. I suppose if I had to categorize my approach, I might include it under "poststructuralism" or "postmodernism," bearing in mind, however, that, with recent critical theory, my approach rejects the absolutism of the arbitrary, the nonrational, and power no less roundly than that of self-transparent subjectivity and of subjectivity regarded as an anonymous function of one sort of structure or another. And if I had to name it, I would call this approach, for reasons that will emerge in the text, situationalism.

If anthropology is to "resolve" the key problems that focus the discipline empirically, it will not do to incorporate analytically other realities into our own (meaning by "our own" the Western idea of reality on which the rise of anthropology as a social science has been predicated), as was the wont of so much early anthropology. Nor is it enough to acknowledge other realities as *simply* other, in the manner of much recent relativism. Rather, it is necessary to do nothing less than redefine the received reality of Western thought. We must not merely put this reality aside, as classical phenomenology teaches, but, in the cant terminology of today, deconstruct it. Deconstructionism notwithstanding, though, we must do so in such a way that we are left with a reality that can at once generate both other and modern realities, and yet come to more than a mere trope, an unreality or aesthetic. The defining characteristic of such a reality can only be *fundamental ambiguity* as between self and other. Needless to say, since in it what there is is also and necessarily not what there is, the resulting sense of reality is deontologized.

In light of such a deconstructed ontology, the ideas of rationality and human agency may be rethought. The first may be primarily construed, not in absolute terms of self-evidence and apodictic proofs, but in relative ones of action and argumentation anchored in ethical (and therefore nonarbitrary) choice. The second may be construed as, not totally autonomous subjectivity, but selfhood, the autonomy of which knowingly depends on its own limitedness.

In developing the argument, both here and in the companion volume to follow, I rely critically on correlative notions of "moral selection," "self-interpretation," and "primordial choice," and deploy supporting ideas of hierarchy, practice, and situation. Doubtless, in today's intellectual environment of acute (sometimes paralytic) reflexivity and antifoundationalism, both "primordial" and "choice" are usages that will put many readers on guard. But I have forged the notion of primordial choice in an effort to emphasize the way in which choice is, *precisely because of its essential heteronomy and uncertainty*, profoundly creative. More than anything else, the creative capacity of choice is what bespeaks the fundamentally ethical nature of the human condition.

As to the ideas of hierarchy, practice, and situation, though they are developed in this volume for the most part diffusely, as imbricated with each other through the key idea of primordial choice, each is important to the attempt to reestablish rationality and agency in terms of basic ontological ambiguity. The first two, hierarchy and practice, enjoy a certain notoriety in current anthropology, through the imposing work of Louis Dumont and Pierre Bourdieu. However, while I have been strongly stimulated by their work, what I have to say here is roundly identifiable with the position of neither scholar. Though the exposition of my usage must wait on the forthcoming companion volume, one may presume that here "hierarchy" and "practice" are defined in terms of each other. As a result, implicitly, the first is given a temporal in addition to a structural definition, while the second is recast in terms of value rather than interest. In this way, the two concepts are tailored anew, being made to fit well with the understanding of society as primarily a question of ethics.

The concept of situation is deployed here in the service of the overall argument. In relation to the idea of human agency developed in the text, the thesis that being human amounts to being situated renders a notion of situation so rich and complex as to suggest the possibility of a situational anthropology. In such an anthropology, human movement is irreducible to any monolithic exterior or interior force, whether one has in mind function, structure, power, or, even, meaning. Because it presents and represents this irreducibility fully, ethics is the only "force" that can satisfactorily key an anthropology. Accordingly, I argue that people are not exactly *moved* (by this force or that), but that, though in an essentially equivocal sense much more complex than the philosophy of consciousness allows, they move themselves.

Naturally, I have not succeeded in stepping outside of the language in which I began my investigations. The reflexive operation is always one of rebuilding one's ship while at sea. But the principal concepts I deploy below are all informed by a picture of reality markedly different from the received picture projected by Western thought. And because they are, they have a radical cast. The picture is, to reiterate, patently nondualist — a picture of *basic* ambiguity. As one result of this picture, the concepts, by contrast to yet another prominent reflexive strain of today's anthropological thought (post- or anticolonialism), are not primarily politicized, but are instead profoundly ethicized. As I have said, I expect that this decided emphasis on anthropology as a kind of ethical practice, in conjunction with my avowedly ontological intention, not simply to deny or set aside the received Western picture of reality, but to replace it with a well-considered, nonstandard (nondualist) one, for better or for worse, sets this study apart.

One

Dualism and Anthropology

A Question of Existence

Though this book is firmly rooted in anthropological fieldwork, it is well outside the mold of standard ethnographic monography. The book is more directly preoccupied with the study of human existence in general than with the particular ethnographic problems arising from the field data. In short, the field community is primarily employed as a vehicle for investigating the existential conditions of human being. Therefore, the book is intended as an exercise in social and anthropological theory even more than one in ethnographic empirical research. I am more concerned to run an argument about ontology and identity than I am to detail the social and cultural operations of a particular way of life. I want to understand the deep workings, the experiential grounds, more than the institutional mechanics and symbolical forms of that way of life. Like a drunken philosopher I once heard responding to his colleague's formal presentation on a comfortable philosophical topic, what I want to know is, "How do you break the bank at Monte Carlo?"

But this predilection for high-stakes inquiry remains a matter of emphasis, not exclusion. While I have brought to the foreground problems that are normally left implicit in more orthodox anthropological analysis, I also aim to elucidate the field community as a particular social and cultural setting. Indeed, since my understanding of the universal human condition includes the paradox that that condition manifests itself only in particular ways, treatment of the field community as it differs from other social settings is important to my designs. I think I throw fresh light on the peculiar character of the community in which I worked; but, as no one should mistake, right from the start I try to plumb that character with a mind to its existential ground.

The Dilemma of Body and Mind

For me the seed matter of social anthropology, as the comparative study of humankind, is the question of what moves people — or, put in a way that does not predispose a deterministic answer, how people move. By "movement," of course, I do not intend simply motion or behavior, but behavior that is also morally informed — that is, conduct or self-movement.

In view of the fact that it is conduct, rather than sheer behavior, with which I am concerned, I am necessarily committed to the study of the correlative dualities of behavior and consciousness, fact and value, process and design. In other words, strange as it may seem from the deeply rooted empiricist bias of modern anthropology, at bottom I am committed to the study of the so-called body–mind question, a question that has vexed philosophical thinkers since antiquity.

Now, that question, even when it is posed without the absolutist trappings of Cartesian dualism (which defines body and mind as mutually exclusive of each other), is, I believe, in fundamental respects intractable. For it is mind or consciousness itself that occasions the question. To ask, then, how mind or consciousness relates to body or behavior is already to answer — one wants to say, "That's how it's done." Conversely, to answer in a manner that is intelligible to consciousness is always to raise the question over again — one wants to ask, "Just how did you do that?" In effect, the body–mind question represents an essential human dilemma.

But this dilemma is not cause to abandon investigation of the question. It does suggest, however, that any endeavor to resolve the ontological question once and for all, in search of an epistemological eschaton, will be an exercise in intellectual futility. Correlatively, it also suggests that, at some point in the course of inquiry, instead of rigorous logic and axiomatic explanation we should pursue thicker description and more contemplative understanding.

I am reminded here of the circus clown who, in the middle of the arena, erects a locked door, which he then proceeds to unlock, pass through, and lock after himself — when all the while the entirety of the arena lies open round the door. But I suspect that, at bottom, we laugh at the clown only because he really is no fool. His performance may be seen as a play on the way in which we humans imprison ourselves by our own constructions, and as such, though it offers no explanation proper, the performance deepens our perspective on our own condition. The laughter expresses an insight with which the intellect alone can never really come to grips.[1]

Socioculture as Trial Solution

If mind or consciousness constitutes its own enigma, then the relation between behavior and consciousness must everywhere be an existential problem, whether or not it is also there a philosophical or conceptual one. In virtue of their ample endowment of consciousness in this world, human beings have no choice but to come to grips with the functional problem of how to relate consciousness with behavior. Considered in its aspect as an organization of roles, and of rules both of and for action, every sociocultural system may usefully be regarded as an expression of, and a *trial* solution to, this lived predicament. It is a trial solution because by nature the problem that it treats is endemic and cannot be perfectly resolved. By "trial," then, I intend both test and tribulation.

Insofar as it is successful, every sociocultural venture treats the problem of behavior and consciousness not by actually undoing it, but by, as the deconstructionists have perceived, deferring it or putting it off. By definition, it does this by transacting the problem onto relatively distinct planes of reality, namely, of course, those we call culture and society. In the case of society, the problem becomes that of the coexistence of the individual and society; in the case of culture, as Claude Lévi-Strauss once made plain, the reciprocation of nature and culture is the issue. Logically these problems are no less paradoxical than the ontological problem they express. Culture and society may be construed, then, as ways of putting, and of putting off or living, that problem.

Transcendence as Conscious Purpose

The body–mind dilemma is thus self-mediated by its reconstitution as the fundamental predicaments we speak of as culture and society. The process is one of protracted recrudescence: an existential problem is made more or less livable by ever shifting it from one mediatory world to another.

Such a process evokes *as limiting cases* two prophetic and complementary understandings of the human condition. Both are deeply embedded in Western socioreligious thought. I have in mind, first, that human existence is futile — "all is vanity"; and second, that final transcendence or "deliverance" is, if not just around the corner, at least in the nature of things. At times, given the vicissitudes of history, these understandings may be brought to light as functional, driving social themes. When this happens, in the case of the first (vanity), the result is some form of anomie; in the case of the second (deliverance), utopianism prevails.

The introduction of utopianism or faultless transcendence as conscious purpose in social life has a number of consequences that may be of interest to the social scientist. Perhaps the most comprehensive of these is the thematization of the basically problematical nature of human existence. In their all-out war on the human dilemma, societies self-consciously bent on transcendence serve, through heightened struggle, to dramatize the problem, making it very plain to see. For this reason, societies of this kind offer especially felicitous conditions for the study of the relation between behavior and consciousness (Evens and Peacock 1990: 4). As a community with an explicit ideology focused on a perfect synthesis between the individual and society, the Israeli kibbutz is such a sociocultural system. But before I proceed to discuss the kibbutz, it is necessary to establish the relevance of ontology to the empirical discipline of social anthropology.

Modern Anthropology and the Body–Mind Dilemma

A Brief but Tendentious History

It may seem odd or even inappropriate for a social anthropologist to concentrate professionally on a matter so patently philosophical as ontology. The present book is here to say that in principle what is odd about such an undertaking is that it should appear odd at all. It seems prudent to set the scene now, though, making a case right from the start that ontology and the mind–body question are as critical to anthropology as they are to philosophy. I can do so with a synoptic glance to the history of modern social anthropology. Naturally, a very condensed history is bound to oversimplify. But, following Jorge Luis Borges's recommended course of procedure, I shall pretend that the history I have in mind has already been written up as a book and that I am just offering a résumé, a commentary.[2]

Taking Émile Durkheim as the seminal intellectual ancestor, it should be plain that his project was essentially ontological. He set out to establish sociology as a scientific discipline autonomous from psychology. To do so, he had to show that, far from reducing to the individual, society is a reality in its own right. In this connection, his demonstration that society is always experienced *as if* it were objectively real remains, in my view, the genial contribution of modern social science. But inasmuch as he could not get beyond an "as if" characterization, his project faltered. For then it always remains implicit that society is in the end reducible to the individual.

The difficulty was that there was no commonsense ontology available to Durkheim that could admit of a certifiable reality that exists in any way apart from, much less over and beyond, the individual. This is because the received construction of the mind–body problem in Western thought is dualist, and as such strongly disposes toward a reductionist view of social reality. By dividing the universe cleanly between a positive reality (body), on the one hand, and a *negative* one (mind), on the other, dualism rhetorically erodes the credibility of those who are inclined to take the latter sort of reality at all seriously. How can "negative reality" be real?

As a result, for all the talk of his "social realism," Durkheim was inclined to hedge his ontological bets. For example:

> On the one hand, the individual gets from society the best part of himself, all that gives him a distinct character and a special place among other beings, his intellectual and moral culture. If we should withdraw from men their language, sciences, arts and moral beliefs, they would drop to the rank of animals. So the characteristic attributes of human nature come from society. But, on the other hand, society exists and lives only in and through individuals. If the idea of society were extinguished in individual minds and the beliefs, traditions and aspirations of the group were no longer felt and shared by the individuals, society would die. We can say of it...: it is real only in so far as it has a place in human consciousnesses, and this place is whatever one we may give to it. (1915: 347)

The passage is no less difficult than it is deep. The idea that in the absence of society and culture human beings could not be identified as such is a revelatory insight, the strongest implications of which anthropology has yet to realize. But if society "is real only in so far as it has a place in human consciousnesses," how then can it be held to afford individuals that which raises them above the rank of animals? Surely, what elevates individuals in this way is precisely their personhood or human consciousness! As a definitively intersubjective phenomenon, society must enjoy a reality that in some sense transcends "human consciousnesses." The passage is deceptive, for while it appears to give — in no uncertain terms — ontological primacy to society over the individual, in fact it is drawn, however subtly and reluctantly, to the reduction of the reality of society to that of the individual.

This state of ontological inconsistency realized itself systematically in the development of Durkheim's thought. In the course of his career, his projection of the nature of society underwent a quiet but major change of emphasis. In his early work, he was inclined to characterize society in terms of its "anatomical" facts — the number, arrangement, coalescence, and distribution of its positive parts. In his later work, however, he was inclined to characterize society in terms of its own representations, its "collective consciousness." As Steven Lukes puts it, "From the initial position in *The Division of Labour*, where he had been tempted to write that 'everything occurs mechanically,' Durkheim had by the time of his latest writings come very close to maintaining that symbolic thought is a condition of and explains society" (Lukes 1973: 235).[3]

What I want to bring out here is that Durkheim was in fact grappling with the mind–body question and, for all his penetrating sociological insight, was sorely constrained by the dualism of the received answer to that question. On the mechanical definition of the reality of society, it is hard to avoid a final reduction to the concrete individual, the hardware of the system, so to speak. By contrast, the symbolical definition probingly evokes the diagnostic essence of human society, namely, its moral nature. Still, even on this definition, given mind–body dualism, one is pointed toward the conclusion that in the end the reality of society turns out to be but a figment of the individual's imagination, an illusory representation. In my view, modern anthropology remains significantly locked into the circle defined by these two reductionisms.

As is well known, though both Bronisław Malinowski and Alfred Radcliffe-Brown were "functionalists," they had conflicting views of the nature of social reality. For Malinowski, there never really was any question but that society reduces to the concrete individual. While the different aspects of culture may hang together in an impressive functional integration, they do so, not in their own right, but by reference to their context of use, which was basically individualistic. As Malinowski saw it, culture is the instrument of the individual conceived of in essentially utilitarian terms.

More roundly influenced by Durkheim, Radcliffe-Brown steadfastly promoted the thesis that society constitutes its own reality.[4] For Radcliffe-Brown, far from social relations being at the disposal of the interests of the individual, these interests are determined by society on behalf of its own welfare. Taking his cue especially from Durkheim's concept of "social morphology," Radcliffe-Brown was inclined to see social relations and the structure they compose as utterly real. However, put in terms of Radcliffe-Brown's vulgar positivism, such an interpretation of the reality of society was even less likely to convince (which perhaps says something about why the discipline seems so inclined today to hold in such poor regard the work of this one of the two scholars who gave social anthropology its modern beginnings).[5] At any rate, like his French master, Radcliffe-Brown too — transcending, as Adam Kuper (1983: 56) puts it, his own "banal prescriptions" — was moved at times to conceive of social structure in terms of symbolic representations. Thus it was possible for Lévi-Strauss, in his landmark work on totemism (1963: 155–64), to find in Radcliffe-Brown's analysis of Australian totemic practices an incipient structuralist enterprise.

Radcliffe-Brown, then, had to come to grips with the thesis of the reality of society in a way that Malinowski, comfortable with his avowed reductionism, avoided. Both men were strongly committed to a positivist approach. But, refusing to compromise the sociologism of his brand of "natural science," Radcliffe-Brown, like Durkheim before him, was goaded — perhaps by the reductionism that tends to shadow a social systems approach — toward a symbolic account of the reality of society. Given mind–body dualism, if one cannot accept that society reduces to the material individual, then one is bound to move toward a view of society as some kind of mentative order. Unfortunately, such is the force of the dualism, that reductionism beckons here too. Thus the "idealist" picture of society in terms of symbolic representations invites reduction of social reality, not to the material individual as such, but to the individual regarded as an order of consciousness. Much of today's "symbolic anthropology" is inclined to this sort of reduction, just as anthropological formalisms remain bound to the empiricist sort. In fact, the difference between Malinowski's atomist and Radcliffe-Brown's structuralist conception of the reality of society set the tone of a great deal of social anthropology to follow.

In this connection, the parts played in the history of the discipline by Max Gluckman and E. R. Leach are neatly instructive. Kuper has argued, most insightfully, that though these two scholars were — famously — outspoken theoretical opponents of each other, in fact their anthropologies tended to converge (1983: chap. 6). This convergence can be better understood if one sees the work of these two scholars in terms of the ontological conceptual framework within which they found themselves.

Following right on the heels of the absolute heyday of the functionalist paradigm, both thinkers were engaged with the problem of how to reconcile the (by then, all too apparent) fact of social process and change with the idea of normative order. Put another way, they were preoccupied sociologically with the relation between process and design, or between flux and norm. Given his Oxford bent, Gluckman focused on showing how social structure takes the social dynamic in hand, virtually employing it as an instrument of the normative order. Seeing the basic principles of any particular society as essentially contradictory, and attending to the play of power as well as to the constraint of norm, he held that conflict is endemic to society. But he was inclined to concentrate his analytical powers, not on the disruptive possibilities of such conflict (which he plainly distinguished), but on the ways in which it could be put to work on behalf of the perpetuation of the social order in its current form.

Gluckman did not rest content, however, with highly generalized ethnographical demonstrations of the point, the sort of analysis that characterized the work of Radcliffe-Brown and even Evans-Pritchard. With a keen eye to individual actors — their victories, defeats, intrigues, mortal strivings, and conflicted feelings — Gluckman attempted to show normative structure at work on the plane of interpersonal endeavor. To this end, he pioneered the so-called case-method or situational analysis in social anthropology.

Given his training under Malinowski, Leach saw the dialectic the other way around. In his view, the normative order was hardly a critical reality in its own right. Rather, the determining reality was the individual, as motivated by the pursuit of power and wealth. And since this implied that individuals were necessarily at odds with one another, the resulting society was always in a state of flux, as represented by the statistical norm of actual behavior. The normative picture of society as well integrated — a picture of equilibrium — was, then, as far as Leach was concerned, a fiction of one kind or another. Either it was the anthropologist's model, devised to fix analytically an intrinsically fluid state of affairs, or it was the interactant's model, constructed in the interest of self-interested manipulation.

Leach was attracted to Lévi-Strauss's notion of structure, in which the representational epistemology of "modeling" was transformed into an exceptionally powerful tool of elegant analytical generalization, a kind of *mathesis universalis* of the human mind. But whereas for the French master, structure in this sense enjoyed the status of reality (a status that could be conferred perhaps only by an intellectualism in which "thinking stuff" [*res cogitans*] is conceivable), for Leach, such structure was *in the end* what British empiricism cannot but take it to be — a merely ideal construct.

What is arresting here is that, despite their forthright theoretical antagonism, Gluckman and Leach produced strikingly parallel accounts of social order. Thus, as Gluckman was quick to point out, Leach's analysis of social flux in his book on the Kachin Hills area of Highland Burma presented a system of "oscillating equilibrium" (1967: 143). And as Kuper says about the two of them: "At the heart of all their work there was a shared concern with the ways in which social systems somehow recognizably persist despite their inherent contradictions, and, despite the fact that individuals are always pursuing their self-interest" (1983: 165). Though Gluckman participated in what Leach called Oxford "idealism," he too saw normative orders as essentially ambiguous and even came to understand the thesis of "equilibrium" as an "as if" proposition imposed for reasons of analysis (1968). Moreover, his critical focus on, not simply the rules of the game, but how the game was played, led to the methodological individualism of rational choice and network analysis, and even bore a Frederick Bailey to Leach's Fredrik Barth.

The parallelism is indeed no coincidence (see Kuper 1983: 165–66). It may be explained in light of the ontological question underlying the work of both men. It is obvious that the problem of the relation between social flux and structural norm is a sociological variant of the ontological question of how mind and body relate to each other. The common concern of Gluckman and Leach to reconcile social process and change with functionalism's stress on normative order, combined with the ontological dualism that implicitly informed their anthropology, gave the two scholars, subtle thinkers both, to produce similar dialectical pictures. Had the two of them not been so acutely focused on the problem of the interaction between process and design, the dualism would perhaps have moved them simply to vulgar reductionism. But granted that focus, the dualism gave each to project a reductionism in terms of a normative order that is to some degree open and a process of interaction that is to some degree subject to the order the individual interactant is always enterprisingly manipulating and bringing into existence. Caught in the gravity of ontological dualism, the two men could only swing theoretically between a social world conceived of as an order of individual interactants and one conceived of as a normative order, all the while depicting a dialectic wherein each of the two worlds is both dependent on and independent of the other.

A genuine concern for the question of the interaction between process and design shows the step between the two reductionisms to be quite small. In light of that concern, the difference between empiricism and idealism does not make the gigantic, acrimonious difference that Gluckman and Leach evidently felt to lie between them. In spite of itself, if it is to provide a credible ontological picture of interaction, each reductionism must afford the side it belittles at least the appearance of a hard and determining reality.

Textbookism: Open Questions and Closed Minds

Anthropology has produced a wealth of imposing responses to the ontological question of the interaction of social process and normative design. To name just a few, in addition to Radcliffe-Brown's "social structure" and Malinowski's "politico-economic man," there is the "rationalism" or "intellectual structure" of Lévi-Strauss, the "symbolical or metaphorical order" of Evans-Pritchard, Victor Turner, and Clifford Geertz, the "practice" of Pierre Bourdieu, the "history" of Marxist anthropologists, and so on. Of course, this list hardly exhausts the variety of responses (or, for that matter, the thought of the anthropologists I have associated with each response). Together, however, as is recorded in the charges their respective proponents level at one another, these responses and their like tend to describe a back-and-forth movement between empiricism, on the one hand, and intellectualism, on the other.

I venture that the reason for this theoretical circularity rests with the fact that all of the responses remain largely caught in the gravity of ontological dualism. As reductionisms, notwithstanding their opposing positions, the two sides of the dualism bear a mighty resemblance to each other. It is for this reason that it is so easy to get from the one reductionism to the other — witness Lévi-Strauss's fluent translation of Radcliffe-Brown's positivist structuralism into intellectualist structuralism; or Dan Sperber's of Lévi-Strauss's intellectualism into cognitivism; or Bailey's of Gluckman's normativism into transactionism; and so on. Given dualism, such circular theoretical motion is in fact logically constrained.

Anthropology's failure to recognize the ontological question as a foundation of the discipline has worked to prevent the discipline from breaking free of the dualism. By failing to break free, anthropology consigns itself to proceed without due regard to its intellectual mission. Avoidance of the ontological question both constitutes and represents the propensity of anthropology to lose sight of the fundamental questions that give it intellectual life. As a result, the tendency is to concentrate instead on questions that give the discipline institutional status and make it "professional." The fundamental questions are those from which social anthropology, conceived of as an inquiry into the social and cultural nature of apparently radical otherness, springs. Having emerged on the basis of the fundamental questions, the professional questions, though they organize textbook anthropology, are distinctly secondary.

Once the professional questions have become blind to their intellectual ground, they tend to take on a life of their own. As they do, they pervert the discipline's intellectual mission. I take it that, in his scintillating attack on Radcliffe-Brownian anthropology, Leach was saying something along these lines (1966: chap. 1). While I cannot embrace (as they stand) his ingenious and valuable recommendations for arriving at sociological generalization, his picture of functionalism as a tautological and self-defeating enterprise of "butterfly collecting" certainly presents an image of an abortive intellectual mission. He was suggesting that, having forgotten the "basic issues," functionalist anthropology had become intellectually sterile — it had "ceased to carry conviction" (1966: 1).

But functionalism in itself is not the problem. Textbook questions in general tend to take the "basic issues" for granted, thus presuming what it is they want to find out. In the case of disciplinary inquiry into the social and cultural nature of apparently radical otherness, what one basically wants to learn bears on the nature of society and culture in relation to the nature of difference and identity. Such matters are directly involved with ontology.

Of the human sciences, anthropology is, I expect, the most implicitly revolutionary.[6] Its constituting interest in otherness renders it intellectually open in a definitive way that no other discipline can lay claim to. By presuming the character of its underlying ontological groundwork, textbook anthropology quite simply perverts anthropology's radical intellectual mission and violates its most basic proscription — the proscription against ethnocentric bias.[7] In effect, by presenting anthropology primarily as a body of accumulated knowledge, rather than as a discipline obliged by the character of its subject matter to continually round up for interrogation the presuppositions according to which it proceeds, textbook anthropology impedes the discipline's epistemic advance.

Toward a Situational Anthropology

Naturally, in a Borgesian synopsis of this sort the picture is overdrawn, designedly "all black and white" (Leach 1966: 1). A less tendentious, more fully proportioned account would show that the circular theoretical motion I have pointed to is more fairly conceived as a spiral, and that the sort of textbook professionalism I have condemned is a matter of degree. Doubtless, a great deal has been accomplished by anthropological research. One cannot help but be impressed, for example, by anthropology's capacity today to yield *as a rule* extraordinarily rich and subtle understandings of meaningful systems. More to the point here, most of the responses to the question of interaction between process and design, though they have been sorely hampered by a repressed ontological consciousness, do not want for a sense of struggle to escape the prisonhouse of dualist thought. This sense is as self-evident in, say, Lévi-Strauss's powerful concept of structure as it is in Bourdieu's directly contrary but equally imposing concept of practice.[8]

In fact, anthropology has not failed to show very deep insight in the struggle against dualism. Although, in the context of his antagonism to things Leachian, I have discussed Gluckman as a normativist who had a keen sense of dialectic, his situational analysis may be construed to point in a different direction entirely. Gluckman was inclined to portray situational analysis simply as a very useful inductive tool. But his inductivism was inspired here in ways he surely felt but was in no theoretical position to articulate. Thinking of social life in terms of situations renders it, not exactly as a dialectic of other-regard and self-interest (as if these two principles precede the relation between them), but as an essential tension from which the two principles themselves emerge as functions of each other. The tension, then, describes the opposing principles as vitally dependent on each other. Thus, being situated is being caught existentially and essentially between the two principles. Under this understanding, what the anthropologist studies is not an individual in his or her social context, but an essential tension with individualistic and sociologistic aspects. In principle, then, situationalism cannot abide reductionism—instead it projects a basically ambiguous reality.

Accordingly, humans are bound existentially between conflicting but equally commanding injunctions. Such a bind—a double bind—epitomizes a certain dynamic of choice. The condition of being insolubly bound between self-interest and other-regard is the condition of moral choice. As there is no way out, creatures who live this bind are condemned to spend their lives putting off the dead-end. They do this by making choices that recognize, in one way or another, the claims of both horns of the dilemma. They are thus condemned to creative and moral choice. In this connection, it is illuminating to recall that, as Sally Moore discerningly essayed, normativism, no less than methodological individualism, pictures human conduct as a matter of choosing (1975).

For situational analysis, then, the reality of society is above all moral. I suggest that in his grasp of the case-study method as descriptive and probing in the way of a novel and psychoanalysis respectively, Gluckman, for all his devout inductivism, was driving at the essentially moral character of the way in which human beings cope with their basically dilemmatic existence (1961).

Another place in which one can find in anthropology an incipient description of the reality of society in terms of situationalism is in Evans-Pritchard's great book on Zande mystical thought and action (1937). The most conspicuous argument in the book is that once one grants the Azande their initial mystical premises, the rest of their beliefs and associated practices appear to follow quite rationally. But, as I see it, the book's most consequential argument is that theoretical contradictions do not necessarily function as contradictions in practice. If the contradictories are invoked only in separate situations, the fact that in the abstract they constitute a contradiction has no bearing. Here, anticipating Bourdieu, Evans-Pritchard features the way in which being situated has to do in the first place with practice rather than theory, with, as Evans-Pritchard put it, "ideas imprisoned in action."

This is a somewhat different emphasis from Gluckman's, on the manner in which social situations manifest the conflicted character of social life and constitute scenes of unfolding ambiguities. But I believe that, like Gluckman's attraction to the case-study method, Evans-Pritchard's insight into the situational nature of social life was — even if he remained unaware of it — connected to his critical understanding of society as a moral phenomenon. As stated above, being situated means being condemned to choice, and therefore betrays moral agency. It is just that the choice to which one is condemned is lived before it is rationalized — that is to say, it is a matter of practice.[9]

Evans-Pritchard's commitment to the idea of society as a moral system received its outspoken expression in his notorious Marett Lecture (1962; see Evens 1982b). This dramatic defection from functionalism is perhaps too easily understood as a call for historical analysis, in the sense of analysis of a course of successive human events, and therefore too easily linked with the general anthropological movement of the times toward analysis of change. Doubtless, Evans-Pritchard's turn toward history was intended in some measure as a remedy to functionalism's excessive concern with synchronic depiction. But far and away, what Evans-Pritchard had in mind was the reconception of society as a moral rather than natural system — he was much more concerned to juxtapose choice to determinism, rather than change to stability. His idea of history, like R. G. Collingwood's (1946), did not equate history with change but with the interpretive study of the life of the mind as this life manifests itself in particular situations and actions. He was, then, interested in human social life especially as it is conditioned by a process of creative choice or, as I call it, moral selection. This idea of history goes a long way to account for Evans-Pritchard's apparent theoretical turnabout, since focal attention to the principles of a society conceived of as moral premises was an abiding feature of his work. The so-called conversion was, as he himself said, more a declaration of independence than a change of heart (see Evans-Pritchard's self-commentary in Kuper 1983: 131–32; cf. Evens 1982a: 385–86).

Finally, I wish to cite in the present connection the work of Louis Dumont. Dumont's controversial notion of hierarchy is, of course, explicitly structuralist, not situationalist. But it is predicated squarely on the idea of society as a moral system. Plainly, in its application to India (1970), Dumont's concept of hierarchy accords the caste system a primarily moral rather than material value. But beyond its application to India, and whether or not one takes exception to that application, the notion of hierarchy tends to recolor in moral tones the intellectualist lines of structuralism's picture of society in general. This is perhaps nowhere better shown than in Dumont's essay "On Value," in which, by taking for granted a hierarchical conception of things social, he is positioned to render value as a given, an authentic measure of the good, rather than as an epiphenomenon of utility (1980).

Given its intimate relation with the idea of society as a moral phenomenon, notwithstanding its origins in structuralism, the concept of hierarchy is perfectly fitting to a situationalist approach. I have described social situations as transcendent, in that they present self-interest and other-regard as an essential tension or ambiguity. As such, any social situation is characterized by a certain openness as to its end. Such openness corresponds to the fact of moral agency — the openness in question is the "space" of creative choice. Gluckman was inclined to emphasize the way in which a social situation constrained participants toward the ends of the normative order. But we can now see that the constraint is above all toward neither order nor flux but creative choice. The consideration that no social situation can be perfectly delimited beforehand, but always remains open and uncontrollable to some degree, bespeaks a certain hierarchical relationship between the situation and its participants — the participant ever relates to the situation as part to whole. The resulting "structure of encompassment" is, however, not primarily normative or intellectual but moral — an open or dynamic structure. Hierarchical encompassment is one (logically liberating) way of describing society as a moral phenomenon.

Thus, prompted by Durkheim's critical sense of society as a moral phenomenon, social anthropology has furnished certain opening gambits in the Promethean-like struggle against ontological dualism. Situationalism suggests that interaction between process and design is not the question, but the answer. That is to say, situationalism suggests that we need to rethink the nature of our reality, so that it begins directly with ambiguity. By doing so, we can position ourselves to refuse as self-imposed illusions the sets of dualistic alternatives, taking up paths other than empiricism and intellectualism.

In social anthropology, the ontological question combines uniquely with the question of apparently radical otherness. As will become clear in what follows, the ontological question (the body–mind question) is of a piece with the anthropological issue of human agency; while the question of apparently radical otherness — controverted philosophically under the heading of "other minds" — has often been posed in anthropology as the problem of "rationality."

Acting on the thesis of ontological ambiguity, the present work will address the question of human agency as well as that of rationality. In doing so, it will begin to develop, in relation to one another, the notions of choice, hierarchical encompassment, practice, and situation.

But the main point of this historical discussion of social anthropology should not be lost. It is that the ontological question is no less foundational to anthropology than it is to philosophy. From Durkheim to the present, that question has underlain not only the way we have answered anthropological questions, but also the way we ask them. Functionalism, structuralism, transactionism, cognitivism, and so on, have not merely interpreted the ethnographic facts but have also helped determine them. If we are to break new ground, if we are to combat facile professionalism, we need to confront the ontological question directly. This is no merely philosophical imperative, of concern only to those anthropologists who enjoy abstract thinking, but bears squarely on the discipline's capacity to conduct, in a critical fashion, its empirical inquiry.

Two

The Kibbutz

The Case Study and the Kibbutz

This study takes as its ethnographic point of departure a set of two incidents that occurred in Timem, an Israeli kibbutz in which I did intensive field research.[1] Together the incidents composed a formal debate over a move to change the rule of voting in Timem's General Assembly, from open to secret ballot. The debate took place in two successive meetings (the two incidents) of this democratic body and arose in response to the members' acknowledgment of serious political apathy and to the question of how best to rectify the problem. Because there was exhibited a propensity to identify the community's second generation with the proposal of secret ballot as well as with the problem of political apathy, the debate dramatized the question of conflict between the generations.

This analysis constitutes, then, a case study. As pioneered by Gluckman and the so-called Manchester school of social anthropology, the case-study "method" recommends analysis of specific, interconnected incidents (a "case") in order to disclose the operation of fundamental principles of the social order. As mentioned in chapter 1, Gluckman was inclined to think of such analysis in terms of a simple logic of induction. But it is crucial to see that it is not simply a method for extracting the general from the particular. Rather, its focus on actual process is meant to reveal the interplay of the general and the particular, the way in which practice and principle interact, to constitute each other in the situational flow of social life. In short, it seems ideally suited to the onto-anthropological analysis of social life as a basically ambiguous reality.

Furthermore, in view of its aim to apprehend social incidents in terms of their deeper, underlying meanings, the method relies strongly on interpretive understanding. In this connection, Gluckman himself pointed out that such studies bring to anthropology some of the penetration and depth one finds in psychoanalysis and novelistic accounts of human social existence (Gluckman 1961). In other words, despite the empiricism that inspired its development, the method is in keeping with an interpretive approach.

In the present study I do not proceed by stringing together a large series of incidents in order to perform an orthodox extended case study. Rather, with a steadfast eye toward the ontological concerns that focus this book, I employ the two key incidents of the debate largely as an empirical occasion to plumb Timem's current political state of affairs in general, its underlying conditions and preconditions, and then to address my theoretical concerns.

In effect, I take the set of two incidents as revealing of what may be deemed the community's overall social situation, the prevailing mood of the community (a mood, as we shall see, of "fallenness"). In this connection, following up an earlier, more orthodox extended case study (Evens 1975), I am interested in digging deeply into the phenomenological core of the community's self-identity, to determine what it means to be a member of the kibbutz.

More radically, though, I take the case also as revealing of the community considered as a social situation in itself. Correlative to this leap of focus — from "Timem's situation" to "the situation of Timem" — I set my sights more broadly, on the determination of what it means to be human. As I suggested in chapter 1, the consideration that as a social situation the kibbutz is specially defined by the theme of transcendence marks this community as uniquely suitable to so anthropologically ambitious an aim.

As a result of this aim, the present case study tends to sacrifice novelistic drama in the interest of theoretical depth. The ethnography is sharply circumscribed, to the point of unorthodoxy, by its theoretical charge; it is less ethnographically round than it is richly pointed in relation to a particular set of theoretical issues. The case study does "extend," however, to cite often and throughout the concrete words and actions of Timem's members, and in this way to document ethnographically the everyday social and cultural life of the community.

Two principal problems arising from my field research on Timem are addressed. The first is what might be called the problem of "utopian fall," especially in relation to the operation of kibbutz democracy. The members' disposition to define their "fallen" state in terms of conflict between the generations constitutes the second problem. The latter is a problem because, as I shall show, it is not the case that the fallenness Timem's members were experiencing is empirically reducible to generational conflict.

As a solution to the first problem, I argue that by virtue of both its explicit and implicit *raisons d'être,* the kibbutz ensured but failed really to take into account the inevitable development of social difference, and that this self-inconsistent state of affairs guaranteed the internal perception of a fall. As a solution to the second problem, I argue that in invoking conflict between the generations to define their situation, the members were at bottom doing nothing less than fashioning themselves.[2]

The Ethnographic Problem-Set

Despite their demographic inconspicuousness (see below, chap. 2, n. 1), as "alternative" but successful socioeconomic enterprises, the kibbutzim have been, and continue to be, the subject of an impressive amount of sociological and psychological research (Schur et al. 1981). In recent years, much of this research has been concerned to address the problem of "counterrevolutionary" change in these communities. Though it remains strongly collectivist in commitment and design, there can be no doubt that over the years the kibbutz has felt increasingly constrained to interpret the principle of collectivism in liberal terms, that is, in terms that stress the relative autonomy of the individual as over and against that of the collective. Most writers take note of this liberalization, but they tend to treat it in view of the question of whether or not it constitutes deterioration. In doing so, they fail to see, I believe, that the liberalization is rooted in the practice of kibbutz ideology and reflects contradictions deeply embedded in the categories of Western intellectual tradition.

In connection with such liberalizing change, I propose to investigate here certain changes that occurred in the conduct of Timem's participatory democracy. These changes pertained to a growing political apathy, as evidenced by poor attendance and low voting counts in the *sichat hakibbutz*, or General Assembly, the chief institutional organ of Timem's direct democracy.

The changes were sorely out of keeping with the ideology's premise of direct and consensual democracy, and presented the members with a crisis of legitimation. The kibbutz is ideologically predicated on a perfect synthesis between the individual and society. This synthesis was originally keyed by the idea of a "new man," a being whose rational and moral superiority guides him to found his own autonomy in the act of transferring it to the community. The problem of political apathy was read, by Timem's members, as a breakdown of this synthesis, a falling out of the individual from society.

Timem's members were inclined to link this problem with increasing social differentiation. From its inception in 1926 to the time of fieldwork, Timem's population had grown tenfold and had become internally differentiated to a marked degree. From the perspective of its own nascent state, Timem had become relatively large and heterogeneous.

Remarkably, then, it would appear that the more the community realized itself on the ground, that is, the more it grew and developed, the more the letter of its ideological ends became difficult to fulfill. I wish to analyze this apparent contradiction between kibbutz theory and practice, paying special attention to the role of social differentiation in the course of events.

More especially, though, I want to plumb the members' experience and self-understanding of their predicament. In this regard, there are two outstanding considerations to be explored. The first is that the community's increasing social differentiation occasioned a growing sense of individual autonomy in the community. The second is that the members seemed predisposed to apprehend this sense of individualism (which they found disturbing), and the community's transformation in general, in terms of conflict between the generations. As we shall see, Timem's members were inclined to attribute their social predicament to such conflict, the founding members, or *vatikim* (lit. "veterans"), being cast as defenders of the collectivist faith and the youth, or *tz'irim*, as representatives of revisionist change and individualism.

The Existing Literature and My Approach

The troubles of democracy and generational struggle in the kibbutz have received substantial sociological commentary.[3] But there exists no really intensive analysis, based on the sort of intimate data elicited by ethnographic research in a particular community, of the impact of social differentiation on kibbutz democracy or, for that matter, of the notorious issue of generational conflict in the kibbutz.

Apart from the matter of ethnographic documentation of the kibbutz and its development, and much more important to my purpose, is the question of analytical character. The literature on the kibbutz ranges from fiction to positive sociology and psychology, from survey work to life histories, and from cultural analysis to psychoanalysis (see Schur et al. 1981). Aside from my own previous contribution (1975), however, there is virtually no available intensive study of the deepest intentionalities and motivations of the kibbutz ethos, what might be called, loosely following Thomas Kuhn's work on scientific revolutions (1970) or Victor Turner's on symbolic systems (1974), the paradigmatic structures of the kibbutz.

It is true that in his study on kibbutz women, Melford Spiro searches out deep, underlying motivations (1979). But far from a concern for paradigmatic structures, his approach is naturalistic — it pictures change in terms of "precultural" causation, as distinct from an experiential dynamic intrinsic to the practice of the kibbutz ethos.

By contrast, the approach employed in the present study, though it knows well the limits of phenomenology, has the flavor of phenomenology, more particularly, existential phenomenology.[4] For my purposes what is critically important about the phenomenological discipline is its relentless exploration of meanings as they are embedded in more fundamental or encompassing meanings and experiences. Phenomenology directs attention, more acutely and systematically than any discipline I know, to the conditions of knowing. Its notorious procedure of "reduction" demands that one put aside ("bracket") what one knows, in order to discern how one knows it, much as one might avert one's gaze from an object to the source of light making possible the appearance of that object. When translated into anthropological practice, this demand becomes a recommendation to isolate and identify the existential points of view or sources of epistemological light through which the everyday events of social life are made to appear. Such points of view pertain to what people take for granted, that is, to tacit knowledge, as well as to the experiential plane of human social life.

Here, then, I aim to dig below both the plane of material motives and the plane of explicit values to determine the existential predispositions of the kibbutz members, the self-understandings without which they would not know who they are and where they stand in the world. Dispositions of this kind are so integrally tied to the members' constitution as human beings that they move them in a manner that appears to be instinctual but is not.[5] Indeed, the host, considered in its aspect of a material and practical dynamic, is intricated in such a way with the dispositions that in the end it is inadequate to speak of structures at all — paradigmatic or not — as *moving* anything. Instead, with Gilles Deleuze and Felix Guattari (1987), we must think of a becoming that lacks a subject distinct from itself and of a reality specific to it. As long as this radical ontological point is understood, it is convenient to retain the terms "paradigmatic structures" and "tacit knowledge." In what is to follow, though, I will eventually come to talk about the (nondualist) reality at issue in terms of "primordial choosing."

This approach departs sharply from what appear to be the two leading approaches to the question of "counterrevolutionary" change in the kibbutz. Spiro (1979) as well as Lionel Tiger and Joseph Shepher (1975) have sought to explain certain transformations in the kibbutz by appeal to naturalism of one sort or another. The systematic focus on tacit knowledge, though, makes it unnecessary to choose between nature and culture in order to account for such transformations. That is to say, in my usage, tacit knowledge is so tightly imprisoned in self-identity and action that it is no less "natural" in force than it is "cultural" in construction.

The other prevailing approach comes from those who explain change in the kibbutz in terms of "modernization" (for example, E. Cohen 1976, 1982). The kibbutz is indeed forced to compete for membership with Israeli society in general, and inevitably this competition has informed the direction of change in this collectivist organization. Nevertheless, when it is considered that the kibbutz has never been anything but an essentially "modern" social phenomenon, the crucial ways the course of its development is implicit in its utopian design and paradigmatic self-understandings demand investigation.

In addition to providing a fresh perspective on change in this utopian community, attention to tacit knowledge and paradigmatic self-identity stands to begin to redress the gap in the literature concerning the rootedness of the kibbutz in Judaism and Western utopian thought. These roots are often paid lip service, and a recent work by Shalom Lilker (1982) seeks to document the distinctly Jewish character of the kibbutz. Even so, when one bears in mind the wide variety of social arrangements revealed by comparative anthropology, a large part of the available literature appears to be at least a little myopic in its overwhelming stress on the "alternative" character of the kibbutz.[6] It seems to me that the flag of "alternative" character has served to blind many students of the kibbutz to the considerations that that character is relative to a culturally limited tradition of possible social worlds, and that the kibbutz shares with the type of society to which it is expressly alternative rootedness in a distinctly Western body of social thought and contradictions.

In particular, the present study lends itself to an examination of the kibbutz ethos in terms of (1) the anthropological logic of world-creation at the core of Judaism — the Book of Genesis; and (2) one logic of social synthesis at the core of the Enlightenment — Rousseau's. Though such attention is selective rather than exhaustive, it points to key foundations of and contradictions in the kibbutz's self-construction.

The Flaw in the Kibbutz Design and Radical Democracy

The consideration that the kibbutz's communitarian ideal appears to have undermined itself in practice brings into conspicuous relief the question of the practicality of that ideal. Naturally, a question of this kind haunts any radical social endeavor, and the kibbutz is no exception.[7] After many years of pondering this question, I have finally come to the conclusion that there is a critical flaw in the design of the kibbutz ideal. This flaw bears on but does not reduce to the (antiutopian) proposition that theory can never finally circumscribe practice. Though I was able to determine the flaw only on completion of this study, it should serve to disclose values and fix ideas if, before embarking on the case study proper, I lay out at the start my thoughts on this matter.

As indicated above, Kibbutz Timem's synthetic ideal appeared to falter in the face of the community's increasing internal differentiation. The latter was associated by the members with the growing expression of individualism and the elaboration of private selves. However, it is not self-evident that pluralism and individual liberty are in themselves bad for community. Indeed, unlike some communitarian ideals, the kibbutz's is acutely sensitive to the ethical precept of individuals as ends in themselves. But if such differentiation is not necessarily inimical to community, why did Timem's growth and development — a process of social heterogenization — lead to a crisis of legitimacy? The answer, I believe, rests with the specific design of Timem's collectivist ideal.

The kibbutz synthesis is ideologically predicated on *basic identity* — that between self and society. The heterogenization of Timem, however, was a process of differentiation — it tended to betray *basic difference* between self and other. The fact that this experience of irrecusable difference or otherness served to threaten the kibbutz synthesis implies that the identity projected by the kibbutz has an absolutist aspect. If the identity were not intended as absolute, the difference entailed by such otherness could not of itself disrupt the successful implementation of the kibbutz synthesis. Therefore, although the kibbutz has always demonstrated a healthy respect for the exigencies of practice, the sought-after identity between self and society is, in principle, colored by absolutism. Even if it is an inconstant pursuit, the critical aim is to establish an immaculate synthesis of the two.

The absolutist aspect of the kibbutz synthesis may be traced to the problem that the synthesis is designed to overcome. The kibbutz began its career in the face of an acute sense of the modern self, a radically differentiated self. As an "alternative" social order, the kibbutz was predicated on the goal of eradicating the profound social problems associated with this kind of self. Put in a way that resonates with kibbutz rhetoric, the synthesis is meant to surmount the bourgeois dualism of self and society.

As a solution, the kibbutz synthesis is keyed critically to the principle of voluntarism. By voluntarily conforming to the community's designs, individuals are presumed to constitute themselves and the community at one and the same time, mediating the dualism. Unfortunately, though, the synthesis fails to take seriously enough the idea of mediation. The picture of self and society projected by kibbutz voluntarism remains ontologically bound by the picture projected by the problem kibbutz voluntarism is meant to surmount. It is a picture of self and society as, not only essentially, but also primarily, separate and distinct entities — a Cartesian picture of absolute rather than relative phenomena.

True, the kibbutz synthesis proposes that society and the individual are in fact critically interdependent. But, as we shall see, when it comes to fleshing out this proposition, the ideology tends to interpret the interdependence as a matter of society's capacity to condition the individual to exercise his or her capacity to choose (volunteer) on behalf of the collective interest — a form of Rousseau's "general will." In other words, the interdependence is seen as political, economic, and moral, but not really as fundamental. There is here a strong affirmation, but no firm idea, of a fundamental mediative identity between the individual and society — some kind of shared identity that antecedes dualism and from which a remedial answer to an exclusive sense of self may take heart. Put another way, for all its intentions to the contrary, the kibbutz ideology lacks a suitable ontology to correspond to its organicist rhetoric and social ideal.[8]

As a result of this "design flaw," the kibbutz synthesis was condemned to subvert itself. As it put itself in practice, creating — in a certain respect, by design — selves thematically centered on their own moral capacities, it necessarily elaborated difference as well as identity between self and society. Indeed, as I shall show, for reasons of voluntarism, the elaboration of otherness and difference was a virtual condition of the attainment of the identity in question. The process of the elaboration of difference (especially in the form of private selves) is in fact a conspicuous feature of Timem's history. But because such difference is not unequivocally admissible in the kibbutz synthesis, it had to be felt, distinctly if also ambivalently, as antinomian. Accordingly, the developed difference between self and society defined these two principles as disharmoniously set against each other. In this quasi-utopian social world, it therewith occasioned a crisis of legitimacy.

The kibbutz was obliged by the absolutist aspect of its ideological design to hold suspect the difference that makes authentic moral choice and therefore, ironically, the kibbutz synthesis feasible. Owing to scrupulous standards, the elaboration of such difference was seen as a falling out of the individual member with the collective, and felt as a breakdown of legitimate order. Under these epistemological conditions, the difference did indeed take the form of political competition between self and society.

To anticipate the case, as especially the proponents of a secret ballot were feeling, the absolute demands of the kibbutz synthesis were making authentic voluntarism impossible. Unfortunately, the call for voting secrecy could only relocate the site of absolutism from that of the collective to that of the individual. Instead of an identity between self and society, a secret ballot, as the opponents of this voting rule feared, would have promoted an identity between the individual and him- or herself. Given such an identity, the openness of one's self to one's neighbor admonished by the kibbutz becomes, instead of a freedom, a compulsion to conform. From the perspective of the individual defined simply as against the collective, a commandment to heed one's neighbor can only be felt as an infringement on one's freedom.

This argument about collective self-subversion needs to be put also in terms of time. The elaboration of personal selves in Kibbutz Timem is critically tied to the historical growth and realization of the kibbutz. What came between the individual and the kibbutz, then, was time — time amplified the difference between them. Indeed, the elaboration of a self that stands apart from the collective may be fairly construed as a *putting off* of the identificatory *stasis* implied by the kibbutz synthesis. In effect, in the kibbutz, the elaboration of such a self *made* time, defining it though as deferral rather than realization of the ideal.

Against the backdrop of the ideal of perfect identity between self and society, the expansion of a personal self necessarily connotes the openness that is time. A failure to exhibit difference between self and society implies a thoroughgoing determinacy and therefore curtails the appearance of the possibility of choice. In turn, where the possibility of choice is not open to view, neither is time. For where there is no sense of choice, there can be no sense of futurity, no sense that things can be otherwise. In the kibbutz, then, the elaboration of private selves could not but be associated with futural uncertainty, and hence time and choice.

Unfortunately, though, just because the kibbutz synthesis attempts to arrest time as uncertainty, time's triumph largely took on a negative rather than positive air. Notwithstanding the consideration that the synthesis is predicated on the autonomous individual, the intensive demand for a complete union tended to define the autonomy of the individual antithetically, that is, in terms of diametric opposition. As a consequence, the development of that autonomy took a dualistic direction, demarcating a private as against a public self.

One *identity* was substituted for another — that of the self for that between self and society.

The uncertainty of time thus manifested itself in terms of the dualism of the private and the public, and of locked combat between self and society. Instead of working to promote each other's creativity, the collective and the individual were moved to seek to restrain each other. As a result, choice came to be associated not with genuinely creative endeavor, whereby together the members construct their own world as keyed to other-regard, but with individualistic calculation. In short, "choice" came to smack of expediency as opposed to principle.

Still, because the kibbutz never lapsed in its ideological commitment to *both* self and society, that is because its devotion to voluntarism is emphatically two-sided, the flaw in the kibbutz synthesis produced — as the debate about a secret ballot plainly exemplifies — principled, not mortal, combat. The annihilation of neither self nor society is thinkable on kibbutz ideology. Hence, no matter how impersonal and detached the collective grew, its power of oppression was rightfully curbed by the precept of the individual's legitimate and essential autonomy. For reasons of this precept, as both the proponents and the opponents of a secret ballot suspected, the expansion of private selves in Timem, for all the ideological trepidation it brought, had something very right about it. The precept of the individual's autonomy is invested formally, however, not in the idea of a private self, but in the fundamental right of voluntary membership. The significance — if I may, the goodness — of this right, to opt out of the kibbutz at any time, is hard to overestimate: this right tends to ensure that the kibbutz remains open to openness, that is, to time and choice.

Nevertheless, that the individual is permitted to pick up and leave at will is insufficient to ensure the realization of the sort of voluntary synthesis the kibbutz hoped for — or, perhaps more to the point here, it is insufficient to impede the development of a dualism of self and society. The right of voluntary membership is essentially a form of *nonidentity* between self and society, an openness in the proposed synthesis, a place for uncertainty. But alone, one such place, however profound, is not enough.

The maintenance of authentic voluntarism depends on a more immediate tolerance of politico-ethical difference. The situation of renunciation of membership is too remote from most everyday situations to prevent the frequent exercise, in one form or another, of coercive conformity. Nor, of course, is it always possible for the individual to exercise the right of renunciation without suffering significant material disadvantage. The possibility of dissent must be backed by more than the caveat "Love it or leave it"; it must also be built directly into each and every social situation. The possibility of dissent, and it alone, is what makes the admonishment to heed the opinion of one's neighbor a call to freedom rather than a condition of power. If "heeding" the opinion of the other *entails* accepting it, then the admonishment betrays closure, not openness. The demand to attend to the other becomes paradigmatically meaningful as a condition of choice when, and only when, the other leaves such attention to you.

To put the point as directly as I can: rather than with the identity of the two, the social ideal of the kibbutz is, to the contrary, most critically consistent with the establishment and preservation of a fundamental and comprehensive *nonidentity* between self and society. The sort of relation I have in mind admits of the identity neither of self nor of society, but instead constitutes these phenomena as finitely identical to each other *by virtue of the fundamental difference between them*. That is, the identity they share is also the difference between them, and because this identity-in-difference is their constituting principle, neither self nor society can ever be truly identical to itself.[9]

Obviously, such an ontological regime gives primacy of place to the other. For each member's identity is always and primordially other to itself. Otherness of this sort certainly makes secrecy possible. It puts members in a position to deceive one another as well as one's self. But the essential way in which members are inaccessible — that is, are other — to one another is not in the first place a matter of privacy, but of uncertainty. One simply can never be sure of, can never really fix, what one's other or, for that matter what one's self, will be. Each member is bound to wonder, with the poet (Emily Dickinson), "what myself will say."

By the same token, under these conditions, although the contrariness implicit in voluntarism can take the form of sheer opposition, what it signifies in the first place is that things can be otherwise. It points to essential futurity, futurity that by definition cannot be known in advance. It points to time as uncertainty and creation. Since time of this kind cannot be reduced to a modality of time-present, since it presents an-other time, it is indeed the time of choice.

On this ontology, the commandment to heed one's neighbor is no less an option than an order. While it commands one to endorse the other, it also leaves one to one's own decision; it thus condemns one to choose and self-construct (or self-destruct, as the case may be). It imposes order, but as anarchy.[10] In this light, the development of pluralism in the kibbutz is basically a positive rather than negative outcome. Indeed, it stands as proof *positive* that the kibbutz has, in noticeable measure, arrived at its ideal of "order without government." Insofar as the kibbutz has managed to realize this ontological state of affairs, it has remained both vital and alternative, a truly radical democracy.[11]

For what is to follow, it is helpful to understand that, in Timem, the ascendancy of time, choice, and the other was glossed, in both of its aspects (as threatening to as well as promising for the collectivist ideal), in terms of the procession and conflict of the generations.

Three

Democratic Procedure and Secret Ballot

The Case

Kibbutz Democracy

The occasion for my argument is a dispute about democratic procedure that took place in Kibbutz Timem. Like all kibbutzim, Timem is dedicated to direct democracy. Indeed, for understanding the case to follow, it is worth mentioning that the ideal process of arriving at community decisions in Timem may be said to surpass even direct democracy — what is projected ideologically is a unanimity of opinion, an expression of the "general will," rather than an aggregation of individual preferences. However, if by "direct democracy" we mean the sovereignty of the people, in the sense that the people as a whole regularly devises and initiates all manner of public decisions through voting procedures, then Timem's members accept this mode of government and believe that it obtains in their society. That the members should themselves, in lieu of elected representatives, assemble to decide public affairs and policy is consistent with the kibbutz's most fundamental ideological precepts, as I will show momentarily.

This strong form of democratic regime is sharply evident in Timem's administrative structure. The following conditions closely approximate Max Weber's (1978: 289–92) "principal technical means" for the attainment of direct democracy. In brief, Timem is characterized by a wealth of functionally specific administrative committees (*va'adot*) and posts (*taf'kidim*). The great majority of administrative staff is elected by ballot, though some committee seats are held *ex officio*. There is a strong tendency to follow a principle of rotation in filling these positions, and tenure is relatively short, ranging from six months to three years, depending on the particular post.

In respect of decision making, all committees and administrative incumbencies are subject to the Secretariat (*mazkirut*), whose scope of authority is comprehensive in respect of the community's functions. This committee normally comprises about twelve persons, most of whom sit *ex officio*, so as to represent the major institutional sectors of the community.

The Secretariat is obligated to submit to the authority of the community's General Assembly (*sichat hakibbutz*) any issue that it finds itself unable to resolve or that is construed as fundamental or principled (*ikarit*). The General Assembly is the apex of the community's administrative hierarchy. It convenes weekly. Virtually all public issues are subject to its decision. This fact, plus the consideration that the General Assembly comprises directly all of the community's members, make this institution the quintessential embodiment of the community's democratic ideal. By virtue of its profoundly democratic constitution, the General Assembly serves, in the kibbutz ideology, to legitimate the very existence of the community. The case that concerns me here centers on a proposed modification of one of the General Assembly's procedural rules.

The Incidents

For nearly all decisions Timem's General Assembly has adhered to a rule of simple majority voting. It has also been the rule to vote by show of hands rather than secret ballot. In 1966, during one of the General Assembly's regular meetings, it was moved that the rule of open-hand voting be changed to secret balloting, at the very least in respect of selected issues. There was a heated debate, and it was decided to continue the discussion at a second convening of the General Assembly.[1] To this end an ad hoc meeting was arranged for the following Friday night (regular meetings of the General Assembly were held on Saturday nights). The fact that an extraordinary meeting was called for suggests that the issue was regarded as uniquely important.

The ad hoc meeting took place as scheduled, but attendance was exceedingly poor (I counted about forty heads; Timem's bimonthly newspaper claimed "about sixty"). After some brief discussion, it was urged that with so few persons present there was little point in proceeding with the debate. This was conceded, and the meeting summarily adjourned. Concerning this meeting, the community's newspaper reported: "The absence of *all* the members from 'the east wing' of the dining hall [which is also the meeting hall] made the continuation of the debate useless." (The cryptic character of the newspaper's comment is full of innuendo, and I shall return to unpack it in the next chapter.) Thereafter, as far as I know (I was in the field some eight months subsequent to these events), there was no further public debate on the issue — it seems simply to have ceased. Voting in the General Assembly continued to be by show of hands.

Now, a debate over a rule of voting is hardly the stuff of high social drama. But that such a debate can be a critical glass through which to study profound social movement has already been amply demonstrated by David Cresap Moore's very imposing historical monograph on the political implications of the adoption of the secret ballot in mid-nineteenth-century England (D. Moore 1976). That poll books (in which the choices of voters were recorded for all to see) became unpublishable was symptomatic of changes of not only social structure, but also attitude about what kind of influence ought to count as "natural" in the determination of the voter's choice. As the leader writer of the *Times* observed in 1872, "Large numbers of voters...are now fixed in the belief that they will be exposed to unknown evils if they have not the power of screening their votes in darkness" (cited in D. Moore 1976: 13). The attempt to introduce the secret ballot into Timem's direct democracy is no less deeply revealing of Timem's social dynamics and a troubled social consciousness. Indeed, as we shall see, though on its face the debate may seem purely cerebral and abstract, in fact it goes right to the heart of the kibbutz ideal.

My data do not permit me to say much about certain particulars of the dispute — questions concerning exactly how, where, and by whom the issue was raised before it was brought to the General Assembly are unanswerable by me. But the dispute's organizational, ideological, and phenomenological conditions can be bought to light through workmanlike scrutiny of the text of the debate.

Text of the Debate

The argumentation of the dispute follows here. In order to fix the main lines of argument and give some idea of the rhetorical flavor of the debate, it is convenient at this point to cite and comment exegetically on the full arguments of four of the eight members who held forth during the formal airing (I record some of the other materials later, as they become relevant). I cite only from the General Assembly's first meeting on the issue, since the abortive second meeting produced nothing substantially new in the way of textual content. For purposes of interpretation it is helpful to keep in mind the following five discursive functions: assertions of problem, cause, solution, justification, and accountability.

> The Secretary:
> I open the debate on the problem of decision making and procedure in the General Assembly. The problem is fundamental. We are confronted with two kinds of relevant questions, namely, procedural questions (such as, What times are best to begin and end the General Assembly meetings?) and essential questions (such as, What ought the nature be of a free assembly of comrades in a modern community, a community in which the various questions arising in everyday life demand for their resolution professional expertise?). The most difficult questions pertain to the number of voters in decision making, to the fact that in our collective decisions we fail to achieve a voting participation of more than one-third of our members. With respect to candidates for membership, we have experimented with a secret ballot, but even this failed to produce truly majority votings. An additional problem (one which the Secretariat cannot evade) is the prevalent feeling that certain decisions, especially ones concerning personal issues (*inyanim ishi'im*), do not reflect the opinion of most of the members of the community.

Explication: the Secretary announces the "problem of decision making and procedure in the General Assembly," and then proceeds to collapse this titular issue into two kinds of substantive questions, namely, "procedural questions" and "essential questions." This dichotomization of procedure and essence parallels that of means and ends or expediency and principle. Thus, the Secretary's example of a procedural question is the merely technical issue of the best hour to begin and end General Assembly meetings, while his example of an essential question is the principled matter of the very nature of direct democracy in a modern community. This dualistic definition of the problem is a critical feature of the whole debate.

The Secretary goes on to assert that the most difficult decisions relate to the problem of insufficient democratic turnout. Although he does not come right out and say so, in his appraisal of this problem as supremely difficult, it is implicit that he regards it as a matter of essence rather than procedure. In this connection his example of an "essential question" is instructive. The example queries the nature of a directly democratic assembly under "modern" circumstances. In other words, he is asking to what extent directly democratic participation is possible under socioeconomic conditions whose efficient operation demands the rationalized and differential knowledge associated with modernity. He thus tags the problem of participation as a matter of ends rather than means. In this fashion, the Secretary tacitly recommends against one kind of solution and justifies another to the problem in question. It stands to reason that a problem of principle requires a principled rather than merely procedural solution.

Indeed, as a matter of fact the Secretary offers explicit justification for rejecting one procedural solution in particular. He takes pains to point out that the rule of secret balloting, which had been employed on a trial basis, did not succeed in producing "truly majority votings." He thus furnishes empirical grounds for thinking that secret balloting cannot resolve the problem of participation.

The Secretary delineates yet another problem, namely, "a prevalent feeling" in the community that some of the General Assembly's decisions do not really "reflect the opinion of most of the members of the community." He airs this problem as an "additional" one, as if it and the problem of participation were related only by way of their common relevance to the titular issue of decision making and procedure in the General Assembly. To be sure, the relation between public opinion (the opinion of the members of the community in general) and public decision (the organized decision of the community) is logically independent of democratic participation. It is possible for public decision to "reflect" public opinion where democratic participation is incomplete and, given insincere voting, for public opinion and public decision to deviate the one from the other where participation is complete. But, as we shall see, for the advocates of secret balloting the perceived discrepancy between opinion and decision was not just another problem but rather the root of all problems. Again, then, the Secretary, whose job it was to open the issue, seems to define the situation to the benefit of those who oppose a secret ballot.

Alef:
>Various personal factors and social pressures prevent members from voting according to their conscience. The General Assembly cannot persist in a state of degeneration [*b'yerida*]. We can surmount this problem by employing a secret ballot for the following kinds of issues: personal issues such as the selecting of administrative incumbents, the selecting of members to pursue external studies, and the granting of leaves of absence from the kibbutz; financial issues which involve amounts exceeding 10,000 Lirot [at the time of fieldwork, about $3,300]; and issues concerning the release of members from work for four or more months.

Explication: Alef lays out two problems. First, that members are being prevented "from voting according to their conscience"; second, that the General Assembly is "in a state of degeneration." The first problem speaks for itself — it is a problem of "political freedom," and it corresponds to the problem raised by the Secretary of a gap between public decision and public opinion. The second problem is implicit in the first: in this radically democratic community, a lack of democratic freedom necessarily bespeaks "a state of degeneration." But in addition, in view of the nature of the debate, it is more than likely that in speaking of the General Assembly's degeneration, Alef has also in mind the fundamental problem of inadequate democratic participation. In other words, Alef's argument suggests that for the most part he regards the problem of participation as a function of the problem of political freedom.

Alef also asserts a cause of the problems. He says that members are prevented from voting as they see fit because of "various personal factors and social pressures." What he means by this is insinuated in the solution he offers for the General Assembly's ills.

Alef maintains that the problems can be eliminated by instituting a secret ballot for certain kinds of issues. He specifies three kinds, which, for our purposes, may be broken down into two: (1) issues involving relatively large sums of money; and (2) issues concerned with the distribution of office, favor, or advantage to particular individuals. As regards the first kind, presumably Alef thinks that such issues are too critical to be determined by an "insufficient number" of voters. Issues of this kind, bearing on the community's rationalized and sophisticated economic sector, recall the Secretary's query concerning the problematics of a need for professional knowledge in a direct democracy. It is not altogether clear to me why Alef believes that a secret ballot will ensure a sufficient number of voters on these issues.

The relation between the solution of secret balloting and the second kind of issues, those involving the distribution of advantage to particular individuals, is more transparent. It is decisions of this kind that the Secretary had in mind when he referred to "personal issues." Here it is implicit that members are unable to vote "according to their conscience" for fear of offending those individuals whose advantages and aspirations are at stake. Analytically speaking, by "personal factors and social pressures," Alef means the interpersonal forces consequent on multiplex relationships.

It can now be seen that implicit in Alef's argument is a pragmatic justification for the solution he offers. It is understood that one necessary condition for the operation of the "personal factors and social pressures" that prevent sincere voting is the open expression of the individual's political choice. Therefore, it stands to reason that voting secrecy will remedy the situation. Moreover, right behind this pragmatic endorsement of secret balloting is the ethical one that what is being eliminated by this procedure are the ideologically intolerable failings of impeded political freedom and "degenerated" democratic participation.

> Bet:
> I speak in virtue of a controversy both comprehensive and fundamental, a controversy that goes beyond any one practical question. I recommend that we do not get enthused over a secret ballot — we will not find in it a remedy. Particularly in a community such as ours is it necessary to pay heed to one's comrades, kinsmen, and neighbors. In addition, there is the consideration of damage [*nezek*] to the kibbutz, damage that already has gone too far; and I doubt that this damage can be dealt with through a secret ballot. The rule of secret balloting promotes formal organization. In a society based on force and duty, secret balloting provides a defense against compulsion; but to bring such a rule to the kibbutz, a free society, is unfitting — here secret balloting can serve only to bring about perverse voting [*hatzba'a m'uvetet*].

Explication: Bet speaks "in virtue of a controversy both comprehensive and fundamental," adding that the controversy transcends "any one practical question." The subject of the controversy is the problem of participation, and the "practical question" is that of secret balloting.

Although Bet does not indicate a cause of the problem, he makes very clear his position on secret balloting ("we will not find in it a remedy"). Furthermore, he is proligerous in justifying his rejection of voting secrecy.

In his very characterization of the problem, Bet adduces broad ideological reasons to reject a rule of secret balloting. By contrasting the problem's "comprehensive and fundamental" nature with the merely "practical" character of the solution of secret balloting, Bet, like the Secretary, marks the problem as demanding something more than a procedural palliative. In the same vein, Bet talks of "damage" to the kibbutz, a consideration that recalls Alef's notion of a "state of degeneration." But for Bet this damage is well beyond repair by a secret ballot, an appraisal that reiterates the characterization of this procedure as a response basically unequal to the problem at hand.

In addition, Bet cites two specific ways in which the solution of a secret ballot fails to grasp the principled dimensions of the issue. First, he declares that in a kibbutz there is an especial need to "pay heed to one's comrades, kinsmen, and neighbors." The ideological import of this assertion is redoubtable. Bet is reminding his comrades that in a community that is meant to be profoundly more than the sum of its parts, collective and universal rather than individual and particular interests ought to determine public policy; in the kibbutz, this is accomplished by means of an open ballot, which gives each person access to Everyman's political opinion.

Second, Bet asserts that secret balloting promotes "formal organization"; that in a society based on "force and duty" it combats "compulsion," but that in a "free society" it can only bring about "perverse voting." Clearly, these ideas presuppose a grand ideology. Briefly, though, by "formal organization" Bet has in mind that kind of rationalized, impersonal administrative structure that, at least in representative democracy, is detached or "alienated" from the source of its authority and is normally associated with constitutional government. In other words, he is referring to bureaucracy and the state, that is, to society based on "force and duty." Under such a regime, he argues, a secret ballot can protect the individual from intimidation ("compulsion") by authority. But in a "free society," he continues, a democracy where the source and the agent of authority are identical, a secret ballot promotes alienation and "perverse voting," by allowing individuals to detach themselves from one another and the social whole.

Gimel:
> Complaints about poor participation in the General Assembly are common to many kibbutzim — the problem is not peculiar to Timem. There are members who simply are not on speaking terms [*b'rog'zim*] with the kibbutz. The problem of poor participation has two sources: apathy [*adishut*] and a failure of communication among members, and both are symptomatic of the times [*m'simeni hador*]. Instituting a rule of secret balloting will do no good, since the members do not lack courage to come and vote when the issue touches on them directly. Therefore, we should continue with the present system. There are things to regret, but we need not make allowances for the apathetic and for those who do not take the trouble to come.

Explication: Gimel starts by acknowledging the problem of participation. But in pointing out that the problem is by no means confined to Timem, he seems concerned to soften its impact for the community. One reason for such concern rests with the solution he offers for the problem — leaving things as they are.

His observation that the problem of participation may be found in many kibbutzim is also tied in, though, with his causal grasp of the problem. He maintains that underlying the problem is that some "members...are not on speaking terms with the kibbutz," and that underlying this consideration are the two factors of "apathy" and "failure of communication among members." In regarding these factors as "signs of the time," he appears to imply that the problem has something to do with the stage at which the kibbutz has arrived in its evolution, and is therefore widespread in these collective communities.

Gimel then proceeds to argue against a secret ballot ("secret balloting will do no good") and to recommend another solution, namely, continuing "with the present system." His justification in this regard is twofold. First, he holds that in any case members come and vote when it is in their particular respective interests to do so ("when the issue touches on them directly"). Second, he admonishes that allowances should not be made for the apathetic. Here, he is concerned to find blame; he seems to be saying that what is needed is a change of heart rather than of rules. Moreover, as we shall see, his target in this regard is the category of young members.

Thus, the text of the argumentation yields a number of considerations.[2] But it is clear that the main discursive points center on the problem of poor participation and the proposed solution of secret balloting. The various causal assertions and statements of justification turn basically on these two matters. The ethically contrasting notions of expediency and principle, as well as the issue of political freedom, are especially salient in connection with the justification of a secret ballot.

Of course, low voter turnout and specialized expertise are commonplace social problems in large-scale democracies. Intuitively, though, it seems not surprising that in a communitarian democracy, such as the kibbutz, to which members commit the whole of their persons, problems of this kind become acutely trying. By bringing out in greater depth the ideological implications of the debate, the force of this intuition can be sharply clarified.

Ideological Context

Like Marxism, kibbutz socialism aims to set humankind free. In its deepest sense, the freedom in question is freedom from unnecessary necessity (see, for example, Marx in Bottomore and Rubel 1963: 260). The end is to afford human beings control over their own being by removing those external controls that by nature they are given to remove. The idea is to enlarge the human being's moral self by contracting his or her phenomenal being, or, more accurately, to bring about a definitive merger of the two. Insofar as the merger is wanting, which is to say, insofar as human beings' mental life remains inordinately subject to their material being, they are alienated from their own nature and from themselves: they are not free.

The antagonism between humankind and nature or humankind and itself may also be read as an antagonism between individuals (see Avineri 1968: 86ff.). Put another way, kibbutz socialism holds that human beings are naturally profoundly social, so that the radical merger of individual with individual is a necessary condition of liberation. Consequently, the kibbutz ideology, with Marxism, enjoins a comprehensive mutuality of individuals, whereby for lack of objective differentia, each person is positioned to identify with Everyman. Through the implementation of such a state of mutuality, the kibbutz aims to effect a radical synthesis between autonomous and heteronomous persons — that is, between the individual and society.

For Marx the fundamental precondition of such a merger was the collectivization of the means of production. The eradication of the political principle and, correlatively, the liberation of the moral life were meant to wait on the establishment of economic freedom. Here the kibbutz deviates sharply from Marx, for it makes no concession, historicist or otherwise, to the political principle. Although it follows Marx in regarding economic freedom or "self-labor" (*avodah atzmit*) as essential, the kibbutz is predicated equally on the principle of self-government or "voluntarism" (*voluntariut*), whereby each person is his or her own governor (see Buber 1949: esp. chap. 2). "In the kibbutz," one of Timem's members told me, "no one tells any one else what to do." In the language of Marx and Engels (1962: 61ff.), by forgoing any compulsion whatsoever, the kibbutz's socialism is "utopian." In this respect, as I will demonstrate directly in chapter 9, the kibbutz is more Rousseauian than Marxian.

Thus, in a very strict sense, the kibbutz's projected merger of the individual and society entails an absence of government. As it was put to me, "In the kibbutz there is no 'government' [*memshal*], there is just 'order and organization' [*mishtar v'irgun*]." Any form of government entailing control of some by others — control that is external to or alienated from the individual — is found repugnant. Thus, all forms of the state, including representative democracy, are rejected, since these entail centralization or relations of sub- and superordination. In effect, the kibbutz eschews "authority."

The kibbutz also eschews legal rules. Such rules are a concomitant of any system of autonomous authority; they serve to define that authority.[3] According to spokesmen of the kibbutz, "Kibbutz democracy...is not based on constitutional rules" (Rosner 1966: 352), and "kibbutz society has no fixed, written laws" (Amitai 1966: 93). Correlatively, the rejection of legal rules entails the exclusion of the organized sanctions that normally serve to back them. To quote the ideology: "There is no place in the kibbutz for any [formal?] system of reward or punishment" (Amitai 1966: 93). Finally, in the absence of legal rules and sanctions, there is no need for institutional means of their enforcement. In the literature of the kibbutz, Infield's observation is commonplace: "Since no institutional sanctions exist in the Kvutza [kibbutz], there are no courts, judges, fines, gaols, orders, titles, or promotions" (1946: 53). Indeed, more than one of Timem's members tried to impress upon me that, although the kibbutz is characterized by order and the absence of "crime," there is no police force in the community.[4]

The kibbutz objects to the rule of law for the very same reason liberalist society embraces it: it entails formal as opposed to substantive rules and justice.⁵ In representative government, rules that are fixed and known beforehand are required to prevent the executive organs from doing what they please, without regard to their constituents. To cite the classical exposition: the rule of law "means, in the first place, the absolute supremacy or predominance of regular law as opposed to the influence of arbitrary power, and excludes the existence of arbitrariness, of prerogative, or even of wide discretionary authority on the part of government" (Dicey, in Hayek 1962: 54, n. 1). But this governmental prophylactic involves a considerable cost, since "every law restricts individual freedom to some extent by altering the means which people may use in the pursuit of their aims" (Hayek 1962: 54). The kibbutz, in theory lacking representative authorities who might exercise arbitrary power, and also unwilling to compromise individual freedom, attempts to do without formal rules. In lieu of such rules, the kibbutz proposes to take each trouble-case as unique, on its own particular merits. One of Kibbutz Ha'artzi's leading ideologists has written:

> Detailed and all embracing regulations, defining everything in terms of obligations and rights, leave no room for group or individual initiative and is [sic] bound to lead to social degeneration.... Primary consideration must be given to the individual and not to the means, however important.... It is not so much... which consumer goods or services a member receives but the spirit in which these are given. A kind "no" very often gives more satisfaction than "the cold, dry and official 'yes.'" As important as efficient and good organization is for large multi-branch kibbutzim, efficiency cannot and must not be allowed to replace the direct social relationships — the "nourishment" of kibbutz life. (Chazan, in Viteles 1967: 350–51 — Viteles appears to have paraphrased)

The emphasis on a "personal" approach runs very deep; the preference for substantive over formal rules has powerful ideological implications. The rule of formal law entails the possibility of a breach between form and substance; it opens the way to the "merely formal" in the sense of "having the form without the spirit." Formal rules imply not only perfunctory, bureaucratic treatment, but also treatment that is devoid of any real substance. Marx seems to have had something of this sort in mind when he distinguished the freedom of capitalist society as formal rather than material, a freedom that applies in letter to the bourgeois and proletarian alike but in spirit only to the former (see Popper 1966: 2:123–24; also Bottomore and Rubel 1963: 255–56).

The kibbutz is keen to ensure that the freedom it grants its members is real and pertains to the substantive world of praxis. This concern is behind the following assertion by a kibbutz economist: "Kibbutz organization originates in custom rather than in law, in usual praxis rather than in a formal constitution" (Shatil 1966: 66). More directly, the Third Council of Kibbutz Ha'artzi, meeting in 1930, expounded: "The desire of democratization should not be satisfied with the formal rights [*zchuyot formaliot*] of equality" (quoted in *Sefer Timem*: 209). Through this commitment to the material realization of rights, or, in Marxian terms, to the unity of theory and practice, the kibbutz means to leave no room for the detachment of society from the individual.

To alienation and the rule of law, then, the kibbutz opposes a radical synthesis of the individual with society, and the rule of morality or self-government. In the realm of decision making, the principal mechanism of the kibbutz synthesis is direct democracy and the institution of the General Assembly. By incorporating all societal members directly as coequals, and by comprehending in principle all issues, the General Assembly ideally makes possible the rendering of social decisions without any cost whatsoever to the autonomy of the individual. As a consequence, there is no question of "external" authority, and no person is subject to the decision of another. From a somewhat different angle, there is no need for formal rules to protect the members from arbitrary decisions; since the supreme decision-making body directly comprises all the members, it could hardly make a decision against their interests. Even should an individual dissent from a collective decision, the question of authorized compulsion should not arise: "Since membership of the kibbutz is a voluntary act and each member is free to leave when he wishes, administrative coercion in securing submission to kibbutz decisions is obviated" (Rosner 1966: 352).

Still, even as a wholly comprehensive and voluntary institution, the General Assembly cannot ensure a complete merger of the individual and society, as mention of the possibility of an individual dissenting from a collective decision suggests. An aggregate of individual preferences does not necessarily yield a consistent social decision. Put another way, it is not always possible to factor a democratic decision so as to fit each component with a given individual.

This circumstance has been described in terms of the following paradox (see Wollheim 1962: 74–75; Murakami 1968: 71, chaps. 5, 6; Arrow 1967: 227ff.). Suppose a community must select democratically one of three policies — A, B, or C. Let us say that A gets 40 percent of the vote, B 35 percent, and C only 25 percent. Obviously, on a rule of simple majority voting (where plurality voting is excluded), A wins. But, as a matter of fact, those who choose B prefer C to A, and those who choose C prefer B to A. Clearly, then, the summation of individual decisions is problematic, for, although A wins, B and C are together preferred by 60 percent of the voters.

This paradox can be approached logically in a number of ways, none of which seems quite equal to the task (Murakami 1968: chaps. 5, 6). But we do not need to enter into this logical matter since all of these ways appear to give less than substantive consideration to the notion of the individual, whereas the kibbutz ideology, as we have seen, will entertain nothing but a substantive notion. In this regard, the ideology seems obliged to take into account not only the order of the individual's preferences (ordinality of preference), but also their intensity (cardinality of preference). A person's preference for A over B may be felt more or less keenly. However, whereas preference orders are subject to objective measurement by means of voting, it seems doubtful that preference intensities can be measured objectively (Murakami 1968: 116–18).

It is perhaps not surprising, therefore, that the kibbutz, again taking a decidedly Rousseauian turn, deals with the paradox of democracy by attempting to go beyond democracy, at least when democracy is defined classically as "the rule of the whole people expressing their sovereign will *by their votes*" (Lord Bryce, quoted in Murakami 1968: 28; emphasis added). "Voting and majority decisions," writes one of Kibbutz Artzi's social scientists, "are not considered sufficient. After a majority decision has been reached, there is still scope for further objections and the reopening of discussion" (Rosner 1966: 353). He continues, "The integrative process of the General Meeting is expressed by free discussion from all sides without a formal time limit. Agreement is often reached without the need for a formal vote" (1966: 359). A second ideological source reads:

> In some countries, like Switzerland (and in Ancient Greece), certain questions are decided by the people directly, in a referendum or plebiscite. But in these cases, the people can express its opinion only by saying "yes" or "no." In the general meeting of the kib-

butz, on the other hand, the important part is the discussion and the exchange of opinion, and very often things are so thrashed out during the discussion that there is no need to take a decision by vote. It might, therefore, be more correct to call the highest forum of the kibbutz a general discussion, rather than a general meeting (in which the participants express their opinion chiefly by vote). (Amitai 1966: 93)

Clearly, the kibbutz is not so much concerned with a summation of individual decisions as it is with a collective decision *sui generis*. This distinction sharply recalls Rousseau's between the "will of all" and the "general will":

> There is often a great deal of difference between the will of all and the general will; the latter considers only the common interest, while the former takes private interest into account, and is no more than a sum of particular wills: but take away from these same wills the pluses and minuses that cancel one another, and the general will remains as the sum of the differences. (1950: 26)

Compare this to the kibbutz's position:

> An attempt is made to find what is common to all the attitudes. Then members must try to work out a position which, in principle, expresses all positions.... The important part is not the actual vote, but the lessening of the differences between all the opinions and suggestions as much as is humanly possible. (Amitai 1966: 65)

I shall save for later (chaps. 6 and 9) further discussion of Rousseau's difficult concept of "general will." What needs to be understood here is that in deciding public affairs, the kibbutz enjoins a process of "political communion," and that it hopes to arrive at a form of general consensus that is regarded as somehow immanent in this fundamentally consociative process. It follows that the general consensus stands for an order of volition and interests that is thought to transcend the individual order. In view of this, it becomes clear that ultimately the kibbutz aims to effect its synthesis of the individual and society, not by the instrument of immediate democracy, but by means of a social compact.

The compact is this: for both rational and ethical reasons, the individual vows to subordinate his or her personal volition and interests to those of the general consensus or social whole. Thus, although "coercion in securing submission to kibbutz decisions is obviated," the individual is nevertheless obliged to submit. Rousseau commonly makes this point in the politico-theological terms of his day: "Each of us puts his person and all his power in common under the supreme direction of the general will" (for example, 1950: 15). The kibbutz, on the other hand, as befits its time and ethos, tends to keep to a more humanistic idiom. Though I heard much the same thing countless times in Timem, I quote from a formal account by a kibbutznik: "There are... various sources to [the] unity within kibbutz life.... The primary source can only be found in the *identification* of the member with the commune" (Leon 1964: 30).

Interpretation: Two Kinds of Freedom

It may now be grasped why Timem's problem of participation was regarded as "fundamental" and "comprehensive," and why it was linked directly with a "state of degeneration" and "damage to the kibbutz." The fact that public affairs were often formally decided by a minority of the members tended to belie the community's claim to substantive democracy and to ridicule its ideal of general consensus.[6] It strongly suggested that the source and the agent of authority had come apart, creating alienation and turning sour an axial political rite. Furthermore, poor participation implied a failure on the part of the members to honor their contractual responsibility for the social whole. In sum, the situation was ideologically indicative of a breakdown in the projected merger between the individual and society, and, therefore, of fundamental and comprehensive failure.

In turn, by contrast to the example of large-scale states and the problems of low voter turnout characteristic of them, the problem of participation in Timem threatened not only the operation of the democratic machinery but also the critical ideological claim to the status of "alternative society."

The problem of participation, once publicly exclaimed, must have been ideologically hard to bear. Doubtless, it was for this reason that the proposal of secret balloting was entertained at all. In fact one of the debaters stated outright that "the motion of a secret ballot should not even be aired as a public issue." The point is that, in view of the kibbutz's crucial stress on the general consensus and on public discussion as the means of reaching this consensus, it would have been hard to define secret balloting as anything but ideologically contrary. As Bet said, "Particularly in a community such as ours is it necessary to pay heed to one's comrades, kinsmen, and neighbors." Another of the debate's participants put it like this: the kibbutz's "most important foundation is open discussion [*hidabrut*] and mutual heedfulness [*hak'shava hadadit*].... We still need to guard over the opportunity for the open expression of conviction." As a deterrent to discursive communion, secret balloting was easily pictured as a direct threat to the collectivist order.

More specifically, by allowing members to keep from one another their political preferences, secret balloting would have exposed the community to determination by private, as opposed to public, interests. Whereas the community is focally predicated on the ideal of the collective or public trust, by definition a secret ballot is a modality of secrecy, that is, privacy.

Take, for example, one member's remark: "A man should not form his decision according to the opinion of his nagging wife." This may seem to contradict Bet's prescription about paying heed to "one's comrades, kinsmen, and neighbors," but, in fact, the two points are similar. In the latter case, it is urged that a member's political preference ought to be informed by others in their capacity as representatives of the social whole, as public persons. In the case of the "nagging wife," it is urged that in coming to a decision, a man should eschew the influence of others in their capacity as representatives of the personal sector, as private persons. That the idea of a nagging wife should be employed to call up the domain of personal interests is fitting to a Western communitarian ideology that has always shown fear of the strong, exclusive loyalties family ties can generate (see Talmon-Garber 1972: chap. 1).[7]

In addition to the dichotomy of private and public, the issue centered on the dichotomy of expediency and principle. Secret balloting was defined as a solution of expediency. Thus, the Secretary and Bet appeared to suggest, respectively, that a secret ballot was a "procedural" and a "practical" question. Of course, secret balloting is indeed a voting procedure. But there was much more to the definition than this.

The secret ballot was presented by its advocates as a practical way of dealing with the problem of participation — a relatively simple, efficient means of getting more members to participate in the making of public decisions. Recall that for Alef the solution of secret balloting was directly justifiable on the pragmatic ground that members were not voting because they feared the interpersonal consequences of the open expression of their opinions. A second advocate of secret balloting — while pressing that the most important problems the General Assembly presented were indeed "practical" — reiterated this point exactly. In other words, for these members it was a matter of adding two plus two — the solution of secret balloting was thought to follow simply in the pragmatic nature of the case.

By pointing out that on a trial basis secret balloting had "failed to produce truly majority votings," the Secretary combated this pragmatic rationale in its own terms. Moreover, the heaviest argument of those opposed to secret balloting did not depend on whether or not this solution really was efficient and practical, but rather on the notion that it had to be merely so. Thus, the Secretary did not simply label the question of a secret ballot "practical," but contrasted it to questions of "essence," while Bet held that, as "one practical question," secret balloting could scarcely meet a "comprehensive and fundamental" problem. Another debater, speaking of secret balloting as "institutionalized efficiency [*misud hay'ilut*] and the shortest path," made the point this way: "The immoderation of relationships in our community yields issues that demand an approach of circumspection and unhurriedness. Instead of this is set before us the intractable summons to objective adjudication [*hachra'a obyectivit*]."

The opponents of secret balloting, then, regarded this rule of voting as a practical or expedient measure in a pejorative sense — the sense in which expediency is opposed to principle and action proceeds without regard to right ends.

In associating secret balloting with "objective adjudication," the member was averring that a secret ballot wholly disregarded the kibbutz's premise of freedom, the ideological basis of the community. "Objective adjudication" was meant to call up the idea of bureaucratic organization, of decision making that is focused on correct procedure rather than just outcome. Put differently, by "objective," the member had in mind "external" — he was talking about alienation. In fact, he leaves no doubt about this interpretation. He concludes his argument this way: "Are we going to take the path of organizing toward alienation [*irgun hahitnakrut*], the goal that follows from the motion of voting secrecy, the path of organizing through unjust means in order to make decisions rapidly and in darkness — if so, then kibbutz life will be impossible."

Recall that Bet argued precisely the same point, using different words. He said that secret balloting "promotes formal organization," that it is appropriate to a society based on "force and duty," but that in a "free society" it can only lead to "perverse voting." In a discussion of ancient Rome, Rousseau captures ever so neatly what these members of Timem must have had in mind:

> As for the method of taking the vote, it was among the ancient Romans as simple as their morals.... Each man declared his vote aloud.... This custom was good as long as honesty was triumphant among the citizens, and each man was ashamed to vote publicly in favour of an unjust proposal or an unworthy subject; but, when the people grew corrupt and votes were bought, it was fitting that voting should be secret in order that purchasers might be restrained by mistrust, and rogues be given the means of not being traitors. (1950: 119–20)

Clearly, the opponents of secret balloting feared an influx of alienation and were ideologically concerned for the preservation of the kibbutz principle of freedom. But the advocates, too, invoked the principle of freedom. Although they were concerned to bring out the practical promise of their cause, at the back of this pragmatic validation stood a problem of political freedom. Members are prevented "from voting according to their conscience," is how Alef put it. A second advocate of the secret ballot elaborated on this theme, saying that it "is a fact that the member is not always free to vote according to his opinion" and that secret balloting "will give to the members a feeling of freedom (*hargashat chirut*) and will prevent the harm in relationships that results from the expression of individual opinion."

This was a serious problem, and the opposition could scarcely ignore it. Indeed, the Secretary felt compelled to introduce it. He said that the "prevalent feeling" of a discrepancy between opinion and decision in the community was a problem that "the Secretariat cannot evade." The problem was serious because, ironically, it directly implied that members were being prevented from engaging in the very process that the opponents of secret balloting held so dear, the process of political communion. Only, in this case the source of alienated constraint was not a matter of bureaucratic or legal machinery, but, in Alef's words, of "personal factors and social pressures." It was argued that the personal or private concerns and forces engendered by the community's social structure were making impossible the open expression of sincere political preference. This circumstance was, I should think, part of what was understood by the claim of "damage to the kibbutz," a claim the truth of which seemed to be taken for granted by all concerned.

Thus, the problem of inhibited political expression could not be readily ignored by the opposition. But since the opposition reasoned that secret balloting also threatened the kibbutz principle of freedom, they could not embrace this rule in solution. The best they could offer in response to it was the admonishment, made by Bet on one occasion, that members should not be afraid to vote as they see fit.

At this point, I can make clear that two different conceptions of freedom were involved. True, in pointing to a problem of constraint on the open expression of sincere political preference, the proponents of secret balloting invoked the same principle of freedom that the opposition held dear. But when it came to removing this constraint and restoring this freedom by means of the secret ballot, a different notion of freedom was introduced. That is to say, although both sides invoked the principle of freedom, the freedom that the one side claimed would be won by means of secret balloting cannot logically have been the same freedom that the other side claimed would be lost by this means.

From the standpoint of the kibbutz's organization of social roles, the rule of secret balloting affords members the freedom of formulating and expressing their political preference without regard to their public person or their various public roles within the community. By precluding the adversity that might follow from these roles upon the publication of political preference, secret balloting makes their political consideration optional. Under a secret ballot, a member may well take his decisions only according to the opinion of his "nagging wife" and other private concerns. In other words, secret balloting gives the individual freedom relative to the social whole.

This sense of freedom seems inimical to the kibbutz ideology. Yet it is positively blatant in the following quotation from the debate. The speaker, who was one of those keen to adopt secret balloting, seems a virtual heretic in light of the precepts of political communion and kibbutz holism. He stated, "The member should be free to choose which meetings of the General Assembly he wishes to attend and what issues he wants to take up. Such a choice testifies to a free General Assembly [*sicha chofshit*]. Members cannot and do not want to absorb all the questions that require resolution."

On the other hand, the rule of open-hand voting is geared precisely to make imprudent such role detachment. According to the ideology, the realization of freedom depends on the individual's identification with the social whole — that is, with his or her public person. As Bet said, in the kibbutz a person's political preference ought to be informed by his or her comrades (*chaverim*). Open-hand ballot tends to ensure that this will be the case. In effect, it affords the freedom that pertains to the individual in his or her capacity as a constituent of the social whole—according to Wetter (1958: 388), "the Marxist ideal of freedom." In less lofty terms, whereas secret balloting promotes the distribution of power in the interest of the individual as such, open balloting promotes the aggregation of power in the interest of the collective as such.

This circumstance, in which for the same cause (politico-ethical freedom), the members found themselves divided according to diametrically opposed senses of this cause, strongly suggests that the community was caught up in a paradoxical social state.

To sum up, the structure of the debate was cleanly bipolar. An open-hand ballot was associated with the public domain and collective autonomy, which were further associated with the rule of principle or morality. On the other hand, a secret ballot, despite its rhetorical linkage with an ideologically legitimate issue of political freedom, was defined in terms of the private domain, individual autonomy, and instrumentalism or the rule of expediency.

However, in the interest of getting the ideological dimensions of the debate clear, I have held back a crucial datum: to complicate matters further, the theme of generational conflict was introduced forcefully into this bipolar structure. As I will now make clear, the consideration of generational tension and the holding to account of the young, in contrast to the veteran, members are positively crucial meanings for the debate.

Four

Conflict between the Generations versus Social Differentiation: The Empirical Picture

Conflict between the Generations as an Explanation of the Situation

The Invoking of Conflict between the Generations

Generational conflict is a salient theme in the sociology of the kibbutz (see, for example, Talmon-Garber 1972: 32; Spiro 1965: 11ff.; Rosner 1982: chap. 8; Rosner et al. 1978; E. Cohen and Rosner 1983). Judging from my own field data, it is also a common focus of discussion and an oft-cited social problem within the kibbutzim themselves.

In the debate on secret balloting, two participants defined the problem expressly in terms of generational conflict. One expounded that "the kibbutz is built on different generations [*gilim*] and therefore on different mentalities." The other, echoing Gimel, said that there was "a lack of mutual understanding among the members," and then proceeded to tie this perception to the assertion that, in accounting for poor participation, the most important factor "is the feeling on the part of the youth [*hatz'irim*] that things are not being managed according to their ideas and that no one listens to their reflections and opinions."

In addition, one of the participants put it to me point blank that the issue of a secret ballot reduced to the fact of "two statuses, the young and the veterans [*vatikim*]." Although she did not air this position in the public forum, it was in fact implicit in her very participation in the debate. Whereas she spoke out vehemently on behalf of secret balloting, her father was one of those who inveighed against this solution. The Secretary later told me: "The conflict between Ester and her father was one of the highlights of the debate." Their contentious exchange must have constituted an iconic, and rather dramatic, representation of generational conflict as a basic source of the issues at debate.

The best evidence, though, that the debate and its issues were defined preeminently in terms of generational conflict is furnished by the events of the General Assembly's ad hoc meeting on the matter and the community's newspaper account of these. As the meeting got under way, the Secretary remarked to me that the discussion would not be successful, owing to the small attendance, and (by way of further explanation) that not one person under his age was present (he was a senior member of the second generation).[1] When one of the speakers offered the excuse that many members had gone that night to a wedding in a neighboring kibbutz, the Secretary further remarked to me that, as far as he was concerned, the reason the members had not attended was that they did not want to. Or, as he added in final explanation, "The young do not come because they are apathetic."

As was noted earlier, this meeting broke up for lack of participation. The community's newsletter reported (I assume the account was the Secretary's) that the meeting was made futile by "the absence of all the members of 'the east wing' of the dining hall." Now it so happens that, at meetings of the General Assembly, the east wing of the hall is customarily occupied by Timem's young members. Consequently, the newsletter was, simply, declaring the young members responsible for the meeting's miscarriage. But this charge tacitly conveyed a more expansive indictment.

The broad reason for the meeting's failure was precisely the problem the meeting had been called to consider — poor democratic participation. Therefore, by holding them accountable, the newspaper managed, by synecdoche, to lay at the feet of Timem's young members the overall problem of participation. Indeed, this abortive meeting must have constituted, at least in the minds of many of Timem's members, a rather timely demonstration of Gimel's thesis that the problem of participation was a matter of commitment rather than technique, and therefore required a change of heart rather than of rules. It is certainly the case that as a result of this meeting the motion of a secret ballot was evidently lost by default — no further action was taken on it at the time. It is likely that the abortive meeting so substantiated the argument of "commitment versus procedure" that the advocates of a secret ballot were left with little room for public maneuver.

In light of this interpretation, it would seem that when, in the debate, Gimel charged that some members "are not on speaking terms with the kibbutz," he was indicting especially the young members. And when he spoke of "apathy" in the kibbutz, he had in mind an affliction of especially the young members (a notion with which the Secretary fully concurred, as he made plain to me at the ad hoc meeting).

It should now be clear that the problem of participation and the remedial issue of a secret ballot became "officially" and, I venture, preeminently associated with Timem's young element. It must follow from this association that the generational dichotomy of young and veteran was fitted into the bipolar structure of the debate. Whereas in the public mind the veterans were linked with public interests and collective autonomy, and therefore with principle and morality, the young members were linked with private interests and individual autonomy, and therefore with expediency and immorality. The association of the world of immorality could not have been put in more graphic terms than those of a member who told me that the proposal of a secret ballot came from "the underworld" of the kibbutz.

The indications are that this definition was, in large part, accepted by all concerned, and not just by the opposition. I have already shown that, in justifying their cause, the advocates of secret balloting made no bones about the fact that they were employing a principle of expediency. They could scarcely have gotten round the fact that the rule of secret balloting entailed promotion of a kind of privacy. But even the charge that the young members were behind the problem of participation was not confined to the opposition. It was a major proponent of secret balloting, herself a member of Timem's second (in contradistinction to "founding") generation, who asserted to me that the whole of the debate reduced to the two statuses of young and veteran. It was also she who formally argued that members ought to "be free to choose" to participate as they like, thus espousing not only a kind of governmental privacy but also, in a way, the very state of democratic participation that was being designated a grave social problem.

I would also argue that, in a very deep and inevitable sense (which I will clarify in chap. 7), the young members acceded even to their implicit depiction as representatives of the world of immorality. But I do not want to risk overstating my case here. For, at this juncture, what needs to be made clear is that the essential question of the debate was precisely the moral one. Though the factual status of the young members' individualism, expediential approach, and even accountability was not actually contested, the ethical nature and basis of these phenomena were entirely at point. Put another way, the debate was less about the facts than the light in which to judge them. To be sure, the problem of participation and the motion of secret balloting occasioned the debate, but the question on which the debate turned comprehensively was that of whether or not more individual autonomy was in the public interest and both right and good—that is, moral.

A question of this kind is not of facts; neither, though, is it entirely of words (see Evens 1978). That is to say, although a satisfactory solution cannot be determined by appeal to the facts, such a solution is also beyond arbitrary definition. To such a question one does not respond, "I shall call this moral," as to a merely verbal question one responds, "I shall call this the theory of X." For the kind of question at issue, people demand a carefully deliberated answer. The ground for this demand is that heavy, lived consequences depend on the answer.

In the case at hand, the consequences were peculiarly heavy. In view of the definition of the situation in terms of generational schism, on the question of the ethical definition of "more individual autonomy" hung the moral, and therefore social, identities of two universal categories of persons in the kibbutz—the veterans and the young.

It is all the more remarkable, then, that, despite the prevailing understanding in Timem, in fact the debate was simply not reducible to these two categories.

The Empirical Validity of Conflict between the Generations

In 1966 Timem's membership (excluding candidates for membership) broke down, by fifteen-year age divisions, as follows: 109 (39.5 percent) between the ages of 19 and 35; 56 (20.3 percent) between the ages of 36 and 50; and 111 (40.2 percent) between the ages of 51 and 70. By the criterion of age alone, then, Timem's population showed a broad bias toward an old/young dichotomization. (The abnormal character of the distribution reflects primarily the facts that during Timem's early years the members were highly homogeneous as regards age, and the rate of birth was quite low.)

In point of fact, there is a significant and peculiar sense in which Timem's categories of "veteran" and "youth" respectively represent different, and even opposed, experiential worlds. I suspect that, if I had polled Timem's population on the issue of secret balloting, by and large the young members would have gone pro and the veterans contra. But "by and large" leaves room for exceptions, and, for empirical purposes, the exceptions can be crucial.

Although it is true that in the debate the two main opponents of a secret ballot were veterans while the two main advocates were young members, it is also the case that the Secretary, whose presentation of the issues was distinctly biased against secret balloting, was a member of Timem's second generation. Moreover, yet another member of Timem's second generation told me that he was dead set against secret balloting (because, as he said, "It would inhibit open discussion"), while, on the same occasion, his father-in-law, a veritable founder of Timem, opined that the rule ought to be instituted. Of course, a few contrary instances might be subject to interpretation as exceptions that prove the rule. But, bearing in mind that I came by these exceptions by chance, they give reason to think that under systematic inquiry others would have surfaced.

However, as regards the problem of participation, I can offer some statistical evidence that it was decidedly not reducible to a matter of generations. Despite the fact that the young were generally given the blame for the poor attendance at general assemblies and seemed to take it, my data indicate that this picture of accountability is significantly misleading. Over 29 meetings of the General Assembly at different times of the year, the average (mean) attendance was 80 (about 28 percent), with a low of 54 and high of 113. Of these 80, in absolute figures, the average number of veteran and young attendants was identical at 25. Since at the time there were 92 "veterans" and 90 "young" members (ignoring for the moment how I determined these categories), this means that on the average some 27 percent of the veterans were attending the meetings, as compared to some 25 percent of the young.

Now, I do not claim that these statistics are anything but crude. For example, should we add to the young element the forty candidates for membership at the time, the participation of this element would then come to about 18 percent only. (I did not include the candidates because, although they are permitted to attend the meetings of the General Assembly, they are neither expected to speak up nor allowed to vote.) In addition, the precision of my information suffered because people came and went at these meetings; there was sometimes a sizable number of members (always young) listening at the open door of the meeting hall; and, on the average, I failed to identify nine attendants per meeting. But, should we grant a relatively large error on my part, the generational account of things would still leave much to be desired.

For the sake of argument, let us say that, on the average as much as 36 percent of the veterans and only 18 percent of the young members were attending the meetings. This would mean that if, so as to bring it up to par with that of the veterans, we doubled the percentage of young members, we would be talking about, at most, an additional eighteen democratic participants — certainly not a sufficient amount to dissipate the so-called problem of participation. We would still need to inquire about the democratic commitment of the relatively many veterans (64 percent) that, on the average, failed to participate.[2]

However, when it comes to speaking up at meetings, there is no question that the young members were substantially less active than the veterans. My data (pertaining now to twenty-one meetings) indicate that the veterans do at least twice as much talking at general assemblies than do the young (cf. E. Cohen 1968: 29). In view of the ideology's great emphasis on political dialogue, this conspicuous circumstance must have generated — as was apparent with respect to the abortive meeting on secret balloting — a feeling about the young, that they were affectively indifferent.

Still, in addition to the considerations of attendance and verbal participation, there is the matter of voting. The degree to which people speak up at meetings was by no means a reliable indicator of the number of persons who actually vote. Although votings were by open ballot, in the time it took for the "presiding member" (*yoshev rosh*) to count hands, I could identify but a few of the voters. It is my impression that, like all the members, the young members voted considerably more often than they spoke up. Furthermore, even more so than the data on attendance, the data on votings oblige one to ask about the nonparticipation of others apart from the young. For twenty-two votings from as many meetings throughout the year, the average number of voters was forty (with a high of seventy-seven and a low of twenty-five) — exactly half the average number of attendants.[3] Obviously, not only young members were abstaining.

However, perhaps the argument that does most to bring into relief the empirical inadequacy of explaining the situation primarily in terms of generational conflict is not statistical at all. Rather, it is an argument that undermines the very possibility of a decisive statistical accounting. I have in mind the fact that the categories "first generation" and "second generation" are situationally indeterminate, not only for the analyst but, in the first place, for Timem's members. In other words, at least in many contexts of everyday use, these categorical designations are employed by the members most imprecisely and lack a set of criteria that can determine unambiguously who belongs to which category. Insofar as the categories are substantively indeterminate, it must follow that a statistical accounting of them is constitutionally perplexed, and their employment as objects of accountability is materially suspect.

To be sure, one can sociologically operationalize these categories. Thus Erik Cohen (1968: 6) speaks of his particular division, by subgroups, of the kibbutz population as "the most economical way to approach the inner division within a kibbutz, and to study the systematic differences between its members." But the fact that for certain sociological purposes such a division may be "economical" does not necessarily mean that it actually divides with a fine cutting edge or, more importantly, that it is phenomenologically veridical, as Cohen reluctantly acknowledges (1968: 6).

For instance, Cohen defines the first generation of members as comprising "both [the] founders and [the] later joiners" (1968: 5). By "later joiners," Cohen intends the members who joined a kibbutz after its founding but before the kibbutz produced its own "children" as members. I am led to wonder, for one thing, just how much later can a "later joiner" join before she or he is regarded as a second- rather than first-generation member. This may seem a hair-splitting ambiguity, but such ambiguities can (and do) count for much in the everyday social life of the kibbutz. Certainly in Timem, many of the "later joiners" who, in the minds of both researchers and kibbutz members, fall into the first generation for sociological purposes, do not so fall, at least not unequivocally, for all lived purposes in the community's everyday social consciousness.

In everyday contexts, when speaking in terms of generations, Timem's members commonly used "the young" (*hatz'irim*) and "the veterans" (*havatikim*). Sometimes, in place of the latter, they used "the adults" (*ham'vugarim*) or even "the old" (*haz'keinim*). These terms are conspicuously imprecise. When adducing my statistical evidence earlier, I had the task of determining, for those present at the various meetings, who was a veteran and who a young member. For many persons I found myself unsure. In respect of the young, despite some doubtful instances, I drew on my general knowledge of whether the person had been born in Timem and/or raised there from an early age (criteria similar to those employed by Cohen to define the second generation). In respect of the veterans, I took recourse to my census cards, where the veterans were identified as such.

Now, of course, having the identifications so recorded gives them an air of objectivity. But I got these identifications originally by going through the cards with two informants, both born and raised in Timem, and asking them to identify the members accordingly. Although in a few cases the informants were themselves uncertain about veteraneity (and other attributes), by and large they identified as veterans all the founders plus those members who joined soon after the community was established (in 1930), but nothing like all of the "later joiners."

Another second-generation member explained to me: "The veterans were veterans when they were thirty years old; veteraneity has nothing to do with how old they are now. Take David. He is fifty years old. But he is still a 'young member' [*tza'ir*]. He joined the kibbutz with Yosef's and Hillel's group, which came some ten years after Timem got started. Yosef and Hillel are not veterans — they are 'young members' [*tz'irim*]." Indeed, I was told by one of those members who did come just after Timem's establishment, and who was labeled a "veteran" by my two census informants, that he was not a veteran because he arrived "some four years after the founders, and those four years make an ineradicable difference."

Similarly, the consideration of time of arrival can make it difficult to determine the category of second-generation members. Up to what age must a youth come to Timem and its educational system before she or he may no longer be regarded as a member of the second generation? Nor is simple time of arrival the sole ground of ambiguity in these matters. What about the status of members who came with the founders but left, only to return at a later date?[4] What about members who were veterans of another kibbutz but took up membership in Timem in recent years? Of which generation are youths who were raised in another kibbutz but, through marriage perhaps, have come to Timem?

My point is not that Timem's members cannot for some practical purposes be unambiguously placed in generational categories, but rather that the accomplishment of this task entails patchwork or ad hoc tactics (see Garfinkel 1967: 96ff.). For the members are substantially marked by differences that in everyday social contexts make differences and that are anomalous from the standpoint of well-defined generational categories. Correlatively, my point is also that, from the perspective of rigorous empiricism, when they employ the generational categories of "young" and "veteran" as if these denote well-defined politico-moral blocs of people, Timem's members are talking, though not wholly unsubstantially, at least loosely. Though it no doubt carried deep rhetorical conviction, the assertion that the matters of democratic participation and secret balloting boiled down plainly and simply to the two statuses of "young" and "old" was hardly an empirically adequate account.

What, then, are the general empirical conditions behind the state of democratic participation found so disturbing by Timem's members?

Heterogenization: Social Differentiation and the Self

When Timem was founded in its present location, its membership was small (about seventy souls) and relatively homogeneous as regards age (most members were between twenty and thirty years old) and ethnicity (most, if not all, were from Poland). At that time, many of the members were still unmarried, and few had children. Family, then, could not yet have served as a significant principle of internal differentiation.

At the time of fieldwork, however, Timem had a population of about six hundred and a membership of about three hundred.[5] In addition to the "standard" principles of age, sex, family, and generation, the members were internally differentiated by the following factors: (1) joining group; (2) age-peer group (kibbutz children are raised in *k'vutzot,* or small, named groups of age peers); (3) ethnicity (ethnic backgrounds include Polish, Rumanian, Czechoslovakian, Yugoslavian, German, Israeli, as well as, to a very small extent, Iranian and American); (4) occupation and/or administrative position (Timem's economy and administration are highly specialized); (5) type and extent of formal education; (6) friendship network (as characterized by visiting and exchanges of goods, favors, and information); (7) neighborhood (there are five residential areas, each marked by a different type of housing); and (8) external ties (links outside Timem). Should we add to these factors, where appropriate, the temporal depth implicit in the principles of age and generation, their capacity to differentiate is greatly amplified. Members were differentiable not only by their current job, friends, neighborhood, and so on, but also by their past ones.

From the perspective of its own nascent state, therefore, Timem's population had become relatively large and heterogeneous. Needless to say, just as in large-scale societies, this development must have been consequential for Timem's social life and, more particularly, for the relationship between the individual and society. To fix ideas broadly, we can use Durkheim's bipolar modes of solidarity as ideal types that delimit an empirical continuum. We can do so provocatively, despite the fact that Durkheim's famous theory was forged with the evolution of civilization in mind. We might well say that Timem had moved from a relatively mechanical toward a more organic solidarity—that is to say, it had moved from a solidarity based on the palpable alikeness of the members' respective structural identities to a solidarity based less on alikeness and more on alignment of these identities. Put differently, taking a hint from Georg Simmel on the "significance of numbers for social life" (in Wolff 1950: 87ff.), as Timem became larger and more internally diverse, the individual members became more abstract and therefore less surveyable to the collective, and vice versa.

Thus, the community's history virtually amounts to an elaboration of the individual defined in terms of structural interests that appear somehow separate and distinct from those of the collective. The result is increasing attention to individuals in terms of their personal rather than social identity, that is, the identity-featuring attributes that define each person in his or her uniqueness. These attributes (personal style, special position, biographical dossier, and so on) differentiate members as individuals, by contrast to the attributes that define them in terms of a particular category of person (male, white, Jewish, Polish, and so on).[6] The attention given to personal identity corresponds and testifies to the play of personal rather than collective interests in Timem's social life. By the same token, as is suggested by Talmon-Garber's important analysis of the attenuation of the ascetic ideal in the kibbutz (Talmon-Garber 1972: chap. 8), the more individuals are defined and define themselves by such interests, the more inclined they are to protect them. Insofar as such interests integrally bear on and constitute the individual's self, that is, insofar as each member identifies with them, the individual may be said to have a comprehensive and impelling "interest" in them.

Though as much rhetorically as descriptively, Timem's members often spoke of this progressive separation of the individual and the collective. As one might expect, they did so in the same idiom in which they talk about the projected merger of the two, the idiom of identification: I heard time and again in Timem that the basic ill of the community was an increasing failure of the members to identify with the social whole.

As I see it, the relative heterogenization of Timem prompted increasing differentiation of social identities and the correlative elaboration of personal ones. In turn, this process led to the development of a conspicuous rift between self and society.

The Uncoupling of the Social System from the Lifeworld

In order to evoke the sociological character of the heterogenization of Timem's population, I mentioned Durkheim's famous evolutionary account of the division of labor in society as well as Simmel's observations on the effects of numerical growth on the relation between the individual and society. For a fuller description, I turn to a recent grand theory of social differentiation, namely, that of Jürgen Habermas (1987). This theory's advanced sociological and phenomenological sophistication makes it a very useful vehicle for picturing more sharply the course of Timem's development, even if, as I will feature in the next section, there is something fundamentally misleading about the picture, something that must not be overlooked. In the final two sections of this chapter, I adduce further empirical evidence of the picture's penetrating power to describe Timem's social situation (notwithstanding the way in which the picture can mislead).

Habermas understands the shift from mechanical to organic solidarity in terms of the increasing differentiation of the social system, on the one hand, and of the lifeworld, on the other. Social system and lifeworld are the two constitutive aspects of society. The former describes society from the point of view of the systemic interconnection of functions, whereas the latter describes it from the perspective of the way in which actors' orientations fit together. In other words, the social system is a matter of the nonnormative integration of society, the integration that has to do with unintended consequences. By contrast, the lifeworld is keyed by the normative integration that follows from communicative or consensual interaction. According to Habermas, as the lifeworld becomes increasingly rationalized, that is to say, differentiated into forms of self, so the social system grows in complexity. What is more, this process entails not only the internal differentiation of each of these two aspects of society but also, and crucially, the differentiation of each from the other — or, as he says, their "uncoupling."

In good part, Timem's social evolution is readily described in terms of Habermas's theoretical framework. The introduction of new principles of social differentiation, and the material enhancement of the old, produced in Timem a systemic integration of increasing complexity. As a result of the growth and heterogenization of Timem's membership, there was a proliferation of social and politico-economic functions. These functions required for their satisfactory discharge the establishment of new organizational institutions and expansion of the old. Thus, the community's economy and polity became increasingly specialized. Such specialization demanded the creation of new roles and the introduction of technical knowledge.

For example, the addition of a factory to Timem's economy required the services of an accountant as well as of industrial engineers. In turn, growth of this kind served to promote the internal differentiation of the Economic Committee, the administrative organ responsible for overseeing Timem's overall economy. Or, take the communal dining hall (*chadar haochel*), a materially and symbolically central institution. Obviously, with growth, the efficient operation of this institution became more demanding. The feeding of several hundred people required specially trained cook-administrators, who know how to plan and supply such large meals. The kitchen itself had to be mechanically equipped for the task. At the time of fieldwork, Timem had installed for the first time an automatic dishwasher suitable to the needs of a cafeteria. With this innovation, members cleared their own dishes, placing them on a conveyor belt, whereas before, the dishes were cleared by members on dining-hall duty. (Many members complained to me that they missed the "family-like atmosphere" of the prior setup.) Or, as the children of the kibbutz grew in number, the community had to create new institutions to cope with their schooling and care — for example, a children's dining hall. Or again, as the generations advanced, the community was forced to acknowledge the political implications of this structural condition, by dividing the office of the Secretary into an older and a younger incumbency — this occurred for the first time during my research.

The endeavor to institute secret balloting was, plainly, another step in the march of differentiation. As especially its opponents were keen to emphasize, the motion of a secret ballot implied the rationalization of the voting procedures, such that Timem's democracy could have operated efficiently even were the goal of normative consensus abandoned. That is to say, the motion threatened to make instrumental success ("expediency") *rather than* moral integration ("principle") the chief goal of the community's democratic process, thus featuring a rift between the social system and the lifeworld.

As Timem's social system underwent internal differentiation, so the community's lifeworld revealed an elaboration of structures of consciousness. As I asserted above, the introduction and material development of principles of social differentiation served to promote in Timem an emphasis on personal distinction. What I wish to emphasize at this point is that by making the members increasingly different from one another, heterogenization also marked such difference for the individual. In so doing, it alerted individuals to the difference between themselves and the collective. In effect, growth and heterogenization moved individuals to distinguish more sharply between themselves as individuals and as members of the community.

This development of the lifeworld bespeaks an uncoupling of the lifeworld from the social system. The member's increasing attention to his or her own individuality entailed the differentiation of the collective as a system in its own right. The sharp differentiation in the lifeworld of self and society tended to render the self as a special domain: the subjective domain of consciousness and reflective activity, as opposed to the objective one of institutional and mechanical functions. As a consequence, the self, in its personal mode, came to grasp itself as the sole sensible mediator of what happens. By the same token, though, society was made to appear as external to the self, giving the social system more room to maneuver separately from the explicit intentionality of the individual member. That is to say, being detached from the member's sense of her or his own autonomy, the social system of the kibbutz was in a certain sense left more and more to run in terms of its own institutional devices. By definition, these devices are keyed to efficient integration, making them matters of instrumentality and power.

The uncoupling of the lifeworld from the social system was not simply a question of the members' perception; the members' reappraisal of the concrete relationship between self and society in Timem helped to make the situation so. As worried both sides of the debate, there was indeed less moral input and more systemic output than had been the case. The failure of democratic participation meant that in fact the degree to which the social system was operating without regard to normative consensus, according to its own functional ends, had increased.

From the standpoint of the individual member, the social system came to look and feel like an imposition. Thus members were moved to propose the ideologically suspect step of changing the voting rule to secret balloting, ensuring that the individual's political preference is protected from the collective scrutiny, and, as I document in chapter 6, they came also to interpret the relationship between the individual member and the social whole more generally as one of growing distrust. No wonder the difference between the individual and the collective had become irrepressibly politically charged. Furthermore, this difference stood not only between the individual and the social whole but also between one individual and another as well as between the individual and her- or himself. Precisely because the social whole was in principle identifiable with the individual, the falling out between the two represented a falling out among individuals as such. By the same token, it defined the individual's self as divided between itself as such and as a member of society.[7] As a result, the redefinition of the relationship between the individual and the collective as strategic, came to define social relationships in general, including the relationship of the self. The members were increasingly inclined to interpret themselves and their interaction in terms of prudence, indifference, intimidation, influence, power, and corruption.

Given the kibbutz's synthetic ideal, the process of uncoupling was hard to bear, creating a crisis of legitimacy. Weak democratic participation implied that the members had departed significantly from self-governance. The source of community authority could no longer be readily regarded as the individual in his or her capacity as member; instead it emerged as the social system in its own right, an order of functional rather than normative integration. The change amounted to a relative shift from government by moral consensus, determined through directly democratic means, to government by formal procedural rules and regulations, directed by instrumental design. The sought-after synthesis between the individual member and the social whole had to be construed as giving way. Hence, the proponents of secret balloting argued that the social system was already, at least in fact, exercising undue control over the individual, while the opposition sought to make plain that secret balloting could serve only to institutionalize the uncoupling it was introduced to obviate. The effort to institute secret balloting was resisted precisely because it sprung from and served to articulate the fact of uncoupling.

The Modern Self as a Founding Feature of the Kibbutz

For all its instructive correspondence, though, the picture of Timem's evolution as recapitulating the path, traced by Habermas (and, for that matter, Durkheim, Toennies, Weber, and others), of societal evolution from archaic to modern, is significantly misleading. For, in fact, an acute, even radical, sense of social differentiation characterized Timem's lifeworld right from the start. The kibbutz project is very well construed as an extraordinary movement to remedy the condition denoted by Habermas's concept of uncoupling. The projection of a synthesis of the individual and society, a synthesis based on direct democracy and moral consensus, is aimed squarely at healing the existential wound to the body-social and body-psychological caused by the removal of the social system from its moral foundations and the correlative instrumentalization of the lifeworld.

By itself heterogenization cannot ensure the development of acutely personal selves. In the absence of an already existing sense of oneself as an autonomous person, an inner, reflexive being, the distinguishing marks made by the process of heterogenization may go, like the sounds of an unfamiliar language, undiscriminated by oneself. In point of fact, however, Timem started out with a keen, modern awareness of the difference between self and society, which makes it easy to understand how the heterogenization of the community brought about a significant material realization of this difference in the community's social life.[8]

For reasons of a relatively small and homogeneous population, in the beginning Timem was able to present an impressive synthesis of the lifeworld and the social system, simulating an archaic or premodern union of the two. But as the community grew larger and more heterogeneous, so this presentation of self became harder to accomplish and sustain. Given the ideological availability of a radical split between the individual and society, the ubiquitous principles of age, gender, and so on, plus the historically more particular principles that were introduced (neighborhood, joining group, and so on), were granted a foothold as instruments of differentiation they would not otherwise have enjoyed. The capacity of these principles to differentiate was given full sway by the radical construction of the difference against which the kibbutz was set up. An acute sense of self was able to elaborate its distinction by virtue of these various principles, constructing itself with strong particular interests that departed from those of the collective.[9]

In fact, the elaboration of the self as against the collectivity was positively promoted by the synthesis the kibbutz hoped to effect between the individual and society. The projected synthesis is based squarely on voluntarism, and it therefore depends on the presence of a strong sense of oneself as an autonomous agent. In the absence of such a sense, the synthesis, as a remedial measure to the uncoupling of instrumentality from moral assent, would scarcely be meaningful. In this way, as I will elaborate in remaining chapters of this volume, the kibbutz synthesis projected its own failure.

Heterogenization and the Problem of Democratic Participation

I am proposing that an empirically adequate explanation of the state of participation in Timem's general assemblies must center on the heterogenization of the community, whereby exclusive selves and personal interests are structurally grounded. It stands to reason that strong personal interests will occasion affective neutrality and abstention from speaking out and from voting openly. For where such interests obtain, any particular member is given good reason to regard some public issues as too "irrelevant" to command his or her attention and others as far too "relevant" to permit him or her to express political preferences openly. The structural elaboration of one's identity as a matter of one's own person impels one to interpret issues overridingly in terms of personal consequentiality. Under these conditions, the only issues that are bound to enjoy a collective, in contrast to merely institutional, relevance are issues that are perceived to affect directly the possibility and security of everyone's personal identity.

Though the amplification of personal identities has received no great emphasis in the sociology of these communities, a thesis concerning a correlation between internal diversity and the state of democratic participation in the kibbutz is by no means new. Cohen speaks of such a thesis as "widely accepted," and both he and Menachem Rosner (a kibbutz sociologist as well as member) have put it to the test (E. Cohen 1968: 3–5; Rosner 1966).

Both scholars find, to use Cohen's words, "that...growth and complexity did *not* essentially impair the workings of kibbutz democracy" (1968: 93ff.). I, too, found that Timem's democratic institutions continue to "work." However, at this juncture my primary concern is not with whether or not these institutions were "essentially impaired," but rather with why they worked as they did. In this regard, I am arguing that the state of democratic participation in Timem's general assemblies, *such as it was,* was in fundamental respects a function of heterogenization.

Moreover, this thesis, when it is informed by the theme of the development of personal interests and exclusive selves, is commonly aired or insinuated in everyday contexts of kibbutz social life. Thus, to recall the Secretary's presentation during the debate, he put the whole matter in the context of a "modern community." He had in mind, of course, a community marked by social diversification and functional specialization and by specialized or, as he stated, "professional" knowledge. Another member observed that "members cannot and do not want to absorb" all public affairs and that they ought to be "free" to attend according to their own interests. Gimel, too, pointed out that, in any case, members come and vote "when the issue touches on them directly," that is, when it is in their own particular interest.

It is a fact that members who normally kept away from meetings could be seen attending some meetings for specific issues. It is also a fact that (as I observed on those occasions when I too failed to go to a meeting of the General Assembly), while meetings were taking place, the nonattendants were engaged in such personal pursuits as hobbies, sports, private parties, and, especially, interpersonal visiting.

To many members it must have seemed anomalous for anyone to have an interest sufficiently broad to impel regular and frequent attendance at General Assembly meetings. Owing to my research, I had such an interest, which made me a target for jokes. For example, just before the convening of one general assembly, a veteran member quipped to me and those sitting nearby that, in view of my assiduous attendance, I was the "most stable member of the community." I protested that certain others attended the meetings regularly — to which he replied by pointing to the Secretary and saying, "Yes, but he has no choice."

In addition to attendance, there are also the considerations of voting and verbal passivity at meetings. Here, again, members made clear, in so many words, that often they choose not to vote or not to say something because personal interests are at stake. As one member observed, "One cannot vote against a candidate for some position or other, because perhaps this fellow's wife minds [is the *m'tapelet* of] my children." Another commented, "In the kibbutz one must be careful to maintain good relations with everyone, since one never knows when one will be forced to rely on someone or other." Still another found, "Because voting is open-hand, it is very unpleasant to vote against someone in a general assembly," and he recounted, talking about one of his fellows, "Once he broke down and started crying in the meeting, it was too unpleasant to vote against him."

These sentiments testify that some abstentions are questions, not of political indifference, but of fear of interpersonal repercussions. To recall Alef, these abstentions have to do with "personal factors and social pressures."

The way in which revotings could sharply reverse a decision, by stimulating a number of persons to vote who had abstained in the initial balloting, lends support to this analysis. It would seem that, upon seeing that things had not gone according to his or her actual preference in the first balloting, a member who had abstained may find it necessary, in order to ensure the political decision of his or her choice, to stand up and be counted — that is, in the second balloting, to show his or her hand and forgo interpersonal prudence. For example, to cite a very dramatic case, one member's wish to take a spouse from outside Timem was put to the vote of the General Assembly, inasmuch as he was stigmatized (as "mentally retarded") and wanted to start his own family in the community. After winning the first voting by a margin of one, this member's father, hoping to cement the victory and preclude the possibility of anyone questioning the decision, called for a revote. As a result, however, the vote was sharply reversed (Evens 1975).

Given an apparent basis for political intimidation, such as current or potential interdependence in respect of personal interests, where one cannot control the publicization of how one votes, one is liable to feel threatened whether or not one actually is (see Schelling 1960: 148). For one's own sense of oneself as a self, a well-developed inner being, entails the understanding that one can appear to be other than what one is, that one's private self need not correspond to one's public appearance. In turn, this self-understanding gives one to picture others as enjoying the same capacity for dissimulation, and therefore as threatening. Although I gathered few details in this regard, I learned that Timem does not lack for strong interpersonal enmities, some of which go back to the community's beginnings, and which had been engendered by the open expression of political preferences. Members can well recall for a lifetime who had voted or spoken against them on such vital concerns as, for example, their request for training in a particular career or, after having left the community, for reentry. Moreover, unlike some collectivist orders,[10] the kibbutz appears to have no regular, ritualized way of expurgating such tensions. Hence, in the kibbutz, voting abstentions are just as likely to reflect prudence as they are neutrality or disconcern.

Similarly, members often refrained from speaking up for fear of offending someone and/or risking their own respective interests. Comments of the following sort evince this fear: "It has happened that, during a general assembly, the Secretary has refused to disclose certain pertinent information on a problem"; "Uri's labor branch voted against his becoming Treasurer of the kibbutz, not because they really were concerned about the loss of his services to the branch, but because it would not have been pleasant if they had readily admitted they didn't care"; "Sometimes in the General Assembly someone will do some soul-searching on someone else's soul, which can be extremely unpleasant"; "In the General Assembly it is often not possible to put your cards on the table"; and the like. The crucial consideration appears to be the acute vulnerability of exclusive selves and personal interests in the context of a collectivist social order.

Personal Issues

The most incisive evidence in this connection pertains to the kibbutz notion of "personal issues" (*inyanim ishi'im*). Recall that Aleph recommended a secret ballot especially for deciding on candidates for administrative positions, external studies, and leaves of absence; he called such decisions personal issues. In fact, Aleph was not the only participant of the debate to single out such issues. Their problematical character is pointed in the following presentation from the debate (as are tacit theses of heterogenization and uncoupling):

> The core of the problem of participation is that over the years the form of the General Assembly has not developed, while the kibbutz itself has developed by leaps and bounds. The General Assembly still concerns itself with issues the likes of which it dealt with many years ago; there is need to allocate the care of these issues to other institutions (committees and administrative roles) and to bestow on these latter the authority necessary to deal with them. It is necessary to work toward a system wherein the General Assembly handles only concerns that pertain to the entirety of the public.

The argument is keyed by the idea of "concerns that pertain to the entirety of the public" (*inyanim hanog'im l'tzibur kulo*). Evidently this debater thinks that all issues that do not bear immediately on the social whole, which is to say, all less-than-public, which is to say, "private" or "personal" issues, should no longer be dealt with by the General Assembly but by lesser decision-making bodies.

"Personal issues" is not a precise notion. Nevertheless, a broad and basic meaning was evident. Any issue that directly bears on a member in his or her particularity — that is, as a personal identity — can be counted as a personal issue. Put differently, a personal issue is one that demands for its reasonable and proper resolution knowledge about some member's personal attributes and interests.

That all internal events be, at least ultimately, matters of public determination is a basic content of the kibbutz ideology. The same organicist principle of holism that describes kibbutz democracy as immediate, plenary, and consensual characterizes it also as jurisdictionally comprehensive. The principle of holism entails no mere aggregation of quasi-autonomous parts, but an absolute mutuality, wherein all parts are totally subject to the regulation of the whole. Consequently, and paradoxically, in the kibbutz, personal issues are also not personal — they are, in principle, collective. The preceptive collapse of the personal into the communal is of course nothing but

Rousseau's "general will" rendered in terms of the kibbutz's synthetic ideal.[11]

So long as personal interests were relatively inchoate and largely confined to the individual's idiosyncratic self (the singular way one walks, talks, and so on) — as at Timem's beginning — this paradox may well have remained more or less latent. But as those interests waxed with the heterogenization of the community, to flow increasingly into the self's social manifold (one's role as worker, committee member, and so on), the paradox became more manifest and sharply felt. As the decoupling of the lifeworld from the social system proceeded, the effort to define the personal as collective became politically jarring.

Personal issues are bound to bring before the public eye knowledge about a member's personal identity. From the public perspective, knowledge of this kind may well constitute an embarrassment for the involved members, an apparent failure to measure up to collective expectations. Thus, for example, some members of Timem were generally regarded as ill-fit for one job or another, on the ground that they were excessively "nervous" (*atzbani*) or "ambitious" (a *shvitzer*). Obviously, such rationales served to discredit the member, and their publicization is bound to prove "unpleasant."

However, in a situation of communitarian living, knowledge about one's private person is difficult to conceal and tends to be available for formal publicization. Furthermore, given that personal issues often involve competition over limited community resources and advantages, some members, depending on the nature of their own particular interests, are given prudential reason to make public the personal embarrassments of the member whose interests happen to be at stake.

Alternatively, members may choose to hold their tongues. It is the case that since all members are formally and, to a considerable extent, actually dependent on collective decisions for the pursuit of their own respective personal interests and security, they all have general reason not to engage in the public "soul-searching of someone else's soul." For a member to do so is to invite comrades to hold up for public inspection her or his own respective personal identity. In point of fact, my observations indicate that many of the General Assembly's decisions were made with regard to highly relevant information that had not been publicly adduced or "put on the table," but was nonetheless common. For example, in the case, cited above, of the stigmatized individual who wanted to take a bride from outside the community, the General Assembly's decision was informed by common opinions that the girl was "ugly" and "idiotic," and that her family was "dishonest" and sexually disturbed; yet, for obvious reasons, none of these opinions was aired in a meeting of the General Assembly (Evens 1975).

Furthermore, in the kibbutz personal embarrassment is by definition also collective (Evens 1975). Each personal embarrassment, marking a performance unequal to ideological expectation, must constitute a special case of the more general failure of the kibbutz's projected synthesis of the individual and society. Indeed, as I argued above, the very presence of pronounced personal interests and knowledge was ideologically adverse. A conspicuous distinction between public and private life marks, by definition, a significant breach between the individual and society (see Suttles 1970).

My principal argument here is that as Timem's population became larger as well as more heterogeneous, such that the members were less concretely commutable with one another, personal interests, knowledge, and embarrassments became more and more conspicuous and therefore socially problematical. I take it that in the debate the special attention proposed for personal issues reflected this uncomfortable state of affairs.

Both the proposal to subject personal issues to secret balloting and the proposal to relegate them to lesser decision-making bodies were meant to mitigate the situation wherein these issues were proving resistant to sincere collective decision. In the first proposal the idea was to eliminate the fear of personal repercussions from sincere balloting; in the second it was to remove altogether personal issues from the public forum, while maintaining, by means of committee decision, the collective's hegemony in respect of them.

Clearly, though, both proposals logically constituted acknowledgments that personal interests had come to enjoy an autonomy they were not supposed to have. Indeed, the proposals acknowledged much more. As the opponents of secret balloting argued, the adoption of this voting procedure would have had the effect of augmenting, for purposes of decision making, the autonomy of the individual in terms of his or her personal interests. The removal of personal issues from the General Assembly's consideration, by protecting personal interests from full public disclosure and by making a radical concession to representative democracy, would have done the same.

Therefore, although both were expressly intended to ensure the collective's authority over personal issues, the proposals, if instituted, would have amounted to "robbing Peter to pay Paul." As such, they neatly manifested the paradox presented by the kibbutz notion of personal issues. The effort to render personal issues absolutely public leads to a paradoxical bind. Genuinely personal issues can be made public only at the expense of their personal nature.

Ontology and Evolution

It is convenient simply to mark here a point that is important to the overall argument of this book. I have maintained that the growth of the kibbutz appears to recapitulate societal evolution as described by grand social theory, so much so that an evolutionary theory such as Habermas's of the decoupling of lifeworld and social system can be very gainfully employed to describe the course of Timem's development. Nevertheless, as I have also featured, the kibbutz actually began its career at the evolutionary point described by these grand theories as an end-stage — that is, the stage of modernity. The heterogenization of Timem cannot be satisfactorily understood outside of the consideration that, though in its early stages the community might well have simulated a society in which the lifeworld and the social system were for most social purposes relatively undifferentiated from each other, even during these stages the culture of Timem was already fully modern and profoundly informed by the social configuration captured in Habermas's concept of decoupling.

The kibbutz notion of personal issues prods me to go beyond this arresting theoretical and analytical hitch, to make a claim very important to my overall argument: the prominent paradoxicality of the idea that the personal is communal seems somehow to point in the direction of the thesis that what Habermas describes as a decoupling of system and lifeworld, even as it sums up much that is ethically disquieting about modern life, corresponds peculiarly to an openness fundamental to human social life and, correlatively, is, at bottom, ontologically predisposed rather than evolutionarily modern. This claim both recalls my discussion in chapter 2 of the design flaw in the kibbutz ideal and anticipates certain key arguments I make in chapter 6 about otherness as irrecusable and voluntarism as paradoxical.

To conclude the present chapter, the state of democratic participation and the issue of secret balloting seem best explained in terms of the growth and heterogenization of Timem's social order. This explanation might appear to bring the analysis to a close. But were the investigation left off at this point, we would be shortchanged. If the processes of growth and heterogenization can adequately explain the events and state of affairs in question, why was "generational conflict" allowed to inhibit and preempt a fully developed empirical account of the debate over secret balloting? To conclude that Timem's members simply lack the training or analytical acuity necessary to secure the scientific truth would be a gross sociological conceit. This question, of why the members inclined to the one interpretation over the other, cannot be so easily explained away. Nor should it be ignored. It is in fact fundamental, both for understanding the case anthropologically and for grasping the nature of such understanding. The apparently straightforward empirical account fails to capture the meaningful essence of the debate.

Five

Conflict between the Generations as a Normative Expectation

The Politics of the Debate

Although in its focus on public affairs, and as a public affair, the contest on secret balloting was highly political, its politics were distinctly ambiguous. By that I mean, it was not at all clear in whose separate interest was a standing rule of a secret ballot, if indeed anyone stood indubitably to gain by it.

In the event of a personal issue such as a member's special request, say, for a loan, secret balloting, as a means of removing inhibitions on negative voting, was likely to be in the interest of the member who wished to vote "no" and in the disinterest of the member whose request was under consideration. If only because every member's personal satisfactions are subject to collective decision, and may arise at any time, no member could be very secure beforehand about the strategic advantage of a secret ballot. Indeed, in virtue of the times (however few) a member's personal needs do come before the public, it may well be that every member is strategically better off with a rule that serves to inhibit negative voting — that is, with open-hand balloting.

Strategic considerations aside, however, there remains something to say about the politics of the contest. I suspect that members who found themselves, in general or for important purposes, feeling relatively powerless were (for reasons which will emerge as I proceed) drawn toward the secret ballot. In this connection the important issue is the identity of these members and the conditions of their felt powerlessness. These conditions are various and complex, and they do not distinguish a category of persons socially uniform in any respect other than felt power. Thus, for example, while some members may feel politically disadvantaged as a result of lacking family in the community, others may find themselves in the same boat as a result of being "late" joiners in the community (see Evens 1975). However, for present purposes I need not embark on an exhaustive analysis of the community's power structure. It will suffice to bring out just one feature of that structure.

For the members whose careers in the community were largely ahead of them, secret balloting must have been especially gravitative. Preeminently occupied with constructing their respective futures, these members must have felt peculiarly competitive over the community's resources. Such members would be keenly concerned about access to particular occupations, professional training, higher education, and so on. Selecting a member to become, for example, a carpenter, or nurse, or cosmetician, or teacher inevitably involved the frustration of those members who felt called but were not chosen. Indeed, claiming that they had been unfairly denied access to certain positions, individuals and entire families have parted with the community. Under these conditions, it stands to reason that the members who were peculiarly caught up in this competition would feel especially anxious about controlling access of their fellows to the community's resources. In addition, they would most likely be concerned about not having to alienate these fellows, who, in turn, under this collective regime, can regulate the access of others.

I am not suggesting that by way of rational choice such members politically engineered the issue on secret balloting. I am arguing rather that, owing to the competitive circumstances described, these members may have found especially painful the necessity to make public their sincere political preferences as well as the pressure to fail to vote in accordance with these preferences. Therefore, they *gravitated to* — as distinct from *decided on* — the secret ballot.

This interpretation fits my impression that the members who allowed that they could not understand why anyone feared to publicize a political preference were members whose careers were largely behind them. On the other hand, the members who stressed to me how "unpleasant" it was to have to announce to the General Assembly one's opinions were members whose adult careers were just getting seriously underway.

I do not wish to suggest that the sole consideration of inchoate career can satisfactorily account for the actual composition of the sides during the debate. However, this consideration does offer understanding of why a number of individuals might have found themselves feeling very strongly in favor of the secret ballot as a solution to the problem of participation. What is more, it gears very neatly into the fact that generational tension became the predominant definition of the situation.

If the proposal on secret balloting was in preponderant measure sentiently engaged and apperceived by Timem's members as I have described, then the issue might well *have looked like* a question of division between the generations. The members whose careers were just getting underway were, of course, principally the "young" members. So that, if these members found themselves preeminently associated with the rule of secret balloting, then the issue would thus have been made available for casting as a matter of the "young" versus the "old." But it is not likely that superficial appearance alone would have sufficed to occasion such a picture. As an additional condition the community would have had to have been predisposed to it.

The Availability of "Generational Tension"

The Kibbutz Ethos and the Idiom of Patriarchy

There can be no doubt that in Timem the definition "generational schism" is on hand and epistemically inviting. As brought out in the preceding chapter, at the time of fieldwork the age breakdown of Timem's membership showed a broad bias toward the dichotomization of the members between old and young. But the presence of generational tension as a salient picture of a general state of affairs depended also on something far more phenomenologically prepossessing than a temporary demographic condition. The fact is that a powerful conception of generational tension is phenomenologically implicit in the kibbutz's basic ethos. More specifically, such a conception is contained tautologically, as an a priori, in the kibbutz's particular ideological commitment to familism, moral choice, and revolution.

In his classic work on the kibbutz family, Spiro (1954; 1963:

110ff.) made clear the kibbutz's commitment to familism. He found that although certain functions of the traditional nuclear family had been curtailed by the collective, the community as a whole was ideologically designed to function as a grand extended family. Correlatively, although it found it necessary, especially in its early years, to recruit members from the "outside," and although it remains a proselytizing movement, the kibbutz, like a biological family, fundamentally is meant to perpetuate itself by means of its own children.

It would be difficult to overemphasize the community's sense of dependence on its children. This dependence is sharply evident in the kibbutz's enormous material and emotional investment in children, a fact well documented in Spiro's intensive study (1965) of kibbutz children. The point is that, because the community has vested itself, in the sense of its perduring self, its succession, in the parent-child relationship, the idea of the generations has a mighty significance for the community.

However, the term "parent-child" is too broad here. It is phenomenologically more precise to speak, instead, of the father-son relationship, emphasizing the male principle and the idea of fatherhood. It cannot be denied that gender equality is a pronounced tenet of the kibbutz ideology. But neither can it be doubted that the kibbutz has found, in basic respects, the institution of this tenet to be exceedingly problematical. As has been well documented for kibbutzim in general, whereas men statistically predominate in the roles of leadership and economic production, for the most part it is women who may be found in the domestic branches of the community, especially the communal kitchen and child-rearing system (Talmon-Garber 1965; Tiger and Shepher 1976; Spiro 1979).

An important condition of this state of affairs is that, the explicit ideology notwithstanding, the kibbutz is, and always has been, characterized by a deep-seated, less-than-conscious male bias, a bias rooted in, *inter alia,* the traditional Jewish family and ethos (Patai 1959: esp. 128ff.). Ironically, in order to see this bias we need not look beyond the ideology. By and large the ideology has intended by gender equality that women should be allowed to perform what were normally regarded as male roles — in other words, that women should become like men. In Timem, I was struck by the fact that a man whose wife has just given birth to a boy is likely to be greeted, as a matter of course, with: "Congratulations, especially because it is a boy." And, though it may seem banal, it is very telling that in this revolutionary community, patronymy has always been taken for granted, so that the self, in the highly significant sense of the *name,* gets perpetuated as a male principle.

In view of this tacit, but deep-seated attribution of superiority to the male principle, I propose that the generational relationship on which the members as a community depend for their continuity is experienced primarily, not in the gender-neutral idiom of "parent-child," but in the gender-biased one of "father-son."

Responsibility for Succession and the Primordial Generational Relationship

Wherever they are found, generational relationships are likely to bear the significance of social succession. In the kibbutz, owing to familistic collectivism, this significance has an additional impact. For, in a palpable sense, it is the *community as a whole* that gets passed on generationally. There is still another consideration that makes the kibbutz's association of social succession with the generational relationship extraordinary, even paradigmatic. I have in mind the community's revolutionary character.

There is implicit in the generational relationship a temporal hierarchy — the son *pre*supposes the father. This temporal priority is present in every father-son relationship, so that, as this relationship is renewed from one generation to the next, so is the hierarchy. In a cyclical sense, then, every father is the first father. But given a context of narrative or linear rather than cyclical time, the temporal priority of the father takes on a fresh relative significance. For under such a temporality, every father must have a unique place in the temporal order. It then becomes possible to speak of a primordial father, from whom all the others ultimately issue. Because the kibbutz was established only recently and is a revolutionary community, in its case we are in fact dealing with the primordial generational relationship.

As Timem was settled only some thirty-five years before my arrival, its population still included many of its first-generation members at the time of my fieldwork. Moreover, as revolutionaries, these persons did not simply situate on the ground another community — they engendered a "new" social order. Therefore, in discussing generational relations in Timem, we must talk not simply of father and son but rather, following Amos Elon (1981), of founder and son.

Clearly, this fact bespeaks a paradigmatic character for the association of social succession with the generational relationship in Timem. In its primordial instantiation, the generational relationship may be said to be representative of all relationships of succession, much as Adam, as the first man, may be said to represent all men. Under such paradigmatic circumstances, the son's burden must be enormous. On him rests the *success*ion of a new world, so to speak. The ability of the sons to carry on constitutes the first critical test of the natural and moral validity of the world that their fathers wrought. This test, like the first critical test of any experimental project, is bound to convey an elevated conative load. In the present case, we might well speak of a maximal load, for the project in question is one on which the "experimenters" literally bet their lives. This implies, at least in a regime based on ethical contract and organic justice (a regime in which one is supposed to *choose* to do the right thing), awesome responsibility and indebtedness of the sons to the fathers.

The responsibility and indebtedness are awesome, not only because an entire social world pertains to them, but also because they naturally admit only of imperfect fulfillment. Their intrinsic problematicity is prefigured ontologically in the fact that, while there is a culturally plain sense in which father and son are consubstantial, there is an equally transparent sense in which they constitute separate and distinct beings. In a generational ontology, the continuity between generations is ultimately predicated on the consubstantiality between father and son. However, that the son is also a being in his own right, a part of but also apart from the father, insinuates the possibility of social deviation, giving reason to suppose that social succession will be less than perfect.

The point may be put in more sociological terms.[1] The founders of Timem constructed their institutional world in praxis, as a function of their pioneering engagement with the natural and social surroundings in which they found themselves. As a result, the founders present for this institutional world no special problems of internalization and legitimation; they need only recollect how this world evolved "naturally" through their own social practice. But for the sons, who have no immediate access to its initial pragmatic circumstances, this institutional world is largely experienced as coming from without. As a result, the presence of the sons poses for this world special problems of internalization, legitimation, compliance, and the like. This is not to say that there can be no blind acceptance by the sons; but rather that, because this world was established in the praxis of another hour, such acceptance can no longer follow in the nature of things. Instead, it must be wrought through myth, charter, and explication.

Thus, ironically, as a fundamental means of social continuity, the sons constitute a powerful condition for change.

The Expectation of Generational Conflict and the Paradox of Moral Choice

That a son is not his father and that social succession from one generation to the next is fraught with difficulty are hardly revealing assertions in themselves. But the essentially paradoxical nature of the generational relationship enjoys an exceptional sociological significance. The projection of discontinuity as a condition of continuity makes the expectation of generational conflict an inexorable conclusion of generational practice.

This picture of the generational relationship's phenomenological dynamics is, perhaps, in no case more true to form than when the paradox is rendered in the idiom of ethical commitment.[2] By emphatically defining generational continuity as discretionary, this idiom serves to focus the paradox in the following way.

Ethical commitment — "voluntarism" — is the chosen idiom of the kibbutz ideology; it is the pivot of the community's proposed synthesis between the individual and society. The principle of voluntarism admonishes that, instead of being compelled to perpetuate the institutional world of their fathers, the sons should be given the option.

But the choice confronting the sons is internally inconsistent. If the sons were to choose (as urged) always to comply and never to deviate, the inference would then be warranted that they do not really have a choice but are instead behaving mechanically. Where the record of conformity is perfect, what evidence can there be for the presence of genuine choice? Where the absence of dissent is complete, how can one be sure that one enjoys the capacity to dissent?

In effect, the sons are caught in a radical bind, a lived paradox. They are urged *to choose* to perpetuate the institutional world their fathers built. But insofar as they do so unfailingly, they cannot but fail to demonstrate that they have so chosen. In that event, since choice is a normative linchpin of that institutional world, the sons' compliance would amount to fundamental deviation. It must follow that in order to comply, they must somehow falter in their charge. That is to say, by the logic of their moral order, the sons are *bound* at once to comply and not to comply.[3]

Plainly, this bind constitutes a dramatic representation of the paradox of continuity implicit in generational practice. I call the bind a *lived* paradox because it bears sharply on engagement in the material world and can neither be tackled nor avoided simply by adverting it to the second-order reality of pure logic. Why this should be so is a point I shall pursue in chapter 7 (where I take up the question of the members' final motivation for employing "generational conflict" as a definition of the situation.)

The point I wish to make here is this. By virtue of this paradox, whereby compliance is effected by deviation, there is in the kibbutz a morally *impelling* expectation of generational tension. As I have shown, such tension is a tacit but powerful directive — indeed, prereflective commandment — of the community's familistic, moralistic, and pioneering ethos.

The Assumption of Dissent

In light of this expectation, it is less surprising that, despite a population that yields only very imperfectly to empirical classification in terms of generations, the meaning "generational tension" is widely dispensed in the kibbutz. Whether the members are disputing a new way for the collective to distribute household and personal goods, or access to a new block of housing, or, indeed, the institution of a new manner of voting, they are inclined to offer "generational tension" by way of explication of the proposed changes.

"The young people don't like to come to General Assembly meetings on or to talk about ideological problems. Perhaps they do not feel strong in the face of the old people's power." This remark, made to me by one of Timem's pioneer members, is packed with the theme of generational tension. It places the responsibility for the problem of participation squarely with the younger members, as a matter of their preference (they "don't like to come to General Assembly meetings"). Moreover, it coordinates the opposition between the generations with the normative distinction between ideological commitment and political apathy (the young don't like "to talk about ideological problems") as well as with the political opposition between the powerful and the powerless (the young "do not feel strong in the face of the old people's power"). By "the old people's power," the speaker had in mind, I suggest, the power the beneficiaries of creative endeavor are likely to feel is held over them by their pioneering benefactors. Such felt-power is amplified by the fact that this particular kind of relationship of unequal exchange is ultimately quite irreversible.

Even more telling here are the statements I recorded that define the putative deviancy of the sons as *deviationism* — that is, as dissent. The following is an excerpt from a discussion that took place at a formal meeting of Timem's chapter of the Youth Brigade (*chativa tz'ira*), a federation-wide organization of the younger members, evidently established in order to elevate and maintain the ideological consciousness of these members:[4]

> *First speaker.* Can we build our home according to our own design, or was everything fixed by our parents? Why aren't we doing what we want?
>
> *Second speaker.* The young members don't know what they want to do; or they don't know how to do it. It is a fact that we don't do anything. This is shown by our absence from general assemblies and other formal meetings.
>
> *Third speaker.* We do not go to general assemblies because we do not believe in the ability of the General Assembly to change anything. The General Assembly is organized today as it was thirty years ago.

The first speaker plainly points to the generational bind in which the sons are caught ("Can we build our home according to our own design, or was everything fixed by our parents?"). The second speaker dramatizes the stultifying effect of being thus caught ("We don't do anything"). In addition, the second speaker accepts responsibility for the problem of participation (he speaks of "our absence from general assemblies"). The third speaker also accepts responsibility, but he introduces a fresh, and remarkable, twist. He opines that the young members fail to participate because the democratic institution in question is ill-fit to accomplish anything in its current form. In so saying, he manages, with dialectical ingenuity, to redefine the young members' alleged democratic passivity into a form of protestant activism — dissent. He thus completes the dialectic, shifting the blame from the putative nonparticipants, that is, the sons, to those who would maintain the General Assembly exactly as it is, namely, the founders.

Another young member made the point to me this way. He told

me of an individual who, when it looked as if the General Assembly was going to refuse him his special (and considerable) request, broke down and cried in the meeting. "After which," my informant confessed, "I stopped going to general assemblies altogether." I interpreted him to mean that such an emotional display so told against the legitimacy of the kibbutz democratic process that he felt justified in ceasing to participate.

Here is still another variation on the theme of generational protest. During a General Assembly meeting, a member, who had been asked by the community to fill a particular office, maintained that owing to "personal reasons" (which she did not offer to reveal), she could not comply at that time. When the vote was taken, it appeared that not a single hand would be raised against her plea to beg off. At the last moment, however, a young member made himself very conspicuous by what seemed an impulsive negative vote. Since it was clearly an exercise in futility, I asked him to explain his action. He replied, "It was necessary to register at least one negative vote." At the time, I failed to take his meaning. I now see that his action was not so much against the member who refused office as against the system that was paralyzed when confronted with the candidate's personalistic excuse. In effect, the vote was a gesture of protest.

In the preceding chapter, I recorded members' reasons for failing to vote at and attend general assemblies. As the reader will recall, these reasons were largely prudential, reflecting fear of embarrassment caused by public exposure of private interests and designs. These reasons are consistent with the thesis of heterogenization and development of personal selves. The data presented here, however, indicate that members resorted also to another kind of reason entirely — the appeal to protest as a reason for deviant activity invokes a normative rather than prudential cause.

These two sorts of reason are the ethical antipodes of each other — to act out of prudence is precisely not to act from normative regard. Yet in practice, it may be just a short epistemic step from the one kind of reason to the other. To close the gap all that is needed is a discursive ground for redefining the one sort of reason in terms of the other, and a normative ambience that selects for such redefinition.

Consider the case of the member who informed me that he was unable to vote against a particular candidate for office because "perhaps this fellow's wife minds [is the *m'tapelet* of] my children." Moving from this prudential concern for personal security to a normative posture, this member went on to say that, in view of such political circumstances, he now refuses to go altogether to "general assemblies on the election of candidates and personal issues." Although it is left implicit by him, there is a discursive ground for his normative judgment. It is that, given the ideology's fundamental concern to preserve the integrity of the individual, the individual in the kibbutz ought to be in a position to vote sincerely.

The normative ambience selecting for this member's shift to a protestant stance was, I propose, the expectation of dissent between the generations. In other words, it took "generational tension" as a prevailing, comprehensive definition of Timem's situation to make this member's deviant action meaningful as protest. The inversion of prudential into axiological concern was not logically or strategically motivated, but was prompted — less than consciously — by the pressing expectation of conflict between the generations.

Six

Conflict between the Generations as a Metaphor

I have argued that the debate on secret balloting was assimilated categorically to the contest between the generations in Timem. So far I have identified two of the objective conditions of this turn of events. First, with an eye to who was pro and who contra in the public arena, the debate did indeed simulate a dispute between the generations. Second, and more important, as a situational definition, conflict between the generations was right on hand as an impelling expectation of the community's basic ethos.

In fact, though, the representational fit of "conflict between the generations" was far more comprehensive and penetrating than mere resemblance of the political composition of the debate. The idea of conflict between the generations could also assimilate, structurally and hermeneutically, the deep logic of the debate's principal contents and conditions.

The issue of a secret ballot was about the troubled state of Timem's direct democracy, and even more basically about the heterogenization of the community and the correlative emergence of highly exclusive selves and strong personal interests. I have described the logic of these contents and conditions as paradoxical. The members found themselves caught between opposing precepts of freedom, neither of which could be unequivocally denied ideologically. Correlatively, as a solution to the social problem Timem's members were experiencing, a secret ballot was no less ideologically correct than it was definitively antinomian. Even as the community practiced what it preached, it found itself falling away from its ideal.

Revisiting these dilemmas, I want now to examine even more deeply their ideological foundations, pointing also to the latter's rootedness in Western thought. At issue is the ideology's approach to the critical questions of (1) the relation between the individual and society, and, correlatively, (2) the element of contingency in social process. After examining the ideological foundations, I analyze the imposing power of the paradigm of generational conflict to represent the paradoxical logic they manifest. The key to the paradigm's capacity to serve in this way is its own logic of dissent and negation.

The Question of the Individual and Society

The Paradox of Democracy

In chapter 3, I discussed the kibbutz democratic theory in terms of the so-called paradox of democracy: although it is constituted as a collocation of individual preferences, a democratic decision need not reflect consistently the individual's choice. In a palpable sense, democratic decisions slight the individual as such. This is perhaps most conspicuous when the intensity (as well as the order) of the individual's preference is considered: although the majority rules, the minority may feel far stronger about their choice. But even when order of preference alone is brought into account, distortion occurs. For example, consider the intuitive and gross distortion of the individual's preference in a democratic decision where the majority prevails by a margin of one.

Now, kibbutz democracy is meant to bring the individual fully into social decisions. It is emphatically direct, attempting to ensure that the preference of every individual is included wholly and immediately in every social decision. In itself, however, direct democracy cannot dispel the paradox in question. Even where every social decision is made by all the people, rules of preference summation may distort the peculiar value of the individual's preference.

The kibbutz confronts this problem by invoking a conception along the lines of Rousseau's "general will." Individuals are admonished to enter into a social compact whereby, in return for the good life, they consent to determine their preferences according to their social self. In other words, individuals are asked to arrive at decisions by taking into account the objective interests of the social whole (that is, the "general will") rather than their separate interests as individuals. Thus, although the kibbutz employs voting rules of preference summation, its ideal projects unanimous collective decisions that are arrived at through public exchange alone — what might be thought of as discursive communion.

In principle, therefore, no individual is denied the exercise of his or her individuality — that is, his or her singular capacity to make a choice. Yet since every individual chooses according to the identical interests, all choose alike. As a result, if all goes well, there can be no discrepancy whatsoever between the individual and the collective decision; the two are identical.

Phenomenologically, however, there is an irrecusable weakness in the kibbutz solution to the paradox of democracy. Where individuals always choose alike, the constant regularity insinuates determinacy rather than choice. That is to say, where difference of opinion is lacking without exception, there is no evidence of individuals defined as autonomous by the power of choice, no evidence of different ethical persons. Observably, there is evidence only of a unitary, overriding control.

Paradoxically, then, were the kibbutz solution to measure up exactly, the individual, whose autonomy kibbutz democracy is meant to secure, even complete, would be defined out of existence. Seen from its other side, this paradox implies that the successful implementation of such consensual democracy depends on the expression of dissent. For only the expression of dissent can make the "will" in the conception of the general will meaningful.

An Anthropological Presentation of and Solution to the Paradox of the Individual and Society

The paradox of democracy may be viewed as a special case of a more general paradox, on whose extirpation the kibbutz is predicated ideologically. I have in mind the paradox of the individual and society, which may be posed in the following way. Every society is the aggregate of its individual members, but also more than this aggregate — which is to say, it both is and is not a matter of individuals. In other words, the individual and society are necessarily defined in terms of each other. Thus each is defined in terms of what it is not. Put in still another way, although society is necessarily made up of its individual members, it does not reduce to them.

In his highly intelligent book *The Foundations of Social Anthropology*, S. F. Nadel thoughtfully addressed the paradox of the individual and society (1951). With a compelling logic (reminiscent of Bertrand Russell's theory of logical types), he warns against conflating two senses of society — the sense in which society is not a matter of individuals and the sense in which it is:

> The group is an abstraction; the individual is a concrete, unique reality; there cannot logically be actual relations (that is, interactions) between them. To say that there are, would be like saying that it is Mr. Gielgud and not Hamlet who has a quarrel with the State of Denmark. (1951: 91f.)

Doubtless, the admonishment not to confuse the two senses of society can save us from making logical nonsense — or, perhaps more accurately, from making nonsense of our logic. However, though "there cannot logically be" interaction between society as an "abstraction" and the individual as a "concrete, unique reality," such interaction is in fact the case, and plainly so.

There seems no denying that every working society constitutes just such interaction, and that this logically anomalous relation is accomplished precisely by basic conflation of actor and role, of individual and person. In theater proper, bearing in mind Nadel's exquisite dramaturgical example, the distinction between actor and role is definitive (theater is theater because of that distinction — witness Hamlet's play within the play). In everyday life, however, at some point of social-psychological penetration, the distinction between the individual and her or his social person becomes opaque and less than empirically meaningful. Put differently, unless we are concerned with bodies wholly as such (as we are not in social anthropology), ordinarily when we apply the notion of "concrete, unique individual," we already have in mind a social being. Society is in fact ambiguous as between its individual member and itself as a collectivity. Social science must try to meet, rather than avoid, this fact.

The Solution of Dualism: The Example of Hobbes

Since the Renaissance, the bulk of Occidental philosophy, taking a cue especially from the thought of ancient Israel (but propounding from ancient Greek thought a radically individualistic ontology), has taken the individual's diacritical mark to be his or her creative or willful capacity.

On this understanding of the individual, the paradox of the individual and society presents itself in the politico-ethical framework of relative autonomy. For their respective autonomies, both society and the individual suppose the autonomous existence of each other; but such autonomy entails that each enjoys a certain power relative to the other and thus implies the other's heteronomy. In other words, individuals' existence as independent, willful agents depends on their social being; insofar as they are social, however, they are dependent rather than independent. The identical conditions hold, *mutatis mutandis,* for society.

For social practice, this condition raises the dilemma of how to guarantee a relationship between the individual and the collectivity, such that each does not radically curtail the autonomy of the other, effectively undermining its own conditions for survival.

The dilemma is very familiar in its Hobbesian formulation of how to get from a state of political nothingness to a state of political society — that is, in Hobbes's words, from a state where men are naturally characterized by "a perpetual and restless desire of power after power that ceases only in death" to a state where, with "the foresight of their own preservation," men introduce a "restraint upon themselves" (Hobbes 1958: 86, 139; see Wolin 1960: 241).

Leaving some room for the social in the state of nature, both Rousseau and Locke mitigated the obvious dualism underlying the dilemma of the individual and society. The sharp individualism of Rousseau's state of nature was cut by his posit of natural compassion (see below, chap. 8), while Locke's picture of this state included an understanding of property as naturally social in virtue of the recognition by others that makes property meaningful *as property* (Wolin 1960: 310). The Hobbesian formulation of the dilemma, though, is patently dualist. It presumes that the individual and society are essentially separate realities, making their union logically impossible. To get round this difficulty, Hobbes was given to reduce the one reality to the other. He took the autonomous, self-seeking individual as ontologically prior to society. As a result, he was moved to picture society as chimerical. Since it is logically impossible to derive a genuine social process from the individual considered as such, Hobbes was in no position to entertain the possibility of a social order that partakes of the reality of its individual constituents but is also autonomous in its own right.

In point of fact, the political society at which Hobbes arrives is not at all real. It is a mere artifice, not only in the sense that it is manmade, but also in the sense that it is feigned. "For a body politic, as it is a fictitious body," said Hobbes (in Wolin 1960: 254), "so are the faculties and will thereof fictitious also." To be sure, Hobbes's sovereign enjoys absolute autonomy. But on close analysis, the autonomy it enjoys turns out to be the kind that *individuals* have in respect of one another, not the kind that an authentic social order exhibits. In Hobbes's philosophy, it is not that inasmuch as individuals are autonomous there necessarily exists a surpassing social power, but that owing to reasons of self-interest alone, individuals agree to exercise their separate autonomies *as if* there were such a social power. As a result, the sovereign's autonomy is completely reducible. To cite an expert commentator:

> The sovereign's powerful body is, so to speak, not his own; its outline is *completely* filled in by the miniature figures of his subjects. He exists, in other words, *only* through them. Equally important, each subject is *clearly discernible* in the body of the sovereign. The citizens are not swallowed up in an anonymous mass, nor sacramentally merged into a mystical body. Each remains a discrete individual and each retains his identity *in an absolute way*. What is suggested here is that the substance of power assigned the sovereign was less impressive than the rhetoric surrounding it. (Wolin 1960: 266; emphasis added)

Hobbes's great Leviathan reduces to an aggregate of individuals, individuals who, though, since they lack any essential social definition, must have the sense and wit of billiard balls.

As they are unequivocally substantive, Hobbes's billiard-ball interactants can share in no reality other than that of the mechanico-physical world. At bottom, their absolute self-identity amounts to the discrete individuality characterizing concrete particulars (see Peters 1967: 41). Relative to them, society must be either a mere epiphenomenon of the mechanico-physical world (as it was for Hobbes) or, alternatively, insofar as its reality is taken seriously, something else again, a creature of another kind entirely.

For our purposes, Hobbes aside, what matters is that an initial premise of ontological individualism logically conduces toward either one or the other of two distinct positions. The first is this:

of the two phenomena, society and the individual, one is real and the other feigned (logically it makes no difference which is which); the second, that both society and the individual are real, but constitute separate and distinct realities. The second position is suggested in Nadel's analytical advice to keep the individual and society logically apart. However, as it is logically foregone that this position can neither describe nor explain any worldly relationship—governmental or otherwise—between the individual and society, it has not been commonly held among students of society and champions of particular modes of political order.

By far the most prevalent position in Western social thought has been the first. Werner Stark (1962) mounts an impressive case that the dualistic tendency to swing between reducing society to the individual and the individual to society has been the characteristic dynamic of Occidental social theory. It is not by chance that the modern world has come to think it must choose dualistically between capitalism and socialism — that is, between alternative modes of socioeconomic organization polarized by reference to the individual and the collective, respectively.[1]

In fact, however, the reductionist position fails really to take the dilemma of the individual and society seriously. By impugning the ontological authenticity of either the individual or society, it marks one of them as categorically incapable of self-government. It thus makes the question of relative autonomy meaningless. If, then, this question is regarded as sound, reductionism may beg but cannot meet it. It seems difficult to deny that the distribution of autonomy as between the individual and society is at least an implicit *problematique* of social practice everywhere.

Dualism, then, formulates the dilemma of the individual and society in such a way as to make it unassailable. Either it projects the individual and society as mutually exclusive or it belittles the one or the other to the point of nonexistence.

The Kibbutz Synthesis

The kibbutz ideology tries hard to avoid dualism and to engage the dilemma of the individual and society in dialectical terms. The kibbutz devoutly sets out to divide up the ethical goods of human practice in such a way that *both* the individual and society may be self-fulfilled. According to the ideology, human individuals' quintessential endowment is their power of creative or moral choice. But the exercise and development of this power is contingent on the individual's existence in relation to his or her fellows. In effect, the individual *as such* is pictured as fundamentally social. Indeed, the ideology would claim that, in proportion as society is lacking, the development of the individual's creative capacity will be duly arrested. It must follow that the way to maximize this capacity is to capitalize on the individual's social coefficient. But, of course, in view of the conceptual consideration that the collective's autonomy is an inverse measure of the individual's, such a design for creative individuality seems perplexingly incongruous.

The ideology thus focuses a paradox, the means to the undoing of which, or so the ideology proposes, is the very capacity at stake — moral choice. Should the individual *choose* to give over autonomy to the collective, granted that this choice remains ever open to the individual, does the individual not deliver the absolute autonomy of the collective and constitute his or her own freedom at the same time? As a kibbutz ideologue has written (in an unpublished, anon. MS presented to me by one of Timem's members):

> I do not know of any other society which owes its very existence and continuation, in quite the same way, to the free choice of each one of its individual members. Each person joins a Kibbutz from free choice and he is free to leave it whenever he wants to. And as long as he is a member of a Kibbutz, he lives and experiences this basic freedom of choice from day to day. The member of a Kibbutz is continually aware of his freedom to opt out of the social contract to which he bound himself upon joining.

Thus the ideology deploys the creative capacity of the individual to mediate the politico-ethical dilemma in which this capacity itself issues.

The crux of this solution to the dilemma of the individual and society is the idea of an ethical identity between the two. The virtual identity between the decision of the collective and the individual's decision to submit to collective rule establishes a unity of autonomy between the individual and society. As I indicated earlier, this harmonious state of affairs recalls the Rousseauian notion of the general will — that commonality of wills emergent on the cancellation of whatever is particular to the will of each individual. Through ethical commitment, the voluntary identification of the individual with the collective, the kibbutz proposes to arrive at and effect the general will.

Kibbutz Naturalism: Ancient Israel and Rousseau

The social contract thus proposed has profound ontological significance. According to this contract, the individual is supposed to choose to comply with the will of the social whole on both rational and moral grounds. The rational grounds are keyed to an idea of objective interests. Given a uniform social structure and homogeneous societal constitution, the objective interests of each member may be seen as identical with those of Everyman. The moral grounds have to do with the values of freedom of choice and other-regard. A choice for the collective is, by definition, a selfless choice. In its concern for the other, such a choice may be regarded as wholly responsible. As such, it smacks of freedom rather than determinacy, of reason rather than instinct. What greater sign of the capacity for choice can be given by a creature that is already endowed with a self than abnegation? Or so the argument goes. "How difficult it is to maintain moral norms and concrete commandments when good and evil are up to you and depend on your own decision.... The mouth that forbids is the mouth that allows," propounds the ideology (*Sefer Timem*: 225).

For all the emphasis on the capacity for reason and choice, though, the projected identity between the individual and the collective is meant to be no less material than facultative. Underlying the logic of this contractual identity rests the idea of a *natural* progression between humankind's sociality and its moral powers. In other words, the ethical basis of the kibbutz social contract is, at least in spirit, grounded in an ontological understanding.

The material nature of the projected identity is expressed in the ideological appellation of "organic society." "If one reads the charter of the founding of the Kibbutz movement," writes a kibbutz member (anon. MS), "one is struck by the repeated use of the concept of an 'organic society.'" The usage is meant as more than merely metaphorical. In view of the ideology's assumption that humankind's sociality is given in its moral capacity, and is, thus, natural rather than epiphenomenal, the ideology does not have to balk at the idea of an *organic* bond between the individual and society.

If this claim — that ethical covenanting in the kibbutz is filled with ontological significance — seems tenuous, it helps to mention here that such covenanting harks back to the contractarian thought not only of Rousseau, but also of ancient Israel.

For ancient Israel, the ethical covenant between humankind and

God rendered the former and society extensions of God, making the individual and society extensions of each other and equally real. In Aubrey Johnson's expert interpretation, the covenant facilitated an "oscillation in thought between the conception of the social unit as an association of individuals...and as a corporate personality" (Johnson 1961: 12). Furthermore, like the kibbutz ideology, ancient Israel took human beings' sociality for granted in their moral nature: "In Israelite thought the individual...is never a mere isolated unit; he lives in constant reaction towards others" (Johnson 1961: 7).

In the case of Rousseau, the "social contract" reduces itself to a *moi commun*, in the following terms: "Each of us puts his person and all his power in common under the supreme direction of the general will, and, in our corporate capacity, we receive each member as an indivisible part of the whole" (Rousseau 1950: 15; see also Wolin 1960: 371). It is true that Rousseau's diagnostic conceptions of "natural man" as absolute and independent, and, correlatively, of human social order as an unhappy disturbance of the natural state of things are less than consistent here (see Charvet 1972). Nevertheless, in his attribution to humankind of a "natural goodness" that disposes to benevolence and justice in dealings with other human beings (Plamenatz 1963: 374), and in his grasp of moral rules as irreducible to considerations of utility and prudence (Plamenatz 1963: 366–73; Winch 1962), it seems plain that Rousseau took — at least for remedial purposes — morality and therefore social virtue to be, *in some sense,* perfectly natural. The sharp contrast between Rousseau's and Hobbes's thought lends support to the point. As contrived and exteriorized, Hobbes's Leviathan is precisely the sort of social order that Rousseau regarded as perverse and in need of radical counteraction.

Otherness as an Impediment to the Kibbutz Synthesis

This contractarian solution to the dilemma of the individual and society is undeniably ingenious. Nevertheless, some of its empirical suppositions are suspect.

The key to the solution is the projected identity of each member's decision with that of Everyman. The achievement of this synthetic identity is predicated on, in part, the establishment of a social order admitting of relatively little internal differentiation. By affording no objective basis for interests other than common ones, this social order was designed to ensure that basically contrary opinions do not take root. But, as I documented in chapter 4, in respect of the ideal of social homogeneity, the practice of kibbutz life is simply not reliable. On the contrary, the unreliability may be counted on.

Even had Timem achieved its ideal of social homogeneity, though, it would not have been in a position to rely on the realization of an absolute identity between the individual's and the collective's decision. For the fact that a person has certain objective or rationally determined interests cannot guarantee that he or she will be guided by them in drawing political conclusions.

Barring physico-chemical modifications that render the individual well-nigh "mindless,"[2] there can be no way to be sure that the individual will make up her or his mind according to some or other specific interests. Indeed, even should individuals affect a decision that duly reflects their "objective" interests, there can be no certainty that that decision is sincere. It is always possible that they harbor contrary, but still unexpressed, opinions.

The point is that in light of the experience of otherness, a phenomenological condition that appears to be omnipresent and that can be mediated only imperfectly, one can never be quite sure what is on another person's mind (or, for that matter, on one's own). This condition necessarily alters the form of the kibbutz's projected identity between the individual's decision and the collective's. Since the only way the kibbutz can know the individual's decision is to ask for it, and since the answer may or may not be sincere, the only such decision the kibbutz can be sure of is the individual's to abide or not to abide by the collective's decision. But it cannot be sure of the individual's authentic preference. Therefore, whatever the kibbutz may hope for in the way of an identity of decisions, logically all it can count on is the identity of the collective's decision with the individual's virtually to comply.

It is true that *for all public purposes* — and therefore significantly — the decision of the individual to abide by the collective's decision and the latter itself are indeed identical. Logically, however, these two decisions are of different types. Whatever the decision of the collective happens to be about, the individual's to conform is in the first place and necessarily about the collective's. In other words, the individual's decision stands in a metalogical relation to the collective's.

The logical difference described by this relation does make a difference to the course of kibbutz social life. For the relation leaves room for the individual to draw and harbor deviant opinions. Accordingly, the individual's decision to abide by the collective's hardly precludes the possibility of the individual holding contrary opinions. In other words, under such a condition, the implied identity of the individual and society may be construed as principally apparent.

The Paradox of Voluntarism

The force of the point becomes clear in reference to the idea of the general will. Like the requirement of social homogeneity, the admonishment of the general will is intended to preclude exclusive political preferences. But here it is revealing to bring out a certain ambiguity in the idea of the general will.

As a process the general will describes a free public debate, a discursive communion wherein individual preferences cancel one another, producing a decision that is social in the strongest possible sense. But note that "cancel" can have at least two distinct meanings here. First, it can indicate that, in the face of reasoned, contrary argument, the individual changes his or her mind. Second, it can mean that, whether or not the individual changes his or her mind, that individual agrees for all public purposes to abide by the social decision.

The first meaning seems to presume that the individual is perfectly rational and, at least on kibbutz ideology, that the community has a thoroughly homogeneous social makeup. Obviously, these conditions are exceedingly strong and more than unlikely. The second meaning presumes only that the individual values the decision of the collective above her or his own — ideally for moral reasons, in practice for any reasons whatsoever. This condition seems relatively weak and, I suppose, likely more often than not.

However, unlike the first meaning, the second admits of a "general will" that is prior to the collocation of all individual contributions. It denotes a preexisting social decision with which the individual can choose to comply. Correlatively, the second meaning does not remove the possibility of the individual continuing to hold an opinion that is contrary to the general will. To be sure, insofar as such opinions remain wholly unexpressed, they can make no direct difference to the public process. However, the second meaning itself gives reason to think that such contrary opinions will eventually out.

That individuals agree to abide by the general will regardless of their personal preferences is a bare-bones interpretation of the kibbutz principle of voluntarism. It is "bare-bones" because under the second meaning, the condition of rational choice is, insofar as this condition supposes complete like-mindedness, unnecessary. Here the kibbutz can be seen to admonish voluntarism on moral grounds alone. The individual is urged to participate in the general will simply because such participation is deemed right and is thought to occasion a moral union between the individual and the collectivity.

However, even this logically less demanding, principally moral sense of voluntarism is not free from fundamental difficulty, for the following reason. Kibbutz voluntarism admonishes not only that the individual ought to *subscribe to the rule of the social whole* but also that he *ought* to so subscribe. In other words, it is a principle of moral optation as well as of collective hegemony. As a result, it comports the paradox with which we are already familiar from earlier discussions, and which is of central importance to my analysis: if individuals follow the collective's lead invariably, they deprive themselves of any means to demonstrate the truth of the existence of their moral capacity. Moreover, since the individual's self is in fundamental part a construction on the model of the other, what I have called the experience of otherness must be intrinsic to that individual's experience of her- or himself. It must follow, then, that as long as individuals' moral capacity remains unexercised to all ostensible purposes, they can no more demonstrate its existence to themselves than they can to their other.

That in the event of unfailing moral choice, the individual must fail to prove him- or herself moral means he or she is caught up in a self-inconsistent demand. In effect, voluntarism exhorts the individual both to abide and not to abide by the general will.

This circumstance must be psychologically hard to bear. My data from Timem lead me to suspect that the resulting psychological pressure is considerable. But my concern here is with one experience in particular. As a lived predicament, the paradox of voluntarism must constitute an intense selective pressure — or, what amounts to the same thing here, a powerful motivation — for, as well as against, the revelation of individual preferences. In turn, to come to the point, a motivation of this kind implies for the kibbutz phenomenology, the presence of a deep-seated, but not necessarily explicit, expectation that such preferences will surface.

The Falling Out of the Individual and Society

The kibbutz solution to the dilemma of the individual and society is thus fallible. The proof that the kibbutz ideology runs afoul of the dilemma at point is, of course, in the empirical pudding of kibbutz social life. If the preceding analysis is correct, then despite its goal of synthesis, the kibbutz must be given to serious manifestations of dualism between the individual and the collective. In chapter 4, I spoke of this dualism, using Habermas's terminology, as a decoupling of system and lifeworld, and traced its development to the heterogenization of Kibbutz Timem. Here, preoccupied with the paradoxical logic of the principle of voluntarism, I am concerned to bring out that the dualism takes the form of politico-ethical dissent.

In ancient Israel, the ironical shortcomings of voluntarism resulted in such conspicuous forms of dissent as defection and merely ritualistic observance of the covenant and its law. Humankind pitted itself against God, constituting a theopolitical dualism the prophets strove mightily to correct (Voegelin 1956: chap. 13).

In Rousseau's work the logical fragility of voluntarism is exhibited in his notorious paradox of freedom: *on le forcera d'être libre*. This paradox has led to the scholarly controversy about the two, diametrically opposed, Rousseaus, one of whom is said to have championed liberal democracy and the other to have spawned collectivist tyranny (cf., for example, Plamenatz 1963: 433ff.; and various essays in Cranston and Peters 1972). The collectivist regimes of eighteenth-century France, revolutionary regimes that set the collective against the individual with a ruthless and bloody absolutism, found their legitimacy and logic in this Rousseauian ambiguity (Talmon 1970).

Defection and ritualistic observance are not unfamiliar themes in the kibbutz, but neither are they salient in the everyday social life. On the other hand, collectivism is a characteristic emphasis. The ideology enjoins the "preference for the needs of the group over those of the individual" (Amitai 1966: 42), and practically all of the individual's social relationships are touched by the kibbutz in such a way as to remind the individual of this.

This is not to say that the kibbutz would be well regarded as a small version of Jacobin or Babouvist France. On the contrary, the kibbutz has succeeded in keeping voluntarism intact as a genuine principle. Hence, although his or her exclusive jurisdiction is relatively thin, the individual person has not been deprived of influence and say. Nevertheless, the individual's autonomy is preserved not in virtue of the synthetic harmony envisioned by the ideology, but at the cost of much struggle between the individual and the collective.

What one finds in Timem is repeated public engagement, even preoccupation, with issues that develop their definitive political charge by means of the problem of relative autonomy between the individual and the commune. In addition to the issue of voting procedure in the General Assembly, other issues were matters of keen, sometimes bitter, political contention, according to the question of what is owing to the individual and what to the collective. These issues include the following: the amount of cash allowance given annually to the members for their personal use; rationing of clothing, cosmetics, and the like; accessibility of kitchen supplies for personal consumption; disposition of the various kinds of private property procured from outside the kibbutz; day-to-day and long-term division of labor; and still others. The fact is that Timem's membership was often divided in the public arena into diametrically opposed factions, of those who defended the community's collectivist designs and those who called for *liberalizatzia*.

Because the constituents of these factions varied situationally, from issue to issue (Evens 1975: 173–76), this politico-ethical polarization was less degenerative of the community's social order than it might otherwise have been. What counts here, though, is that, despite the situational shifting of individuals from one pole to the other, the polarization itself was pervasive and constant. Such polarization is, by definition, indicative of a discrepancy between the perceived interests of the collective and those of the individual. Under these strained social conditions, the collective's demands on the individual, far from being readily construable as a boon to the individual's freedom, must have been felt to prescind and belittle it.

In effect, though it had never been complete (the ideological picture notwithstanding), the synthesis of the individual and society had come appreciably apart, flagrantly remarking the antithetical force that also serves to define these two phenomena. The collective reacted to this relative ideological undoing by pressing ever harder for the principle that it inherently supposes — collectivism. Vis-à-vis the individual, this principle had become imposing and oppressive in spite of ideological design. Under these conditions, the individual could do little else but protest what had become an intolerable threat to her or his autonomy. In this atmosphere of exigent and doctrinal collectivism, the individual's protestations on his or her own behalf were necessarily synonymous with basic dissent.

The Question of Contingency and Social Order: Time and the Kibbutz Synthesis

I have so far discussed the paradoxical nature of the kibbutz's solution to the problem of the relation between the individual and society as a matter of logic. I have argued that the solution of voluntarism is no less deceptive than it is ingenious. Since full voluntary compliance must fall short of demonstrating a capacity for voluntarism, the solution actually exerts a force for noncompliance or deviance.

Now, since the solution is logically formidable, the force it exerts as against itself cannot operate as logic qua logic — instead it must operate covertly, as a tacit and, for this reason, very powerful condition. In this way, it appears to act more like a force of nature than of logic. In point of fact, the paradox is not driven by logic alone, but receives its most critical impulse from practice.

I mean here more than the trivial observation that the paradox cannot unfold materially, to exhibit a confrontation between the individual and society, unless the attempt is made to practice it. I mean, rather, that the paradox *as a paradox* virtually hinges on practice.

As I have analyzed the paradox, the reason why the commandment to comply voluntarily amounts to its own counterorder is that in the absence of at least one instance of observable noncompliance, there can be no assurance that compliance is in fact voluntary. Whatever one's thoughts, if one has never actually done otherwise, then there can be no certainty that one can actually do otherwise — that is, that one really enjoys the capacity to choose. Under these conditions, one must always be plagued by doubts about the voluntary character of compliance. Above I glossed this state of doubt in terms of the experience of otherness, of the uncertainty as to the state of "one's own" mind or an-other's.

The paradoxicality of the commandment of voluntarism is critically conditioned, then, by the uncertainty attaching to the question of agency. Were it not for the element of uncertainty, the commandment to obey voluntarily would entail no logical inconsistency. Now, while it is true that the uncertainty can be mitigated by an act of apparent noncompliance, it can never be abolished. A contrary act can serve to differentiate oneself, thus engendering a sense of one's own agency — the feeling that somehow one is given to choose one's own place in this world. But it cannot thereby *guarantee* that any act of compliance thereafter may be counted as voluntary. Even if one enjoys a strong sense of oneself as an agent, the degree to which that self-identification informs one's acts must always remain open to interpretation. For it is precisely that openness, an ineliminable uncertainty or otherness, that calls forth the construction of the sense of self. Put differently, the uncertainty presents a kind of vacuum, which we call human existence, the interminable filling of which *is* self-fashioning.[3]

What this means is that, even before one may be *commanded* to choose to obey, one is always already *condemned* to choice. The paradoxicality of the commandment arises from the condemnation to choice. What is most diagnostic about human practice is the fact that it is always open as to its projectory and meaning — it is always in fundamental measure uncertain and other. The commandment to choose to obey constitutes a play on the condemnation to choice, such that choice as such or self-projection is made thematic and brought sharply to consciousness.

This thesis, that we are condemned to choice, calls for further development (Evens, forthcoming). What I wish to bring out here is that the dilemma of the individual and society is no less a matter of practice than of logic — put another way, it is intrinsically temporal. On the kibbutz's approach to this dilemma, the individual represents the element of otherness and uncertainty, in an otherwise normatively fixed and self-enclosed order. The solution of voluntarism aims to arrive at the synthesis of the individual and society by incorporating the individual as such into the objective social order. But in this ideological scheme of things, the individual stands for the uncertainty that is time, the otherness that always moves beyond the sameness of the holistic ideal. Hence, the kibbutz's approach to the dilemma of the individual and society betrays a specific attitude toward time and contingency.

The Practical Erosion of the Kibbutz Ideal

It is unassailable that in its goal of punctilious synthesis between the individual and society, the kibbutz is well described as utopian — nowhere. It is equally true, however, that the kibbutz is characterized by a strong pragmatic bent.

The kibbutz has always strenuously denied that it is utopian, if by that term one intends "impractical." The ideology has stressed the capacity of the kibbutz to respond adaptably to the concrete exigencies of human social existence (Leon 1964: 3–4, 21–22; Amitai 1966: 19f.). As Martin Buber wrote about this enterprise (calling it an "experiment that did not fail"): its ideal motive "joined hands with the dictates of the hour" and "remained loose and pliable in almost every respect" (1949: 142).

There is no denying that actual practice is a central concern of the ideology. But neither can it be refuted that as a result of this concern the kibbutz has had to subject its ideal of synthesis to forces that are in a plain sense both external and indifferent to it. These are the forces of the world of practice. Relative to the normative fixative of the world of kibbutz ideality, these forces are necessarily contingent and uncertain. They introduce the flux and chaos of time and history into an impeccable and necessary order.

It must follow that, in the interest of practice, the kibbutz ideal has had to compromise its integrity and autonomy. To speak here of compromise is, of course, another, less happy, way of putting that the ideal is "loose" and "pliable." But whether we employ "compromise" or "pliability" to describe how this ideal world relates to concrete practice, there is in the usage a distinct implication of a fundamental incongruity between the two worlds. And this incongruity implies in turn the limited practicality of the ideal.

The implication of limitedness holds, in a sense, for all ideal endeavors. But what matters here is that for an ideal such as the kibbutz's, one that is explicit and aspires to scrupulous realization, coming to terms with the world of practice is peculiarly fraught with existential peril. Owing to its complete outspokenness, every time an ideal of this kind is subjected to the forces of contingent reality, the exercise is bound to be construed as a test for validation (or, depending on who is doing the testing, invalidation). So that, despite devices to absorb or explain away shortcoming, in the final analysis these "tests" are going to lay bare the ideal's limited practicability and conventional nature. And where the ideal at stake asserts its own scrupulousness, making the absorption of failure hard to bear and accomplish, the ideal's limitations will be exposed all the more readily. Thus, ever hiding right beneath the endeavor to live an ideal such as characterizes the kibbutz is a revelation of futility.

It would appear, then, that despite a genuine sensitivity to the exigencies of practice, the kibbutz can put itself into practice only by pointedly facilitating its own destruction, in the sense of eroding its own *ideological validity*. The processes of growth and internal diversification were the products of the engagement of Timem's synthetic ideal with practical reality. As such they introduced into the punctilious order of that ideal the fundamental incongruity that is *implicit* in all human practice, thus insinuating the *ultimate* insolvency of the ideal.

In order to run its institutions and ensure its material survival, naturally Timem found it necessary to recruit members. At first, it was forced by circumstance to rely on groups of immigrants, groups whose backgrounds varied in respect of important social considerations. Later, it came to rely primarily on members' children, who with time grew increasingly differentiable, not only by reference to age and generation, but also by reference to family of origin, marital status, friendship network, and the like. The processes of recruitment gave rise to considerable increase of size and internal diversity. From the perspective of Timem's normative order, however, this course of development was in a certain sense downright contrary.

In effect, whereas what I referred to earlier as an ineluctable experience of otherness ensured a phenomenological gulf between the individual and society, the material processes of growth and internal diversification fixed that gulf substantively, helping to transform it into politico-ethical schism.

A Matter of Trust

I have already noted how the community was fairly rife with concrete politico-ethical encounters between liberalizing and establishmentarian forces. I have also documented how the debate on secret balloting neatly instantiated this state of dissension and polarization. But beyond this openly embattled state, in priming the separate interests that are only implicit in the quality of otherness, growth and heterogenization occasioned still another antinomian condition. While dissent and its prospect broadcast shortcoming, the condition I have in mind lent to such ostensive unsuccess the affective air of ethical insidiousness; it drove home the ideological lesson of moral harm in the event of decreasing approximation to the synthetic ideal. The condition I have in mind is lack of trust.

As one of Timem's members has written, the kibbutz can achieve its ideal state only when "one's opinion is heard" and when "one's every move is not accompanied by excessive hindrances and suspicion and fear of insult" (*Sefer Timem*: 241). The kibbutz's social order is ideologically predicated on unencumbered openness among the members:

> Criticism in the kibbutz is voiced so frequently and so openly that a casual visitor might think that the membership was on the point of breaking up. The reverse is the truth... and nothing could be more healthy than such open criticism. While outside the kibbutz such a procedure might lead to damaged social relations, within the kibbutz framework it actually cements the general social relationship by bringing disagreements out into the open. (Ben-Yosef 1963: 59)

The prescription for probity stands on all fours with kibbutz democracy's critical emphasis on open, discursive exchange as the means to arrive at the general will. I suspect that the immoderate worry, found in the kibbutz, over the evils of gossip is sharply promoted by the normative weight placed on this prescription. Whatever its social functions and psychological ends, gossip tends to connote suspicion and intrigue, not uprightness and honesty (see Gluckman 1963a; Bowes 1989: chap. 4).

That there should be no want of trust is a crucial prescription of the ideology, and one that serves to certify the community as exceptionally moral. Indeed, this prescription is a corollary of the synthetic ideal. The identification of each member with Everyman should effectively eliminate any problem of other minds. Where minds fail to appear significantly other to one another, there can be no grounds for distrust. Under such conditions, the self that one is, is the self that one seems to be.[4]

In point of fact, however, the contingent course of Timem's development gave the members good reason to suspect one another's presentation of themselves. Once the member is defined as having private, as well as public, dispositions, the telling of the sincerity of a member's public face must become less secure. Put another way, the greater the gap between the private and the public domains, the stronger is the possibility of hypocrisy and dissimulation (Suttles 1970).

That Timem's members were experiencing their social state in such terms is well borne out by the dispute over secret balloting. One of the critical features of the debate was the claim that the current situation made it difficult to vote sincerely. It was argued that "personal and social pressures" entailed great risk to members were they to express openly their authentic preferences. To quote a member who put it point blank: "The present system promotes hypocrisy."

The judgment that Timem's democratic process had become less than frank was not contested; even the Secretary felt compelled to introduce it in the debate, though the condition it described might well have harmed his efforts to depreciate the motion of a secret ballot. Voting dishonesty could not be ignored. Its existence called into question the kibbutz's capital claim to the practice of substantive, in contrast to merely formal, democratic freedom. Insincere voting mocked the community's admonishment of political communion.

It is no wonder, then, that this state of affairs gave the members to regard the community's moral state as "degenerated." When members of a community, whose order is predicated decidedly on moral consciousness, come to a point wherein, as was publicly proclaimed by one of Timem's members, they "fear to criticize their comrades on moral grounds," the disingenuousness involved is a very serious matter. It pertains not only to the consideration that one's comrades cannot be trusted to criticize their fellows in moral terms. It pertains also to the reason for this consideration — to wit, that one's comrades cannot be trusted not to make instrumental retaliation. A waxing world of private concerns had occasioned in this collectivist universe a general vulnerability to social disapprobation, and therewith a pervasive state of distrust. Although the detractors of secret balloting seemed stymied by the problem of insincere voting, it was one of their heavier arguments that a secret ballot could effect a remedy only by giving institutional warrant to the more inclusive state of distrust that lay behind the voting problem.

The theme of distrust was readily apparent in Timem's social life. During the course of everyday discussions and gossip, it was usual to hear misgivings expressed about the trustworthiness of other members. No doubt the expression of such misgivings characterizes most any community. More importantly, though, distrust was thematic also in Timem's public forum. For example, during the period of fieldwork, at least two senior members of Timem, both of whom were responsible for the distribution of essential consumer goods, were formally accused of showing favoritism in the performance of their tasks. In the one case, the accused managed to publicly exonerate herself and turn the tables on her accuser, whereas in the other, the kibbutz felt compelled to impose additional controls on the accused in relation to his job. These were serious matters, and they necessarily exhibited to all concerned — perhaps with even greater impact than the debate over secret balloting — that distrust had become diagnostic of the community's social process.

Nor was the public manifestation of distrust confined to interpersonal events that had escalated into collective issues. Distrust was a distinctive feature of the relationship between the individual and the collective itself. A striking case in point was the community's attempt to institute a formal (though not legal) contract between itself and members whom it was sending, or planned to send, to study to become teachers in the community's schools. I was told that the kibbutz feared — and by past example had reason to fear — that after qualifying as teachers these persons might well decide not to return to the kibbutz. Consequently, the kibbutz sought by means of the contract to ensure their labor for a number of years (to be exact, twice the number they took to study) subsequent to the completion of their training. I do not know the number of persons involved. But at least two of them refused to sign, on the grounds that, as one put it to me, "the whole business is not fitting to a kibbutz [*lo kibbutzi*] and implies that I am not trusted."

That the distrust was reciprocal is implicit in the example. The very attempt to impose the contract served also to convey that the community is in a position to thwart the individual member's own plans. "As a nonmember there is one thing you cannot experience here," an informant explained to me, "and that is the damage the kibbutz can do to you."

A word of caution is in order here. It is not my intention to depict the community as a hotbed of suspicion and deceit. My general experience of Timem was certainly not in such terms. It would be far from the truth to think that distrust is the singularly representative quality of social intercourse in this community. My point is, rather, threefold: (1) Timem's members were indeed suspicious of one another's intentions, to a degree that is analytically impressive; (2) by virtue of the contingent development of the private domain, Timem's social order, which had been programmed to rely preponderantly on the superogatory social controls inherent in open frank interaction, had grown sharply conducive to social suspicion; and (3) such suspicion had become a significant representation in Timem's social life.

Liberty, Equality, and History

Thus, owing to the contingent course of practice, Timem has manifested its ideal also by belying it. In giving itself to Buber's "dictates of the hours," the kibbutz ideal, being also explicit and scrupulist — which is to say, unconditional — might be described, paradoxically, as nonutopian utopianism. Divisiveness and distrust bear witness to the deeply paradoxical constitution of Timem's social process.

The debate on the secret ballot communicated this constitution even more directly, in relation to the question of "personal issues." To recall, on the one hand, the institution of secret balloting would have preserved the collective hegemony over personal issues only by institutionalizing the force of personal interests in Timem's political process. On the other, the proposal to restrict the General Assembly's jurisdiction would have kept personal issues public only by making a substantial move away from immediate and toward representative democracy. In the case of either solution, then, the paradox of "personal issues" would have been addressed only to take hold in another place.

Another conspicuously paradoxical content of the debate in question emerged through the main ideological justifications offered by the contending sides. The advocates of a secret ballot supported their cause by invoking the warrant of "freedom to vote according to one's conscience," while the detractors appealed to the principle of "open discussion." Although, as was elaborated in chapter 3, these two justifications represent the values of individual and collective freedom respectively, both enjoy a fundamental legitimacy in Timem. The former is keyed to "voluntarism," the latter to "holism." These two ideological dogmas stand at the heart of the kibbutz's projected synthesis of the individual and society. In effect, therefore, Timem's members were at odds over distinct ideological principles, both of which were unassailably legitimate and neither of which could take absolute precedence over the other.

The dilemma centering on the question of personal issues as well as the dilemma centering on the question of freedom appear to be variations on a common paradoxical theme in Western social theory. I have in mind the theme of how to satisfy the call for commonality with the demand for absence of restraint. In more usual terms, this is the question of how to reconcile liberty with equality (Dahrendorf 1968: chap. 7).

A perfect synthesis of these two principles seems feasible only so long as the uncertainties of human existence are kept at bay. Once "liberty" and "equality" are opened to the exigencies of history, their coexistence becomes problematical. At times, a choice must be made between them. As Dahrendorf writes:

> The harmonious or discordant counterplay of liberty and equality, indeed these very concepts and values, become meaningful only if natural as well as social inequalities substitute history for the terrible perfection of constant equality and thus expose man's freedom, his efforts toward self-fulfillment, to the threats of the world. (1968: 189)

In Timem, their exposure to membership growth and diversification forced these two principles increasingly apart. Waxing social differentiation resulted in the elaboration of discrete selves, selves significantly different from one another as well as from the collective "self." This state of affairs placed a terrific burden on the kibbutz's radical principle of equality. While in itself difference does not entail inequality, because it poses the question of commensuration, difference does make the institution of equality essentially problematical: as it calls for a *standard* of comparison, difference appears to stimulate, if not necessitate, evaluation. As a result, in order that it might preserve the equality that is its hallmark, Timem was moved to attempt to circumscribe individuals' liberty by treating them, now rather *uncommon* or detached selves, as means to the collective end rather than as ends in themselves. In other words, with the circumstantial sacrifice of equality for liberty, and the resulting substantive redefinition of these two principles as discordant, the community was forced to compensate by attempting to restrain the individual's liberty. In so doing, however, it underscored the new definition of the principles as out of keeping with each other.

This conflict of principles — an expanding conflict in the wake of the substitution of "history for the terrible perfection of constant equality" — was doubtless implicated in certain of the debaters' remarks. It was said that Timem had "developed by leaps and bounds" (to outstrip its organization), and had become a "modern community" given to "professional" (specialized) knowledge and to public issues that can no longer "touch on" (interest) all the members directly. And it is this expanding conflict, between liberty and equality, that accounts for the public unraveling of the ambiguous precepts of personal issues and collective freedom. Under the influence of this conflict, these two precepts broke down into the concrete and consequential political oppositions of personal versus public issues and of individual freedom ("voluntarism") versus collective freedom ("open discussion"), respectively.

The Paradigmatic Apposition of Conflict between the Generations

Generational Conflict and the Dilemma of the Individual and Society

At this juncture, I can show that, by virtue of its own logic of negation and dissent, "generational conflict" is eminently fit to *represent,* both structurally and hermeneutically, the profound dilemmas in which Timem's members found themselves caught.

The issue of secret balloting was both demonstrative and constitutive of a falling out between the individual and society. By raising to political contention the problem of participation, this issue brought into bold, public relief (1) an active difference between public and private planes of interest in Timem, (2) a pragmatic opposition between resolutions that are moral and ones that are merely expedient, and (3) a teleological antagonism between the goal of collective hegemony and that of individual autonomy. Thus, the issue was a representative evolvement of the logic of the community's answer to the dilemma of the individual and society. As such, the issue directed the public attention to the (ideologically perverse) irony of the practice of voluntarism and to the (ideologically unhappy) gulf between collective and individual decision.

The bipolar constitution of the issue characterized the social problem underlying the issue, the proposed remedies to the problem, and the justifications propounded on behalf of the remedies. Significantly, the issue's dualistic compass reached also beyond these functions, to include accountability. By holding the young members to account for the unhappy state of political participation, generational conflict was tacked on to the other bipolarities. In this way the generation of the young members was linked to self-interest and instrumental design, and that of the veterans to other-regard and moral principle.

It would, however, be misleading to think that the division between the generations received these character associations afresh by virtue of the dispute over secret balloting. In a universe whose thematic center is moral discourse, the kind of universe the kibbutz defines, these associations belong to that division as a matter of course. As we are now in a position to see, the dualism that is enfolded in the logic of the community's ethical approach to the dilemma of the individual and society did not so much impose itself on the generational relationship as find in this relationship an approximately coordinate structure of meaning.

There are at least three critical ways in which the generational relationship could assimilate and represent the dualism in question. First, the paradox of voluntarism, whereby resolute conformity amounts to fundamental deviation, is common to both the generational relationship and the community's contractarian approach to the dilemma of the individual and society. Since lettered conformity by the sons would fail to demonstrate the paramount principle of voluntarism, the sons can effect continuity with the fathers only in the breach.

The paradox of generation and the paradox produced by the kibbutz's solution to the dilemma of the individual and society are formally homologous. In both cases, strict conformity amounts, ironically, to fundamental deviation, while, conversely, essential conformity requires deviation. As a result, in both cases dissent qua dissent constitutes a tacit but normative theme.

There is between the two paradoxes, then, that of voluntarism and that of generation, a compelling synecdochic presence — in a substantial and specific sense each is representative of the other.

Second, the generational relationship is eminently capable of expressing what I described as a resistant logical difference between individual and collective decision. The *logical* vacuum obtaining between these two kinds of decision permits the establishment of preferences that are merely personal. As it thus implies the limitations of the kibbutz's organicist ambition, the logical difference in question enjoys a far-reaching practical significance.

Given a moral universe keyed by the idea of generation, this consequential significance is projected also by the father-son relationship. Though the substantive identity between a father and son is biologically plain and considerable, no one is likely to claim it is complete. There stands between a father and son an essential phenomenal difference. However, the phenomenological nature of this difference varies from the perspective of the father to that of the son. In this moral universe, normally, whereas the father experiences the son as an emergent part of his own world, if not as his own issue, the son experiences the father as an imposition from without. In effect, for the father the son's otherness is cut by experience, while for the son the father's is essentially unadulterated. To be sure, the son will eventually learn that he and his father are somehow part and parcel. But such learned knowledge is precisely not experience, and its use here, to mediate the father's otherness, must serve to mark even more emphatically that that otherness is experientially unmitigated. As Levinas writes, filiality designates "a relation of rupture and a recourse at the same time" (1969: 278–80).

Speaking phenomenologically, then, the son's is a world of self and other, and the father's of self-and-other. The difference is that obtaining between a dualistic and a synergetic world, respectively. Put another way, the son's world thematizes, in phenomenological principle, the nonsocial and, in this sense, the amoral, while the father's evokes especially the social and the moral. Whereas the father's experience of the son is basically from within and holistic, the son's of the father—like one's experience of society—is basically from without. Translating into terms of relative autonomy, it must follow that, representatively, the son's is a world of individual governance and the father's of social dominion. Thus, the generational relationship assimilates the logical gap between collective and individual decision.

Third, because the lines it draws in the social world seem easy to read, the generational relationship can supply the kibbutz with a culturally appropriate framework of meaning for the experience of fundamental schism. The kibbutz must be hard-pressed to find a meaningful place for this experience. For the kibbutz the final arbiter of meaning is moral discourse. But the highly situational politics of the kibbutz, wherein each issue tends to occasion a different set of political divisions, makes the assignment of consistent moral accountability difficult. By featuring a dualistic population breakdown that seems cognitively and morally unambiguous, the generational relationship can make kibbutz-sense of a divisiveness that is, to use a kibbutz turn of phrase, *lo kibbutzi*—not fitting to the kibbutz.

Generational Conflict and the Dilemma of Time and Social Order

In assimilating the falling out of the individual and society, the idea of generational conflict not only reflects but also refracts the situation. This is quickly seen in relation to the question of temporality. In representing the dilemma of the individual and society, the generational relationship converts a spatial configuration into a temporal one. For while the relationship between individual and collectivity may be construed as simply a matter of form, that between father and son cannot but be regarded as also a question of process. Thus the generational relationship gives to a fundamental dilemma, that of the individual and society, a processual cast as well as a perspicuous meaning. In doing so, the generational relationship can serve as a gloss for the way in which the development of individualism in the kibbutz brought time to bear on the kibbutz synthesis.

I have linked the development of individualism to the condition of contingency in kibbutz practice. The debate on secret balloting may be regarded as a kind of gloss on the antinomian impact of contingent growth — that is, of time — on the projected union of the individual and society. As I argued above, the manifestation of politico-ethical division, distrust, and paradox in Timem's social order reveals the impact of the essential uncertainty of practice on the kibbutz ideal. The generational relationship is richly capacitated to represent this temporal influence and its particulars.

To start with the distrust that had become so prominent a feature of Timem's social relations, generational conflict constitutes an iconic representation of this feature. Recall that the debate's divisiveness centered on the cause of liberalization and was keyed by the motivational antithesis of self-interest and other-regard. As I have just shown, the phenomenological asymmetry of the father-son relationship tends to define the father by association with collectivism and the son with individualism. The identical phenomenological asymmetry can be shown to be coincident with the appearance of distrust.

Phenomenologically, for the father the son issues basically from within, whereas for the son the father first appears from without. From the father's perspective, the son originates from a world with which the father identifies implicitly; but from the son's, the father emerges from a world in which the son only happens to find himself, a world into which he has been thrown. It must follow that the experience of radical otherness is implicit in the generational relationship — that that relationship projects, with the figure of the son, the appearance of an exterior world. In more familiar terms, the generational relationship implicitly conveys a distinction between a subject-world and an object-world. As this distinction naturally defines a communications barrier, so it defines the possibility of dissimulation and distrust.

But the generational relationship determines more than the possibility of distrust — it leads one to expect the emergence of distrust. Given that they include moral choice, the father's demands on the son for compliance are self-inconsistent. In view of these conflicting existential demands, the generational relationship must constitute at least the tacit understanding that deviation is as likely as not. In which case, both father and son must come to "know" not only the possibility but also the expectation of the son's contrariety. In other words, that the father cannot trust his own son is an intrinsic epistemological moment of the relationship between them.

To turn now to the paradoxical nature of the political alternatives that characterized the debate, Timem's members found themselves subject to incompatible, but equally exacting normative principles. On the one hand, kibbutz voluntarism left open the possibility of entertaining personal interests, while on the other, kibbutz holism sanctioned public interest alone. Though the community was predicated on the comprehensive union of these two principles, in actual fact it seemed possible to neutralize their opposition only in piecemeal fashion. Far from eliminating the opposition, the proposed solutions to the problems facing Timem's democracy would have served, in one way or another, to institutionalize the opposition. In effect, Timem's members found that, as a result of the contingent course of the community's development, the principles of liberty and equality had broken apart, and all the community's good intentions and political devices could not put them back together again.

The generational relationship can well represent the opposition of liberty and equality. From the principled association of collectivism and individualism with the figures of the father and the son, respectively, it must follow that, phenomenologically, the father enjoys a privileged connection to the principle of equality (as defined here by identity), while the son enjoys a similar connection to the principle of liberty.

The generational relationship captures iconically not only the two principles as such but also the basic incompatibility between them. In this connection, the crucial consideration is that there is no way to eradicate the tension of asymmetry in the relationship between father and son without destroying the relationship itself.

For as I have argued in depth, the son cannot yield fully to the father's authority without defining that authority as basically absurd. On the other hand, the father cannot fully relinquish his authority without becoming something less than the father. Given a phenomenological association of the father-son pair with the duality of liberty and equality, the basic incompatibility between these two principles is phenomenologically implicated in the fundamentally hierarchical nature of the generational relationship. As the son, in order to satisfy the father's demands, draws away from the father's authority, so the principle of liberty establishes itself in increasing opposition to the constant equality of the father's world, an equality defined by unadulterated identity or homogeneity.

Finally, the generational relationship neatly comprehends the involved material ground of this momentous dividing of principle — namely, the role of contingency in the course of Timem's development. I have just described how the generational relationship, considered phenomenologically, insinuates a distinction between a subject-world and an object-world. This distinction bears with it the operation of essential uncertainty.

Owing to his experience of the father as an external phenomenon, the son is representative of the emergence of an objective reality. Such a reality is entitative, for ontological purposes at large. It describes individuals, in the sense of basic particulars — things that are materially distinguishable from one another (see Strawson 1963: pt. 1). That is to say, in Cartesian terms, by contrast to its subjective counterpart, objective reality comprises things that extend in space and stand as differentiated from each other by reference to the (material) limits of their extension. The precondition for the appearance of such relations of extension and difference is a distinction between a subject-world and an object-world. Any such distinction serves to define not only Subject and Object but also Difference per se. Clearly, then, the generational relationship is constitutionally provided to represent relations of difference.

But, of course, in question here are not simply relations of difference — the advance of such relations is an even more critical feature of the course of events. It is *progressive differentiation* that inserted so substantial a wrench into Timem's ideological works. In which case, the generational relationship must be equipped to provide an analogue of social difference as a temporal, not merely spatial, phenomenon.

The temporality of the generational relationship varies perspectivally. As a First or Fundamental, the father stands peculiarly for the side of the relationship defined by Principle. The son, however, as a Derivative, is especially representative of the aspect of the relationship projected in terms of exigent circumstance rather than principle.

Taking the primary perspective of the father, then, the generational relationship enjoys the atemporality of a principled universe. From this perspective, the two terms of the relationship entail each other *in principle,* so that at *no time* can there be a "father" without a "son" or a "son" without a "father." Correlatively, from this perspective, the hierarchical nature of the relationship is a question of principle. That is to say, the authority of the father over the son is defined here as a matter of rightful domination.

Taking the primary perspective of the son, however, the generational relationship looks quintessentially temporal. From this perspective, the point of view of practical existence, the father is seen in his creaturely aspect, as a genitor. As a consequence, now the son *pre*supposes the father, and there is, necessarily, change through time. Not only that, owing to the asymmetry of time — that is, to the fact that there are traces of past but not of future events (Grunbaum 1964) — generation appears now as a contingent rather than necessary relationship. Accordingly, the hierarchical nature of the relationship becomes a question, not of domination, but of origination. It conveys the creative but uncertain authority of authorship rather than that of principle.

It should now be apparent that the son, as an emergent phenomenon, representatively enfigures the contingent aspect of social existence. This figure has an especial capacity to represent the side of the opposition between the individual and society that found its expression in the antinomian aspect of the course of Timem's history. It is this capacity that empowers the generational relationship to picture in linear-temporal terms structural difference.

Phenomenologically, the emergence of the figure of the son from that of the father can well represent the movement from the timeless design of the world of principle to the exigent process of the world of practice — in a word, the movement from order to history. It is the apparent and ideologically frightening inevitability of that movement, which the issue of secret balloting, as a social problem, evoked.

Metaphor and Metonymy

I have argued that the relationship between father and son makes an apt representation of the issue of secret balloting in respect of at least two critical areas of kibbutz theory and practice. These are (1) the kibbutz's ideological solution to the problem of the opposition between the individual and society; and (2) the kibbutz's approach to the intrinsic uncertainty of social life. In each of these areas, the issue of secret balloting conjured a logic of paradox and theme of dissent, a theme and logic that are prepossessingly paradigmatic in the generational relationship.

Before concluding this phase of the argument, there remains to make a brief, but arresting, point. My discussion about the tie between the generational relationship and the issue of secret balloting has so far pictured that tie exclusively in terms of representation. By "representation" I have intended metaphorical assimilation — relations of homology, analogy, and the like. But the generational relationship's imposing power to represent the circumstances lying behind the issue of a secret ballot should not be allowed to blind us to the consideration that the procession of the generations did *for a fact* contribute to those circumstances.

As was documented in chapter 4, demographically the division between the generations in Timem was abnormally marked, and politically it did indeed demarcate a categorial power differential. It is the case that when Timem got its start over fifty years ago, the families in the community were, relative to what they have become, scarcely visible. Moreover, Timem has had increasingly to rely on the reproductive function of the family as the primary means of ensuring and replenishing community membership. In view of these facts, it is plain that one salient factor of the growth and internal differentiation of the community has been the procession of the generations.

Therefore, the generational relationship was not only representative but also constitutive of the dilemmatic state of affairs in which Timem's members increasingly found themselves. In more meretricious terms, the apposition between the generational relationship and the dispute over secret balloting was metonymic as well as metaphoric. That there stood between the generational relationship and the dispute a material contiguity needs to be borne in mind for the analysis to follow in the next chapter.

Seven

Conflict between the Generations as a Primordial Choice: The Paradigm of Genesis

Theoretical Prologue: Anthropological Options

The main ethnographical question at issue in this book is why Timem's members failed to pursue an explanation in terms of heterogenization, choosing instead to define the debate in the empirically less adequate terms of generational conflict. At this juncture, taking certain standard lines of anthropological inquiry, at least two seemingly compelling answers suggest themselves.

The controversy about a secret ballot brought near to public consciousness the understanding that the community's realization had proceeded by putting farther from everyday reach the ideology's most central goal—the perfect synthesis of the individual person with society. Through the medium of the debate, the processes of growth and internal differentiation threatened to expose the relationship between the individual and society as being disharmonious in some fundamental measure. By the same token, the debate threatened to define the kibbutz, on its own (ideological) terms, as an exercise in futility.

Consequently, if the members had attended the empirically more precise explanation to its logical conclusion (of heterogenization), they would have had to end by raising to doubt the reason for their singular social being, their ideal of synthesis. For it is distinctly implicit in the empiricist explanation that their ideal, though perhaps more practically informed than most utopian ideals, is in the final analysis faulty — which is to say, not perfectly in keeping with the world as given.

Therefore, for the moment taking for granted that "generational conflict" leaves room for hope in a way that "progressive heterogenization" does not, the members' selection of the former explanation over the latter served to deflect the realization of ultimate disjuncture or anomie. Put another way, in this community of scrupulous design, their selection put off sociocidal interpretation. Put in the way most familiar to anthropological discourse, the members' definition of the situation functioned to maintain the social order in its current form.

One answer, then, to the question of the members' choice derives from orthodox structural functionalism. The hypothesis that generational conflict in the kibbutz is a situational belief cloaking an even more threatening disjuncture sharply recalls the classic anthropological explanation of ritual and mystical beliefs in tribal society, as modes of containing "fundamental disharmonies of social structure" (Gluckman 1967: chap. 6; see also Nadel 1952).

I find this structural-functionalist position ingenious. But it leaves at least one important question unanswered and raises another. It leaves unanswered the question of why "generational conflict" in particular was selected as the alternative to "heterogenization." Would not "witchcraft," say, have served equally well to define the situation and mask the fundamental disharmony?

In addition, the structural-functionalist position raises the question of the psychological bearing of such a society-serving choice. Just how does the social order get its individual members to make such a choice? Clearly, under the thesis of masking one conflict by another, it does not stand to reason that the members made their choice in order to put off the bad social end. If it did, we could then infer that Timem's members had already arrived at the conclusion of the kibbutz's essential faultiness. In that event, just who is it that they try to deceive by covering over the flaw with a hollow figure? These questions suggest that the structural-functionalist position is, to say the least, too simple.

In addition to the structural-functionalist position, my analysis of Timem's development especially disposes to another, less dated, kind of answer to the question of the members' choice. The analysis showed the logic of the dispute and the logic of the generational relationship to be dramatically alike. This striking correspondence is, surely, in itself reason to account for what happened. In other words, a second response to the question at issue is that, as an apt metaphor, "generational conflict" served to codify the problem-situation, or, more generally, to impose meaning on it.

This response corresponds to a number of analytical strategies, most notably, certain forms of structuralism as well as of hermeneutics. The thesis that "generational conflict" was selected for its metaphorical might brings to mind the proposition, in the structuralist mood, that ritual is a symbolic or semiotic mode of labeling difference and structuring events (see Leach 1964: xiv, 14). The thesis also brings to mind the proposition, now in a hermeneutic vein, that culture is an assemblage of texts, an artful work of self-reflection (see Geertz 1973: 25f.).

These two approaches are not exactly bedfellows in the literature. Yet there can be no doubt that each does its main analytical work by educing a metaphorical or symbolical order, of one kind or another. Both of these approaches are analytically powerful. By means of exegetical technique and some conception or other of the unconscious, both can address the questions of the differential selection of "generational conflict" and of the mentative bearing of such selection.

Still, if only for a somewhat transparent reason, neither structuralism nor hermeneutics seems adequate to account for motivation. Even should we dwell in ivory towers, when we regard our own lives *as they are lived*, it is plain that we live neither by thought nor by imagination alone. We are not only in the world, but also of it. If this is so, then to take motivation exclusively, or even basically, as a matter of intellection or aesthetic enterprise is to reduce it overmuch. To describe our worldly engagement as, for all important purposes, a mental exercise in metaphorization is, I should say, an immense intellectual conceit, whether on the part of the rationalist or of the aesthete.

It is true that, unlike structuralism, the great power of which resides in a Cartesian heuristic of symmetry, the hermeneutic or interpretive approach is not necessarily focused on geometrical rationality, but can well take into account the arationalities of affect and novelty proper. But insofar as hermeneutics treats of meaning only as it is detached from everyday practical affairs (that is, as symbolic form pure and simple), failing to grasp it as it is enclosed in practical activity, it too takes the life out of the meaning. Such an aestheticism is really too precious to get into the thick of things, descriptively or otherwise.

When it comes to understanding basic motivation, the ground

wherein we are moved, I can find as little reason to espouse a monolithic concept of "cultured man" as I can to embrace one of cerebral or of "normative man." Each of these aphorisms has much to offer the study of social life, but none can suffice. Whereas normativism tends to take for granted the psychological bearing that could enable it to show just how the social order does (and does not) inform itself, structuralism and hermeneutics tend to assume the practical course of social life that could enable them to show just how meanings do (and do not) construct themselves.

The sort of selection of definitions that took place in Timem was no more a function of symbolical or metaphorical design than it was of social utility. To grasp the nature of that selection it is indeed necessary to investigate meaning, but meaning that is lived before it is metaphorized. The sort of selection that pertains to such meaning may be called moral. Moral selection, as will become clear, describes behavior and consciousness in terms of primordial choices and of essential or ontological ambiguity.

The Paradigm of Genesis

It has been shown that "generational conflict" is readily available as an implication of Timem's ethos. Furthermore, in virtue of a striking and many-sided iconic homogeneity, such conflict proved an apposite definition of the situation.

But apposition alone cannot explain why "generational conflict" was selected as a definition of the situation. The kind of selection in question is not reducible to metaphorical design. Rather, it was motivated by concerns that were both tacit in the situation and at the root of the members' experience of themselves and the world. Such concerns pertain to *basic* self-identity. Accordingly, to explicate the kind of selection in question, what I am calling moral selection, it is necessary to undertake analysis of first or primordial choices.

In chapter 6, during the discussion of the duality of the individual and society in relation to kibbutz ideology, it was illuminating to refer to Rousseau's account of the origin of moral order and his contractarian solution to the flawed state of affairs characterizing that order. His account is, of course, a staple of Western social thought. But it presupposes another such account, namely, the story of the creation and fall of man in the Book of Genesis. As one scholar has put it:

"Rousseau's hypothetical history of mankind reads like a secularized version of the fall of man" (Cantor 1984: 7).

Genesis 2–3, which may be read as an account of the eventuation of moral order, bears a stunning logical resemblance to the kibbutz's self-understanding of the relation between the generations. Leaving aside for chapter 9 the question of just why it should exist, let me draw this resemblance. The marked character of this resemblance and the paradigmatic nature of the Genesis story point the way to a fuller understanding of the motivational relevance of generational conflict as a definition of the kibbutz's situation.

For this reason, it pays here to digress deeply and at length into the anthropological significance of Genesis. The meaning of the story is virtually inexhaustible and wonderfully rich. Needless to say, in the present reading, I seek to develop only those themes of the story that directly serve to illuminate Timem's explanatory focus on the idea of conflict between the generations.

Creation and Fall

The chapters of Genesis in question, 2 and 3, center thematically on the nature of man's creation and expulsion from paradise. The story may be seen to present a number of pointed responses to a host of questions — questions pertaining to the relationships between man and woman, man and earth, man and beast, man and work, woman and child, parent and child, and, of course, man and his maker.

But there is still another question, one that strikes me as less obvious but no less central than that of man's relationship to God. I have in mind the question of man's relationship to himself — which is to say, of his moral identity. This relationship is characterized by a set of transformations of states of man's being. Even before the move from paradise into the worldly world, and from a situation in which death has no dominion into one in which it becomes imminent, there occurs a shift from innocence to guilt or from simplicity to duplicity.

Each of the relationships in question is ultimately referred to the relationship between man and God, and is occasioned by an alteration in that relationship. The relationship between man and God is pictured, however, as basically ambiguous. On the one hand, as man's creator, God enjoys the absolute authority of an author over his creation; on the other, man enjoys a certain authority in his own right. The ambiguity is clearly implicit in the fact of man's capacity to disobey God's commandments. That God's instructions to Adam are given in the imperative mood bespeaks this capacity of Adam.[1]

Thus the relationship between man and God is characterized, paradoxically, by both determinacy and choice. In connection to choice, the relationship is based on trust. It is man's breach of this trust, this Edenic covenant, that in one sense constitutes the so-called fall.[2] In exercising his own authority, man falls away from God's dominion.

Genesis 2 opens with the fecundation of the earth by a mist that "went up from the earth and watered the whole face of the ground."[3] The consideration that in a sense the earth generates its own mediating agent is deeply significant. It pictures immanence as inherently self-transcending, thus anticipating man's act of self-mediation, the act of disobedience.

After the earth is fructified, God forms man of "dust from the ground" (the name "Adam" derives from *adama* — "earth") and gives life to him by means of divine inspiration: God "breathed into his nostrils the breath of life; and man became a living being." Thus, right from the start man has a dual nature — he exists tensionally, as between body and soul.

God then makes an authoritative pact with Adam. He commands him that of the trees of the garden he planted for him, Adam may eat of every one but "the tree of the knowledge of good and evil." This tree he forbids to Adam on pain of death: "In the day that you eat of it you shall die." Evidently, the fruit of this tree, though not exactly unfit for human consumption, presents a grave risk to mankind.

Owing, however, to the serpent's guile (the serpent being "more subtle than any other wild creature"), and then to Eve's essential concupiscence (being inclined to give way to her appetites, "The woman saw that the tree was good for food, and that it was a delight to the eyes, and that the tree was to be desired"), Adam too proved unequal — or, perhaps better, more than equal — to temptation.

For his transgression Adam is punished. They all are. Before it is possible to adequately comprehend the nature of the punishments, though, it is necessary to attend to something else that befalls Adam as a result of his act of disobedience. Adam becomes god-like ("Man has become like one of us," says the Lord), which of course is just what the serpent said would happen ("You will be like God"). As I will elaborate momentarily, the character of their punishments has much to do with this new elevated status of Adam.

It is crucial to see that the woman is literally part of the man: "The rib which the Lord God had taken from the man He made into a woman." "This at last is bone of my bones and flesh of my flesh," proclaims Adam. Therefore, remarkably, Eve's temptation of Adam must amount to Adam's temptation of himself.

There is more to this point. Plainly, as "bone of his bones and flesh of his flesh," the woman represents one side of Adam's dual nature especially — the bodily side. A psychoanalytical interpretation of Adam's "rib" as a euphemism for his penis is inviting here. But even if one does not wish to entertain this sort of psychoanalytical conjecture, the one-sided identification of Eve with Adam remains textually compelling. Perhaps the most authoritative gloss for *tzeila,* the Hebrew for "rib," is "side" (Rashi 1949; Brown, Driver, and Briggs 1975). It would appear, therefore, that Adam's temptation of himself by way of Eve amounts to the seduction of his more spiritual by his more carnal nature.

The significance of the serpent also becomes clear here. It is only fitting that this distinctly phallic figure, whose earthly character could scarcely be more complete (it is predisposed to go on its belly and eat dust), should tempt the woman. In a crudely formal sense, it is the serpent to whom the woman is fit. This sense was not lost on Rashi, who held that the serpent actually desired Eve (Rashi 1949).

Yet as a phallic figure, the serpent also shares in the identity of Adam. And since it partakes of the identity of both the man and the woman, it naturally obtains between them. It is thus a mediatory figure par excellence.

Furthermore, since the serpent is identifiable with Adam, as in the case of Eve's temptation of Adam, so in the case of the serpent's cunning deed, it is Adam in his dual construction inciting himself. Hence, as the serpent obtains representatively between the man and the woman, so it obtains between the two sides of Adam's nature, the spiritual and the material. It must follow that the kind of mediation at stake here is self-mediation, reminding us of the earth's capacity to generate its own fecundating fluids.

The punishments for the act of disobedience also take their meaning from the tensional dynamic of Adam's dual makeup. The serpent is cursed and condemned to a thoroughly tellurian existence: "Upon your belly you shall go, and dust you shall eat all the days of your life." The identical meaning is given in God's determination of the relationship between the woman's and the serpent's "seed": "He shall bruise your head, and you shall bruise his heel." In other words, there is the prognosis of a malicious opposition (an "enmity") between a being that stands upright and one that has no distance whatsoever from the ground, and thus, more generally, between the two poles of creaturely existence.

For her part in the act of disobedience, Eve is made to suffer much in childbirth, but also to want the precondition of her pain — her mate ("In pain you shall bring forth children yet your desire shall be for your husband"). In addition, she is subordinated to her husband's will ("He shall rule over you"). In effect, her limitations as a contingent, creaturely being are given added emphasis. Her autonomy or capacity for creation is limited to a painful physical process, to be compared with her violent ejection from the garden, and contrasted with her benign delivery from a slumbering Adam. And in its governmental mode, her autonomy is subjected to the temporal authority of the object of her desire — Adam.

Finally, because he "listened to the voice of [his] wife," Adam is condemned to struggle with the earth — his very ground (*adama*) — for a living ("In toil you shall eat of it") and then to return to it ("You are dust, and to dust you shall return"). In his case, too, then, the punishment consists of the amplification of his material limits. He is made to work for a living, a contingent activity that is prefigured in Eve's labor pains (the Hebrew words for Eve's "pain" and Adam's "toil" are both derived from *atzav,* "to suffer"). Furthermore, he is condemned to die. The material limitation of his autonomy could not be given more absolutely than in his sentence to death by reduction to the dust from which he was formed.

Thus, in all three cases, the punishments are formally identical. For their failure to observe the limits God originally set for them, the man, the woman, and the serpent are all brought down to earth, so to speak. Human beings' spiritual nature, or, what amounts to the same thing, their capacity for self-determination, is fixed absolutely according to the limits of their material nature — ironically, the very nature that prompted humankind to exceed its god-given limits in the first place. Measure for measure, the punishments fit the crime.

Such irrecusable fixation of the limits of human beings' creative capacity is likely to be experienced by them in punitive terms of alienation and debasement. For even in a nondualist universe, one in which spirit and matter are only relatively separate and distinct, the spiritual pole of the equation still enjoys a certain hierarchical primacy. It enjoys the primacy of inclusiveness and, therefore, of generation. In view of this consideration, and despite the fact that one is irrevocably included (in the whole of things), the apprehension of ultimate material limits on one's spiritual being and creative imaginings is bound to give one an acute sense of exclusion and inferiority. Under a hierarchy of value, this sense amounts to the experience of falling.[4]

Ascent

As we have seen, an act of disobedience against a founding father on the part of his son, an act experienced as a falling away from an ideal state of being, is a central phenomenological theme of Timem's apprehension of its own situation. But before we can extract the lesson from this parallel, it is necessary to attend to another side of the Genesis story.

The act of disobedience betrays a certain limitedness intrinsic to Adam's creaturely nature. It is just this expression of limitedness (plus the punitive fixing of such limitness), that in good part defines the fall. But it is crucial to see that the very same act of disobedience describes an ascent: "Behold," says God, "the man has become like one of us," and, so that he does not "put forth his hand and take also of the tree of life, and eat, and live forever," God expels him from the garden. Evidently, as the serpent divined, for reasons of his transgression, Adam becomes god-like, and he does so to such an extent that he poses a substantial threat to God's dominion, moving God to drive him from the garden.

What, then, is this god-like capacity? The diacritical difference between Adam and God in the story may be apprehended in terms of the capacity to create. Whereas God creates absolutely, Adam does so only relatively, on behalf of creation. This difference is given irremediably in the fact that Adam could not have created himself in the first place. Therefore, an increase in Adam's likeness to God must indicate an increase in Adam's capacity to create on his own behalf — that is, in his autonomy relative to his maker.

The power to create is nothing but the power to decide on possibilities. In effect, then, at stake is Adam's power to determine his own world, to choose for (the sake of) himself, precisely the power that is circumscribed by the penalties inflicted by God, especially the penalty of capital punishment. The fact that the fruit of the tree is a matter of good and evil — that is, of axiological alternatives — makes it clear that in contention is the power of choice in relation to ends, to possible worlds. The serpent's words, "And you will be like God, knowing good and evil," may be taken to mean, says Rashi, "Creators of worlds."

What Adam wins in the way of choice, though, cannot be a material addition to his nature. As he had been created with a certain autonomy relative to God, he must have come equipped with a capacity for choice. The consideration that although God formed the beast of the field and the birds of the air, he left it to Adam to name them, implies that Adam was already creatively endowed (God "brought them to the man to see what he would call them; and whatever the man called every living creature, that was its name").

In its nontrivial sense, the sense in which it confers basic identity, there is a great deal in a name (see Kripke 1980; Benjamin 1986). To identify something in this way is to bring it to the mind's eye, to make it appear in consciousness. It is, then, to select it out. Naming is thus a form of choosing. Put another way, to select something out by baptizing it is to disclose the difference between it and what it is not. In so doing, naming opens the world to choice; for in the absence of awareness of difference, there is nothing to choose between. Therefore, that God left it to Adam to give names to all the creatures implies that Adam was already a conscious being capable of telling difference and making choices. Indeed, it intimates that Adam stands to these creatures in somewhat the same way that God stands to Adam, his creature.

In becoming god-like subsequent to his act of disobedience, then, Adam must have acquired not the capacity for choice, but the power to exercise that capacity more extensively. Put differently, if choice presupposes consciousness of difference, then Adam must have experienced a rise in consciousness. This rise can have been brought about solely by an awareness of a further difference, but one that had the power to expand his capacity for choice exponentially. For logical reasons, the distinction between "choice" and "nonchoice" makes just such a difference. Because this distinction is itself about choice, it defines all differences in terms of choice, making them a matter of choosing. Thus, in becoming acutely aware of the question "To choose or not to choose?" Adam had his horizons of choice expanded mightily.

This is a difficult point, but it can be put in more concrete terms.

As long as Adam was not fully aware that he could make choices, which is to say, that he could do otherwise, in a plain sense he really had little choice. Consider: when you proceed down one of two paths but are not fully aware that you could have chosen between the two, a choice has been made, but was it you who made it? It is implicit in such a state of affairs that the choice was, in a sense, determined for you, not by you. In Adam's case, God's commandment to avoid the fruit of a certain tree on pain of death scarcely gave him a choice. It defined Adam's situation in such a way as to suggest that he had open to him only one *viable* path. Prior to his act of disobedience, then, what Adam lacked in the way of power of choice was developed awareness that he could fruitfully exercise that power.

That Adam's transformation bore peculiarly on his consciousness is given directly in the name of the forbidden fruit. The tree "in the midst of the garden" bears the fruit of "the knowledge of good and evil." The tree takes its name, then, not only from the possibility of choice, as represented by the alternatives of good and evil, but also from the knowledge (*hada'at*) of that possibility. The serpent's promise too is of enlightenment: "For God knows that when you eat of it your eyes will be opened, and that you will be like God, knowing good and evil." And when he reiterates the serpent's words, proclaiming, "Behold, the man has become like one of us, knowing good and evil," God himself acknowledges the equation of godliness and consciousness.

Duplicity and Insurgence

That man's fall is concurrently a leap of consciousness is evocatively cast in the story's treatment of Adam and Eve's nakedness. Before having eaten the forbidden fruit, "The man and his wife were both naked, and were not ashamed"; but after, "The eyes of both were opened, and they knew that they were naked." Plainly, it is not the nakedness per se that is significant, but the awareness of it: "Who told you that you were naked?" God asks. God wants to know how Adam and Eve became self-conscious, how they arrived at an acute sense of self. His question insinuates the capacity of naked or simple creaturely existence to transcend itself, reminding us of the earth's capacity to do the same. As has often been noted, the word for the serpent's cunning, *arum*, is a play on the word for the primordial couple's nakedness, *arumim* (see, for example, Cassuto 1961: 143–44).

Evidently, concealed within their nakedness, their innocence, was a cunning, a serpentine potential for duplicity.

The emergence of their selves is revealed in the act of their coming to know their own naked state. The transition from a state in which they were not ashamed to one in which they could experience shame testifies to this emergence. Shame can be felt solely by creatures who are aware of their own acts as originating in themselves, and of demands being made on them in virtue of being responsible agents.

According to Gerhard von Rad, "To appear naked before God was an abomination for ancient Israel" (1972: 91). To be sure, Adam is afraid and ashamed because a naked display of self is a patently defiant gesture. But the fear and shame are rooted in a deeper phenomenological consideration: Adam's nakedness cannot but remind him of his creaturely limitations and therein the ultimate vanity of his defiant act. Specifically, his naked body makes plain to him that he is not wholly self-contained but inevitably requires an other to complete himself. Adam's sexual anatomy must alert him to the fact that in the final analysis he cannot create, but only procreate. It is for reasons of this constitutional embarrassment that Adam and Eve "sewed fig leaves together and made them*selves* aprons," taking steps to cover themselves and hide their shame.

Clothing, however, hides shame only by pointing to it; it directs attention to what lies beneath. But in pointing to what it hides, clothing also signifies the dissimulation it is. Thus, implicating a difference between appearance and reality, clothing realizes the possibility of duplicity. As that which somehow puts off nature, all things cultural do the same — they play on "reality" in such a way as to make it appear to be otherwise. As one scholar has put it, "Clothing sums up all the dissimulations that make social life possible" (Dubarle, in Ricoeur 1967: 247 n. 6).

The possibility of duplicity emerges along with the self. To have a self is to be self-conscious. To be self-conscious, however, is to have at least two selves, one to think with and one to think about. As a consequence, human conduct is ever open to question and the charge of deceit. For, given the self's basic duplicity, it is always possible to judge the self-on-view as but a deceptive cover for the self-behind-the-scenes, the "true" self. And this possibility holds not only for the observing other but also for the attending self. Descartes notwithstanding, without the prospect of self-doubt, there can be no sense of self. Under these (cultural) conditions of existential suspicion, even nakedness can be worn, like clothing, to conceal a knowing self full of worldly desires.

With their awakening to their naked state, Adam and Eve take a natural turn toward the practice of deception and, correlatively, the avoidance of guilt. Upon learning of their revelation, God fires the question at them, "Have you eaten of the tree...?" The man responds, "The woman whom thou gavest to be with me, she gave me fruit of the tree"; and the woman responds, "The serpent beguiled me." In effect, each attempts to shift the blame onto another. Consequently, they introduce distrust into their relationship not only with God but also with each other and with themselves.

Put another way, they attempt to conceal from God and from themselves that they themselves made a choice. More exactly, they try to conceal that they chose for the sake of their selves. Hence, when they heard God walking in the garden, "The man and his wife hid themselves," and when God called to Adam, and inquired, "Where are you?" Adam replied, "I hid myself." The point of these passages, as I read them, is that in endeavoring to conceal their newly found selves (the Hebrew is *chavah*, "to withdraw or hide oneself"), Adam and Eve are guilty of failing to come to grips with the issue of guilt and accountability implicit in the power of choice.

It would appear, then, that Adam's failure to observe God's explicit command describes no accidental neglect but, though not a fully conscious act, a truly insurgent or revisionary one. For Adam's act of disobedience constitutes a leap of consciousness and conscience no less than it does a fall into more creaturely circumstance. It is as much a development of man's autonomy as it is a wayward movement from God's dominion. In effect, the story of the fall into a greater mundanity is also a story of the eventuation of that world as a moral universe. It is only in such a universe, where, in view of self-consciousness, there obtains a rift between subject and object and between appearance and reality, that such cultural phenomena as nakedness, clothing, dissimulation, distrust, and responsibility may be found.

A Host of Paradoxes

The emergence of distrust in social relations and of an acute consciousness of self on the part of the sons is, as I have documented, a salient feature of Timem's history. Indeed, the paradigmatic value here of the biblical tale is especially pointed in the account of disobedience as a necessary condition of the appearance of a moral universe. Whether in the Hebrew Bible or in Timem, only at risk of his own moral being (in these traditions, his very humanity) can the son fail to negate his father's order. In order to explicate the motivational basis of such negation, though, it is necessary now to direct attention to the paradoxical logic of the Genesis story.

On the face of it, it is a striking paradox that Adam's moral identity, the identity given in his creative, god-like consciousness of the difference between good and evil, should be grounded in and occasioned by an exemplarily negative act. In fact, however, a paradoxical makeup pervades the story and stands at the heart of its semantic logic.

Consider, virtually every relationship the story treats — including that between man and woman, woman and her issue, man and animal, and man and earth — is rendered as basically ambivalent. Although woman is literally of the man, she brings about his downfall and his separation from God and from himself. Although man is the object of woman's desire, he is the cause of her confinement, whether in childbirth or governance. Although woman takes her identity from her capacity to procreate ("The man called his wife's name Eve [Hebrew *chava,* from *chai,* or 'life'], because she was the mother of all living"), her issue makes her suffer and is the cause of her life's labor. Although the animal kingdom, as represented by the serpent, relates but the truth to man, it remains his antagonist and its promise of self-fulfillment his burden. Although man is fashioned from the earth, in order to eat of it he must struggle with it and eventually be reduced to it. Clearly, these relationships are constituted paradoxically. Each describes man and woman as essentially dependent on precisely that which runs contrary to them.

The fact that these relationships share a paradoxical constitution is more easily understood when it is remembered that each of them is a variant of a more encompassing relationship. It has already been shown that the woman, serpent, and earth are elements or aspects of the man — respectively his rib, creaturely cunning, and substance. The woman's issue must also be part of the man, since they are part of her and she is in a sense an alienated part of the man. Thus each of the relationships constitutes a specific manifestation of the relationship between man and himself.

Man's relationship to himself is made out to be a matter of his essentially dual makeup — he is at once both spiritual and material. Since, in principle, each of these properties is precisely what the other is not, it must follow that man presents a paradox. Insofar as spirit and matter define a single creature, they define each other; in which case, each is being defined in terms of its antithesis.

But the paradox runs deeper still, to pervade the story's dynamic. This can be told by attending more closely to the question of accountability as regards the act of disobedience. I pointed out above that both the man and the woman attempt to shift the blame away from themselves. Although this is a fair description of their conduct, their protestations of innocence are not without foundation. Eve did tempt Adam, and the serpent did tempt Eve. And, in any case, who are Eve and the serpent but aspects of Adam, of man's relationship to himself? But who is Adam? He is an extension of his maker — it was God who brought Adam into existence, forming him from the ground and breathing life into him. This consideration is not lost on Adam, who, in blaming Eve for tempting him, speaks of her to God as "the woman whom thou gavest to be with me."

Apparently, man's relationship to himself, his identity, is itself a specific manifestation of a relationship more encompassing still — the relationship between God and himself. Who, then, after all is to blame for Adam's incontinence?

> You can blame it onto Adam,
> You can blame it onto Eve,
> You can blame it on the apple,
> But that I can't believe.
> It was God who made the devil and the woman and the man,
> And there wouldn't be an apple if it wasn't in the plan!

As this Protestant Sunday school jingle suggests (never mind its New Testament message of "the plan"), the figure of God contains unavoidably the paradox in which the story is rooted. The paradox may be expressed in terms of the Absolute: if the Absolute is absolute, then it must include everything, including that which it is not, namely — the relative.

The Absolute as a Double Bind

I have shown that kibbutz practice also reveals a host of paradoxes — for example, the paradoxes of democracy, personal issues, and voluntarism — each of which presents a variation of the basic dilemma of the individual and society. In the kibbutz this dilemma is posed in terms of the problem of how to implement the full autonomy of both the individual and society at the same time. The kibbutz's response is keyed to the principle of voluntarism. This principle, as we know, yields a profound irony in its own right. Should individuals invariably follow the collective's lead, "voluntarily" or not, they necessarily deprive themselves of any means to demonstrate to others and to themselves the truth of the existence of their moral capacity.

The paradox of kibbutz voluntarism closely parallels the paradox of the Absolute. To grasp the son's act better, to see how he is moved, it is edifying, then, to inspect the paradox of the Absolute for its motivational implications.

The paradox in question is not simply a logical or epistemological configuration, but an ontological one. In effect, it implies its own concrete, evolutionary dynamic, its own unfolding in time. Put differently, it portrays the translation of itself from a form unto itself into a form of life, a worldly perspective from which the paradox may be experienced as such.

The goal of making perspicuous the mediatory "mechanism" of the unfolding of this paradox stands at the heart of the story of Genesis. The paradox of the Absolute is initially expressed in the act of Adam's creation as a two-sided being. As was brought out at the beginning of the exegesis, God created Adam such that the relationship between them is basically ambiguous. In making Adam in his own image, to resemble a self-sufficient deity, God created a being who is both dependent on and independent of him. The selfsame ambiguity is given elementally in Adam's dual construction, from the dust of the ground and from the breath of life.

The point is that, in terms of governance, Adam is granted a double mandate. Insofar as he is God's creature, he must conform to God's designs; but insofar as he is a facsimile of God, he must create for the sake of himself. Clearly, then, in order to conform, Adam must exercise his capacity to create, which, after all, is god-given. The trouble is, in so doing he necessarily effects his independence from God, and therefore, paradoxically, from God's designs.

Clearly, Adam is caught in a double bind. God's word to Adam effectively translates as, "You are damned if you do and damned if you don't." Though, on the one hand, this predicament deprecates the possibility of choice, on the other, it presents a paradigm of what it means to choose. For only a choice that is intrinsically difficult to make, one that can guarantee neither its outcome nor its rectitude, can ultimately capture what it means to choose. Alternatives between which one can choose by virtue of certain knowledge, do not present a thoroughly elective situation.

Adam's double bind makes the "choice" between the paths of conformity and nonconformity less than certain. Since the path of nonconformity is also in keeping with God's designs, albeit his implicit ones, the constitutional availability of nonconformity as a genuine (even if apparently lethal) option casts a certain doubt on the rectitude of God's explicit commandment. Epistemologically, the very possibility of nonconformity vitiates the certitude of the world of conformity, insinuating that the hinges on which that world turns are not the only hinges on which to hang a world. Thus, Adam's double bind implicates the possibility of movement from a world based on security, at the cost of total conformity, to one based on uncertainty, to the benefit of choice.

Adam's violation of God's commandment serves precisely to transform a situation of apparent certainty into one of uncertainty. Before his insurgent act, it was as if there was only one viable (though, owing to the possibility of another god-given choice, implicitly suspect) alternative open to him. But by choosing death over conformity, even if his choice was not perfectly witting, Adam informed his world with the uncertain component of certain death. That is to say, he brought to his awareness the indefiniteness of death's "when." By doing so, he made his choice of ends critically meaningful. Taking a death-defying action, he altered his situation in such a way that the world became uncertain for him and hence accessible to his elective manipulations. His change of residence, from the extraordinary world of the garden to the ordinary one of mundane human existence, signifies just this sort of epistemological sea change.

Thus, by calling up an act of transcendence, the double bind promoted a liberating choice. Adam's response to the predicament into which he is thrown is to take a choice that in a sense puts off the bad end, setting time (indefiniteness) between him and his finitude. In other words, his crime may be a capital offense, but his punishment is a life-sentence — that is, a life-toward-death. In effect, his solution is to confront the dilemma head-on, taking just one of its horns, the high-risk one, thus instituting that moral form of life we live primarily as discrete selves and speak of as history. As it makes his dilemma livable, Adam's solution is not only foolhardy but also profoundly creative. As such, it testifies to the worldly wisdom of the serpent, who, intuiting this turn of events, planted the seed of doubt in Adam's benighted consciousness.

The principal development in Genesis 2–3, then, describes a lived paradox, a paradox promising its own evolution into a form of life. Such a paradox unfolds neither by chance nor by necessity — instead it supposes a universe that is *both* directed *and* indeterminate. Ambiguous existence as between chance and necessity is part of what it means to say that the paradox is lived. Like God's act of creation, which, though an act of will, is nonetheless implicit in his absolute nature, Adam's act of disobedience, though also willful, is implicit in his paradisical state of being.

Put another way, Adam's act was both motivated and unmotivated. On the one hand, as he was constructed on the model of his creator, Adam was predisposed to strike out on his own, to create, so to speak. His motive was self-fulfillment or completion. Just as Eve is ineluctably drawn toward the serpent, so Adam is drawn toward Eve. The sexual nature of such attraction indicates the motivated aspect of the act. The tree of knowledge is, after all, a tree, a fruit-bearing tree at that — a powerful, organic symbol of generative and hence appetitive nature (see Eilberg-Schwartz 1990: 149ff.).

On the other hand, although Adam is predisposed to transgress God's prohibition, he is not predetermined to do so. His act is genuinely self-propelled, which is to say, creative. Put differently, Adam was not moved, but moved himself to transgress God's order. In Adam's case, the attraction of completion is the attraction of self-generation as well as generation simple, of creation as well as procreation. The fact that the fruit of the tree is knowledge evokes the creative and unmotivated aspect of Adam's act. An appetite for food for thought is in principle not really an appetite, but a willful and factitious need.

The decided ambiguity of the motivational character of Adam's act may also be told in terms of his consciousness. Though Adam was not unaware of the contrary nature of his act, it was not a fully conscious act. The tree of knowledge had been plainly prohibited to him, and he had been directly forewarned of the consequences of failure to observe that prohibition. Therefore, his act was truly insurgent. Nevertheless, precisely because he had not yet partaken of the fruit of that tree, Adam could not then have *known* right from wrong! In effect, then, Adam both knew and did not know what he was doing, an equivocal state of consciousness corresponding to the ambiguity of his motivational state.

Genesis and the Kibbutz

Generational Conflict and Primordial Choosing

The ambiguous nature of Adam's act in relation to the question of motivation is an outstanding finding. Adam's act presents a primordial choice, a choice obtaining directly between cause and reason, and that therefore is analytically reducible to neither. Such a choice is irreducibly creative and ultimately can be understood only in terms of itself.

The creative character of Adam's choice is revealed also in the consideration that his choice made choice *as such* possible. By taking the course of action he did, Adam transformed himself from simply a function of his maker to a veritable maker of himself. In effect, he created himself. Such primordial self-fashioning cannot be finally understood by appeal to motives external to itself, for by definition it constitutes its own motivation. Indeed, Adam's was an act of self-identification. In violating God's order, Adam identified himself as the sort of being who identifies himself — that is to say, a moral being. Put another way, by striking out on his own, Adam defined things in such a way that his action could no longer be immediately referred to his other. He thus established himself as an identity, a being who is identical to himself.

How, then, does this picture of Adam as a primordial chooser throw light on the question of motivation in the case of Kibbutz Timem? We have seen that in fundamental respects the story of Genesis is paradigmatic of Kibbutz Timem's situation. As in the biblical tale, Timem's members were experiencing themselves as having fallen away from an ideal state. They were inclined to apprehend their newly created community as under attack from within. The deterioration of democratic participation and the remedial recommendation of a secret ballot were construed in terms of this fallen state, as was the development of distrust as a thematic feature of the community's internal relations. In effect, this utopian undertaking was caught in the throes of a punishing awakening to its own limitedness.

In the abstract, Genesis may be read as an attempt to explicate and cope with the problem of the coexistence of the one and the many. The story provides a model of how the one produces the many, and, correlatively, of the desirable relationship between the one and the many. In the kibbutz, the paradox of the one and the many takes a sociological rather than theological form. Here the concern is how to produce the one from the many. Accordingly, the kibbutz is predicated on a certain synthesis of the individual and society. By voluntarily subjecting themselves to the collective will, the individuals are supposed to effect both their own and the collective's freedom at one and the same time. As in Genesis, then, the kibbutz synthesis describes a contractual relationship.

However appealing this synthesis may be in the abstract, though, in practice it proves flawed. For, most basically, in the absence of any visible expression of a will different from the collective's, there can be no evidence of the existence of the individual person. To be sure, it is possible to decide according to the collective will but, preserving one's sense of oneself as such, feel sure that one could have decided otherwise. However, certainty of this subjective kind presupposes self-consciousness, which, as the story of Genesis powerfully proposes, requires a willful distinguishing act. Such an act is necessarily observable and negative, an act that distinguishes by contraposed agency. Just as Adam in Genesis distinguishes himself as such by standing against an encompassing other, so the individual in the kibbutz distinguishes her- or himself by standing against the collective. In order to know one's own will as one's own, one must first differentiate oneself from what there is.

The more concretely identifiable the individual with the collective (the limiting case being a collective made up of just one member), the easier it is to approximate the kibbutz synthesis. Correlatively, the larger and more varied the collective's membership, the more difficult it is to effect an identity of the individual and society. In Timem the growth and heterogenization of the membership actually exerted pressure on the individual to deviate from the position associated with the collective. Under these conditions of de facto differentiation, by projecting a synthesis that guarantees the integrity of the individual, the kibbutz itself moved its individual members to dissent. Thus, in Timem the paradox of the individual and society was elaborated in terms of an increasing gap between these two poles of existence in the practice of kibbutz democracy and social relationships in general. This falling out between the individual and society was conceived of in terms of a failure of the individual to identify with the collective (that is, a failed contract), and experienced in terms of a falling from an ideal state of affairs defined by that contract.

In Genesis, the paradox of the one and the many is not presented as an abstraction but in terms of an evolving relationship between a creator and his creature, a founder and his son. Strikingly, as I have documented, the falling out of the individual and the collective in Kibbutz Timem was also assimilated to the relevant founder-son relationship. That is to say, as in the biblical account of the paradox of the one and the many, the kibbutz paradox of the individual and the collective was apprehended as a paradox of generation.

As we have seen, the founders of the kibbutz imposed on their children a set of fundamentally conflicting demands. The children were expected to perpetuate the utopian venture. But since voluntarism was one of the axial principles of this venture, the sons were put in a terrific bind. Voluntarism entails a capacity to make autonomous decisions, that is, a moral capacity. For obvious reasons, in itself compliance cannot finally demonstrate such a capacity — only difference or dissent can. Thus the children of Timem virtually were bound to oppose their parents' demands. By virtue of the demand imposed on them to conform to a given order, the children were predisposed to revise that order. In so doing, they not only opened their situation to their own designs but also, as Timem's *tz'irim* (youth) made plain, became acutely self-conscious of their limited ability to live up to the expectations of their parents.

Clearly, the predicament of Timem's sons parallels Adam's double bind. Both are bound at once to conform to a parental order and, by virtue of the creative place given to them in that order, to establish an order of their own. In both cases, thus, the children are predisposed to revisionism.

Nevertheless, no more in the kibbutz than in the story of Genesis is the violation of the given order predetermined or compelled by logic or symbolics.

It is true that there is something patently formal about the sons' role in Timem's counterrevolution. In the case study the sons are inclined to shoulder the blame for revisionism even though the empirical picture of things does not altogether bear out this attribution. In point of fact, as in Genesis, it is firmly implicit in the logic of Timem's situation that the founders too must be held accountable for the falling away from the ideal. For it was they who doubly bound their children to carry on what had been established in the utopian moment, but, paradoxically, to do so as founders themselves.

It is more than tempting here to read the community's self-interpretation in terms of filial disloyalty as a sacrificial idiom. In the story of Genesis, it seems plain, in view of the finding that Eve constitutes an aspect of Adam, that in her role as temptress she is also a sacrificial victim. And just as the female principle is thus sacrificed on behalf of the male, so the anthropological one is sacrificed on behalf of the theological one; humankind is made to take the fall for the imperfections of God's designs. Just so are the sons of Timem held responsible for the community's backsliding, blinding the members to the paradoxical nature of the order imposed by the founders.

Timem's counterrevolution has something considerable about it of a merely ritual enactment and portrayal of hostility and divisiveness — what Max Gluckman called a "ritual of rebellion" (1963b). Only, in Timem substantial change of a kind was intended and wrought (moral selves, in the modern sense, were enlarged, occasioning concrete organizational revision); the "ritual" component of things was largely confined to the question of accountability. Furthermore, it is crucial to see that this ritualistic turn of events was not fueled by a societal need to conceal an irresolvable conflict of fundamental principles, as in Gluckman's concept (though in part it did perform this function). Rather, the ritual was fueled by a passionate quest for self-identity.

The sons' assumption of responsibility for the counterrevolution in Timem corresponds to the achievement of their moral majority and of a key succession — the first! — in the life of the community. Timem had reached the point in its evolution where the founders, for reasons of age, were slowly stepping down, leaving the everyday leadership of the kibbutz to the next generation. To cite a conspicuous example, when I arrived at Timem, the position of Secretary (*mazkir*), the community's "highest" administrative post, had for the first time in Timem's history been divided between two occupants, a veteran member (*vatik*) and the son of a veteran.

What needs to be understood in relation to this transition is that, at the same time as it defined the community's current moral status as fallen, the sons' willingness to assume responsibility for the revisionary turn defined them as fitting successors to the founding fathers. The revisionary turn identified the sons as self-creators, and therefore, ironically, as equal to the enormous moral task imposed on them by their fathers.

But the irony runs deeper still, as it doubles back on the identity of the fathers. By bringing to realization the sons' self-identity as moral creators, revisionary change dialectically confirmed and fixed in perpetuity the fathers' self-identity in the very same terms. As the story of Genesis propounds, morally endowed sons are but mirror images of their fathers. In a sense, then, the sense in which revisionary offspring entail founding fathers, the sons gave birth to the fathers.

Of course, the transumption of the fathers is incomplete, an aspect of the ritualism displayed by these events. By definition, sons can never position themselves finally to overcome their belatedness in relation to fathers. As in the case of Adam in respect of his creator, however radically Timem's sons deviate from the designs of their fathers, they can never do so radically enough to erase the consideration that they could not have created themselves in the first place. In the present ethnographic context, this lesson is given nowhere more revealingly than in the case of the founders themselves. Their revolutionary break from their own fathers, as this analysis of profound connection between Timem and the myth of Genesis suggests, was far less radical than they supposed, and even less radical than meets the eye.[5]

To come to the main point here, it should be evident by now that the sons' assumption of the role of transgressor in Timem was an act of self-constituting along the lines of Adam's act of disobedience. Therefore, their act was in a certain sense and in crucial measure unmotivated. At bottom, the sons took the role of transgressor, not because doing so deflected blame away from the community's ideological foundations, nor because it imposed structure and meaning on a normatively perplexed social situation (though, to be sure, it did these things). At bottom, the sons identified themselves in antinomian terms "because" that is what sons as sons are given to do. Outside of the act in question the sons would have been significantly less secure about their identity as sons, that is, about who they are and where they stand in the world. By differentiating them from their fathers, as moral choosers in their own right, the act defined them as "sons," and, correlatively, it defined the world in terms of generation.

Generational Conflict and Moral Selection

To understand the nature of such an act, an act of self-constitution, it is futile to attempt to determine beforehand all its conditions, since these are developed in the course of the act. Thus, paradoxically, while putting on the antinomian drama that served to identify them more perfectly as true sons of Timem, the sons as sons could not have been fully determined. The act of assuming the role of transgressor was a crucial condition of the greater realization of the sons' filial identity. As a self-constituting act, however, it had to be itself in a certain sense unconditioned. In effect, as a means to the goal of self-identity, the sons' act was not altogether distinguishable from their goal.

The logical scandal that the connection between act (means) and goal (ends) is internal rather than external points to another consideration here. Self-identity is necessarily lived before it is cognized. By definition, the sons could not have been as self-aware, as acutely conscious of their selves, before, as after, their antinomian transformation. The fact that the motion of a secret ballot was not adopted is irrelevant here — for the transformation to occur all that was necessary was *the act* of making the motion. As is told in the story of Genesis, the emergence of self-consciousness must itself be less than self-conscious — it is forged, rather, in a blatantly existential act, an act of defiance and violation.

Neither, however, could the act have been merely mechanical, a product of the material forces that be, even if these forces are conceived of as essentially social. As the story of Genesis implies, mechanism per se simply does not suffice to account for the existence of choice and of self-constituting.

In effect, the sons' revisionary action(s) described a choice that was neither caused nor reasoned. I have spoken of this sort of choice as primordial. In so speaking, I do not intend — as perhaps Genesis does — first occurrence. Rather, I have in mind existential path taking. Such path taking is reducible neither to mechanical law nor to intellectual exercise — though it can, depending on the path taken, foster choice in the standard sense of conscious selection. The sons' revisionary posturing ostensibly opened the world of the kibbutz to their own designs. By apparently freeing them from certain comprehensive taboos laid down by their fathers, the sons' antinomian turn oriented them toward the mediate and the possible. This orientation enabled them to enter more paradigmatically their fated role as *kibbutzniks,* that is, utopian pioneers, though, relative to their fathers, second-rate or belated ones.

At this juncture, in view of what has been learned from our reading of Genesis about the motivational character of the sons of Timem and their revisionary posture, we are able to offer a direct response to our central question of the community's selection of a definition of its situation. In assuming the role of transgressor, the sons were simply advancing a prevailing definition of the situation, namely — conflict between the generations. In other words, their social perversity was a form of participation in and compliance with a particular moral selection current in the community at large. Through the attribution of responsibility for the community's fallen state, the fathers and sons together colluded, in a strange dialectic of negative continuity, to define themselves in terms of a conflictful generational relationship. And just as the sons' movement to this definition of the situation enacts an identity quest, so the fathers arrived at it as an act of self-constitution.

Conflict between the generations, then, presents and represents a primordial choice, a less than self-conscious choice to identify oneself in terms of a generational universe. Its selection cannot be satisfactorily accounted for as a function of societal needs or of intellectuo-symbolical designs, antithetical forms of reductionism. To be sure, generational tension was an especially apt metaphor for Timem's troubled situation and served the community well as a psychological and sociological defense mechanism. Doubtless, these features selected for the employment of this metaphor as a definition of the situation. But its baptismal selection, its emergence as a selection, is a matter of, rather than figurative thought or language, creative and semiautonomous choice. It is the product of a creature whose lot it is to create him- or herself, to constitute his or her own identity.

Primordial Choice and Human Existence

Remarkably, the action of human beings supposes an understanding on their part of who they are and where they stand in the world. Put differently, human action is always, inter alia, self-identifying (see Taylor 1985a: chap. 2). The distinctive ambiguity of living things — that they constitute individuals who depend on, but do not reduce to, their character as material collections — reaches its apogee in humans. Here nature doubles back on itself with such a luminous intensity that the ambiguity of form and matter may effect the appearance of a dualism of mind and matter. In human beings the "needful freedom" of organic form from gross matter becomes self-conscious and therewith mindful in the sense of thoughtful.[6]

The story of Genesis attempts to describe and comprehend, with an abiding primitive insight, just this leap into self-consciousness. It does so through an implicit theory of a diagnostically ambiguous nature endowed, by its creator, with a capacity for self-mediation, a capacity for rebegetting itself.

But the paramount consideration here is that human action is, in a sense not plain but indubitable, no less "naturally" self-identifying than it is instinctive. In the case of humans, form has achieved autonomy from its own matter to a stunning degree. This radical autonomy is expressed as self-consciousness or, in Descartes's arresting trope, "thinking stuff." In effect, the outcome amounts to an inversion of the usual order of form and matter. Instead of the human being serving as a mere carrier of material processes, his or her appetitive drives are drawn up into the service of a quest for self-identity. In other words, human beings' vital existence comes to be mediated by self-consciousness, and their bodily actions to depend on an articulatory sense of self, a transcendental construction.

If human beings' vital activity is necessarily mediated by their sense of self, if such mediation is diagnostic of their sort of being, then their sense of self must be critical to their survival. Indeed, it can be no less critical than their instinctual manifold, which it has transumed. Strikingly, therefore, their search for identity can be no less naturally impelling than their drive to satisfy their appetites.

Now the ontological shift to the refined independence of the human form from its own matter logically entails an originary self-identification. This self-identification remains tightly and ostensibly rooted to its material constitution, but looks forward to completion in self-consciousness. It is a form that obtains betwixt and between instinct and option, having emerged from a preeminently material universe, but having emerged self-begotten. I have referred to such a form as a primordial choice, a choice lived rather than deliberated, but a choice from which deliberated choice can spring.

Clearly, this kind of choice constitutes a cultural radical or first principle. Therefore, there is a certain futility in trying to account for it entirely in genetic terms, whether "because" or "in order to" terms.

A choice of the kind in question is significantly creative. At some point of inquiry into it, understanding must depend on recognition of its novel character. Such understanding must be effected simply by picturing, as perspicuously as one can, the world — the definition and arrangement of parts — according to the standpoint presented by that choice.

Generation, History, and Practice

I arrive at my argument's central claim: that the selection by Timem's members of "conflict between the generations" as a definition of the situation presents and represents the primordial choice of "generation" as a self-identification and standpoint in the world. Given the primordiality of this choice, at bottom the members moved to it — just as Timem's youth moved to negate the founding fathers and embrace the role of revisionary — in a manner so spontaneous and bodily as to promote and disclose a second nature. The kind of selection at issue, then, is in the first place neither sociological nor tropological, but existential and expressive — in a word, phenomenological.

The community's interpretation of its revisionary turn in terms of generational conflict betrays — as the story of Genesis spells out paradigmatically — a world in which difference, or manyness, or plurality, or individuation, is principally attributable to a creator-creature or father-son relationship, a relationship of generation. Since the creator, the father, is by nature self-generating, his son necessarily partakes of his identity. The son, then, who, if only by reason of his posteriority, must also be unlike his father, is both different from and identical to the latter. In effect, the relationship and the universe it keys are profoundly ambiguous and paradoxical.

The ambiguity of the relationship sets up a remarkable dialectic. As he shares in his creator's capacity for self-generation, the son is able to make choices. But in view of his indelible creatureliness, his faculty of choice serves to catch him up between heteronomy and autonomy. In the concrete, then, the ambiguity manifests itself as a moral and governmental dilemma. Whether he chooses to comply with the limits set by his creator or to embark on a career of self-aggrandizement, he must in a sense be less than true to himself. He always remains caught fast between alternatives both of which leave something critical to be desired. As a consequence of his dilemmatic condition, his choices are ever open to question; the moral judgment on them is never finally in. These are choices whose resolution does not yield to logic alone and is forever and essentially perplexed. As such, they epitomize the notion of choice, entailing a world whose axis is peculiarly voluntary.

Even so, the son's choices must be as natural as they are factitious. Though his world is definitively voluntary, the alternatives with which he is confronted are givens, aspects of an essentially ambiguous constitution. Put differently, both are predispositions of a kind; both are performative before they are deliberative.

However, should the son take the alternative of filial resistance, unequivocally choosing for the sake of himself, he can effect *the appearance* of unrestricted, fully cognized choice. By negating his creator's negative commandments, he takes a choice for choice itself. In so doing, he appears to emerge from a state of ignorance and innocence in relation to his capacity for choice.

Emergence into self-consciousness makes the generational dialectic overtly historical. "Generation" refers at once to begetting; to a body of persons born about the same time; to a step in descent; and to the average period of time it takes children to replace their parents — a replacing time. Furthermore, in ordinary and dictionary (OED) usage, its reference reaches beyond procreation to include "artificial" production, that is, creation as such. As a consequence, the replacement of the parents by the children is a moral as well as a material process; it proceeds also as a matter of choice. Therefore, the time marked by it pertains to a course of events that could have been otherwise, in a word, to a history.

As is insinuated by the very idea of replacement, this historical dialectic is keyed by negation as well as continuity. Since the choice of self-development can be enacted only at some cost to the creator's world, revision and dissent are characteristic moments of generation and the course of moral events.

This world of generation is culturally highlighted by the idiom of patri-filiation: the creator and creature are conceived of as father and son, respectively. Doubtless, the choice of the father-son relationship as the idiom of generativity betrays a critical anxiety over priority of gender and indicates a powerful usurpation of the female principle.

Perhaps, also, the mother-child relationship does not bear so easily the factor of separation crucial to the dialectical sense of generative movement. Phenomenologically, relative to the father-son relationship, the mother-child bond smacks of incorporation rather than separation. Indeed, in the West we are inclined to measure autonomy, and hence creativity, as a function of distance from the mother. The more independent of that relationship one becomes, the more mature one is deemed to be, making maturity a male privilege (see Gilligan 1982). In other words, as is stunningly implicit in Genesis, moral progress is defined by the developmental metamorphosis of the mother-child bond into an all-male relationship — the relationship between father and son. The idiom of patri-filiation serves to radicalize the distance from the mother.

The crucial point is that this generational formula implicitly expresses a dialectical shift from procreation to creation, from begetting as such to *creatio ex nihilo*. By sublimating the generativity of the female principle and shifting attention away from the mother-child to the father-son bond, the formula manages to evoke the mystery of creation lying on the horizon of every act of procreation. Relative to the child's virtual enclosure by the mother, the distance between father and child is great right from the start, giving the father's act of reproduction an air of begetting at a distance. Such begetting simulates the magical or unmediated begetting *that is* creation. Thus, as becomes a primordial choice, "generation" makes a play on the ontological ambiguity of begetting as an act of creation as well as of procreation, therein conveying the idea of moral development and the identity of man as a self-generating or moral being.

"Generation," then, identifies man as that being who re-creates his own identity, and it describes the world corresponding to this identity in terms of a developmental sequence of replacings or re-creations. As this sequence is set in train by creative choice as well as by procreative urge, it marks historical time. Historical time describes not simply difference, but difference reflecting different self-understandings. Furthermore, since such difference always presupposes a prior point of view from which it differs, it is inevitably open to interpretation as a falling away from an ideal *or* as a creative leap in its own right.

"Generation" is the ontological center of gravity of Timem's sociocultural world. It sums up the originary self-identification on the implicit basis of which the radical enterprise of the kibbutz was projected. Timem's revolutionary ethos presupposes the world of generation before it does kibbutz ideology. In the final analysis, that ethos is unintelligible outside of the creator-creature or founder-son relationship. As Spiro put it, invoking Freud's Oedipus: "The ideology of the kibbutz..., in its unconscious psychodynamics, rests on rebellion against, and the ultimate banishment of, the father" (1965: 381).

As a biological process, generation is not left intact but is conventionally informed. Still, it is not an ideology. It is, instead, a form of existence or practice. That is to say, in the kibbutz, generation is inseparable from its performance. As principles of identity, the ideological tenets of kibbutz voluntarism, collectivism, and Zionism run distinctly secondary to the principle of generation. Though members can leave the ideological universe of the kibbutz and still retain their sense of self, they cannot leave the world of generation without losing sight altogether of who they are and where they stand in reality.

Eight

Primordial Choice and "The Universal": Kibbutz Familism and the Sexual Division of Labor

In the preceding chapter, in conjunction with an intensive reading of the myth of Genesis, I argued that self-identification through the biblical notion of generation is a primordial choice for Timem's members. As such, though it served to define the situation, it did not move the members as if it were a cause or, even, reason of their conduct. According to this understanding, "generation" cannot be exactly distinguished from the members themselves, from who they are. It is a key component of their self-identity. Therefore, the conduct associated with it was, in a certain, critical sense, self-founded — it was in fundamental part its own end.

Such an account of the members' conduct — ultimately an account without "why" — supposes a nondualist ontology, one in which cause and effect, or reason (in the sense of logical premise) and behavior, enjoy an essentially intrinsic rather than extrinsic connection with each other. In effect, then, the account is implicitly predicated on a nondualist ontology, one in which "the universal" (simply, that which is irreducible to particulars) may be said to obtain still, but, paralogically, as basic ambiguity rather than a substance or absolute essence — no-thing rather than something.

I was led to this approach, in significant measure, by my reading of Genesis, a story whose ontological claim to universality is given in its name. Genesis has served me not only as a paradigm for understanding Timem's preoccupation with the idea of generational conflict but also (notwithstanding that I do not regard the story as absolute and find important features of it objectionable) as a kind of anthropology from which to learn.

In the present chapter, I want to comment reflexively on the role played by Genesis in my approach and to expand on the concept of primordial choice. I shall do so, first, by applying the thesis about "generation" as a primordial choice to an empirical matter in kibbutz studies other than that of secret balloting and direct democracy. I have in mind the reemergence of familism and the sexual division of labor in this revolutionary community.

"Some three generations prior to the rise of the contemporary women's movement," writes Melford Spiro, "the founders of the kibbutz movement proclaimed as one of their historical missions the total emancipation of women from the 'shackles' — sexual, social, economic, and intellectual — imposed on them by traditional society" (1979: 5–7). This emancipation included as a crucial desideratum the "abolition of economic sex-role differentiation," which in turn entailed revolutionary change in "two core institutions of traditional society, marriage and the family." Evidently, however, very early on, if only with the appearance of the first families and the realm of privacy they introduced into the collective life, this emancipatory mission was threatened with revisionism. For instance, in an article published in 1924, we find the following troubled description:

> Until today, the kibbutzim struggle with the family as with a difficult adversary.... As compared with love in general, the love of two people for each other is a matter of the most private choice. That is what separates couples from the rest of the members, and encloses them as an "isle of the happy," against whose shores beat the waves of collective living. (cited in Hurwitz 1965)

Unsurprisingly, analyzing and assessing the significance of this "counterrevolutionary" course of change became a preoccupation in kibbutz studies and has produced a rather extensive literature that has had a real impact on social theory (the psychoanalytic variant of which is of special relevance here).[1] It seems fair to say that the counterrevolutionary return of familism and the sexual division of labor are perhaps the most highly vexed issues in kibbutz studies.

The approach taken here casts the issues in a fresh and different light. If this is so, my account of the issues, even though it is far from full, will serve to back up significantly the interpretive power of the thesis of "generation" as a primordial choice. Such support seems reason enough to treat the issues here. But, in addition, analysis of the reemergence of a more traditional family and sexual division of labor, at least as this turn of events has been controverted in kibbutz studies, raises directly the question of "the universal." Indeed, the very ideas of the family and the sexual division of labor enjoy a special connection with the Judaic idea of generation and the story of Genesis, and, therefore, since this idea and that story are universalizing, lead straight to the question of what, if anything, is universal about them.

Having treated the empirical matters of the family and the sexual division of labor, I shall then turn directly to the theoretical concept of primordial choice, remarking on the connection of this concept to the myth of Genesis and developing the concept further with reference to the way in which it obviates the dualism of the universal and the particular. I will also comment on the concept's implications for the standard anthropological question of traditional social settings, settings to which the idea of choice has often been thought to have little if any relevance.

Is, Then, the Family Universal?

The Reemergence of the Traditional Family

For reasons of its primarily existential bearing, the idea of generational conflict arises spontaneously and recurrently among Timem's members to define and inform the community's revisionary movement. Though I have concentrated here on a certain development in Timem's political life, the implicit commitment to generation is crucial for understanding revisionism in other areas of kibbutz life. In particular, it is worth essaying the sociologically celebrated return to a more traditional family and division of labor.

Already at the time of fieldwork, during the mid-1960s, there was a conspicuous sexual division of labor, according to which women largely filled the "domestic" branches and men the "productive" branches of the economy. Furthermore, though prior to and during those same years the children of Timem lived in the community's "children's houses" (*batei y'ladim*), in recent years the family has become a singularly residential unit.

In order to understand these "counterrevolutionary" developments, it is not necessary to appeal to naturalistic explanations, as do Spiro (1979) and Tiger and Shepher (1975). Rather, given the phenomenological backdrop of a primordial commitment to generation as a principle of existence, they are expressions of the general process of internal differentiation accompanying Timem's growth or "routinization." In other words, bearing in mind that, at least in any human context, generation does not exist apart from its conventional coefficients, these developments present a representative form of the procession of the generations.

As Genesis makes plain, both the family and sex-role differentiation are integrals of the world of generation. Generation is nothing but differentiation of a kind, describing a doubly helical shift from identity to difference or from the rule of law and order to that of desire and rebellion. A doubly helical shift is one that advances, but whose direction of advance is essentially ambiguous as between the two poles.

In this historical dialectic, the identities "wife" and "son" are distinguished by their especial association with the pole of difference and rebellion. That "wife" and "son" are made to represent fragmentation and axiological inferiority is legitimated ultimately by suggestive reference to the functional difference between creation and procreation. This difference is spatially one of containment, and temporally of priority: in view of their marked limitedness and belated arrival, the son is pictured as naturally disposed to a creaturely willfulness, and the wife, whose concupiscence triggers "the fall," as outstandingly symbolic of this willful disposition.

In result, differentiation is apprehended as that specific dynamic form we call the patriarchal family. Thus, in the world of generation, the patriarchal family is inherent and also is the form of differentiation.

In principle, the kibbutz eliminated the patriarchal family. According to kibbutz ideology, the bond between the individual and the collective, rather than family ties (which are thought to detract from that bond), is the critical axis of social organization. In the interest of the primacy of the collectivity, then, certain functions of the family, chiefly economic activity and child-rearing, were appropriated by the collectivity. This rearrangement of functions was also meant to destroy the basis of the traditional division of labor.

In practice, however, even the principled opposition to the institution of the family was implicitly predicated on the world of generation, and, thereby (a stunning irony, to be sure), on the family. The human self-identity on which this revolutionary enterprise is founded is unintelligible outside of the principle of generation. That identity, the *chalutz*, or pioneering rebel with a cause, a quintessentially moral mission, has deep roots in Adam's fall and rise from the Garden of Eden. In its initial stages of development, the kibbutz was able to reallocate certain functions of the family. Try as it might, however, it could not eliminate the bare-bones form of a socially sanctioned and presumptively enduring relationship between a man and a woman, the special charge of which is reproduction *in the sense of generation*.

In an article of some notoriety, published in 1954 under the title "Is the Family Universal?" Melford Spiro attempted to demonstrate, against the received anthropological opinion of the time, that the family is not universal. Spiro argued that the kibbutz had eliminated the family as a structural phenomenon. He found that the functions of the family had been appropriated by the collectivity, and that the latter performed and apprehended itself as a family. Four years later, however, critically questioning his earlier interpretation, he concluded that "parents and children comprise a distinct and differentiated social group within the kibbutz" (1960). In effect, shifting away from the prevailing functionalist definition of the family, he recognized that something like what I have called the bare-bones form of the family does indeed exist in the kibbutz. As Yonina Talmon-Garber made plain (1972), it always has.

Their ideological aspirations not fully comprehending the implications of their own project, the pioneers envisioned the kibbutz, in its perpetuity, as a procession of generations. As we have seen, the world of generation comports the social centrality of the family as, among other things, a set of sex/gender roles based on the general superiority of the male principle. Conceived of in any other fashion, "generation" would be another name. I mean by this, not of course that the term cannot be intelligibly defined otherwise, but that the relevant cultural idea presents not simply a concept, but a phenomenological universe. The axiological furniture of this universe includes a representative association of the male with creation qua creation and of the female with creation on behalf of the male, which is to say, with procreation.[2]

There is no doubt that in the beginnings of the kibbutz, the ideological fear of the family engendered strong pressures against overt expression of family ties. The community not only took from the family's charge the functions of economic endeavor and socialization, but also saw to it that the very presence of "marriage" (such as it was) and the family went unsung (see Spiro 1963: 11ff.; Talmon-Garber 1972: 8–9). For example, as Timem's members often related to me, husband and wife would avoid sitting together during communal meals, thus symbolically subordinating the marital bond to the collectivity.

What needs to be seen about such behavior, though, is that while its emphasis on the family is negative, it *does* emphasize it. It plainly substantiates the presence of this institution as an operative social principle. Avoidance behavior of this kind proceeds no less according to the principle it means to reject (familism) than to the principle it means to endorse (collectivism).

As long as the community grasped its posterity in terms of generation, the family, ideological designs notwithstanding, was ineliminable as a structural phenomenon. Granted that as a basic form the family has always been a component of kibbutz social organization, why did it reemerge as a key, thematic component?

Presumably, the removal of politico-economic functions from its purview deprived the family of any competitive goal by which it might distinguish and develop itself. In point of fact, however, its simple existence in this revolutionary social setting constituted sufficient basis for its self-realization. Ideologically, the wellspring of self-identification in the kibbutz is the collectivity. The individual is supposed to realize him- or herself through the collectivity and to identify with it before any other body, especially the family. But as much as the kibbutz continued to rely on the family as its most important source of recruitment for the long run, there was a presumptive, material identity between the kibbutz and the family. This identity was bound to grow with the generations.

The ideology proposed a synthesis of the individual and society so complete that for sociopolitical purposes it would be impossible to distinguish between them. But as a result of the 'natural' — that is, generational — growth of the identity between the kibbutz and the family, the latter vied with the individual for primacy of place in the proposed synthesis (see Talmon-Garber 1972: 42). In important, but publicly unstated ways, family came to mediate the individual's relationship to the collectivity, and in certain ways to enjoy the individual's place in the kibbutz synthesis.

In this connection, it should be borne in mind that the kibbutz never attempted to overcome its ancient legacy of patronymy. For all the talk about "children of the kibbutz," the family continued to serve as a — indeed, if my analysis of the ontological world of the kibbutz is correct, *the* — fundamental source of self-identity for the individual. Though its effects were varied and subtle, the consideration of a member's surname, that is, of *who he or she is,* played as an important backdrop to all sorts of decisions made in respect of the individual's relationship to the collectivity. These decisions pertained to the allocation of such goods as type of work, quality of housing, and even marriage.

In another place (Evens 1975), I have documented how the consideration of family entered consequentially into a case (mentioned earlier) of stigmatization and tacit expulsion in Timem, in which a member's desire to marry and to pass on his family's name were at stake. The member was generally regarded as mentally defective, and though the issue was publicly debated in terms of the suitability of his choice of brides as a candidate for membership in the kibbutz (she was from outside), close analysis revealed that the community was more fundamentally concerned with the suitability of him and his family as members in perpetuity. Indeed, the fact that his father too was stigmatized, so that his family of origin had little real political clout in the community, ensured for this member certain defeat in his bid to get the community to accept his plans to marry and bring his wife home.

Moreover, considerations of family influence were keenly felt by members who were not particularly well placed in this regard, and these considerations became part of the rhetoric of political negotiation in the community. For example, one young member of Timem, who came from abroad and married into a family of little influence, argued publicly that for reasons of his lack of family "connection," his request for a personal loan from the kibbutz was treated by the Secretariat (*mazkirut*) less receptively than that of another member.

The kibbutz's collectivist social arrangements effectively barred the family from direct access to politico-economic authority. But these arrangements could not, short of abolishing it altogether, bar the family from access to differential power and influence, both as regards relations among families and between this institution and others. In point of fact, the family enjoyed a peculiar access to power and influence, the access furnished by its uniquely dynamic and material identity with the kibbutz. According to the ideology, the kibbutz is basically constituted or run by individual persons (albeit ones whose character has been tempered by a collectivist upbringing and social context). But in order to generate these individuals, the kibbutz relies primarily on the family.

The kibbutz synthesis is predicated on the utopian proposition that the individual and society should share alike in the hegemony of the social whole. But insofar as it is the family rather than the individual that enjoys identity with the collective, and within the redoubtable limits set by the formal barriers against the assumption of power by the family, it must be the family that shares in the control exercised by the collective. Of course, many kibbutz institutions, including preeminently the various administrative committees and branches of the economy, share in this control. But whereas the family, like the individual, is characterized by a substantial and fundamental autonomy, these institutions are wholly derivative of the collective.

The family's warrant for existing stems from an ontology of generation, not from the kibbutz, whose revolutionary character also presupposes this ontology. The family's independence makes the family's identification with the kibbutz, like the individual's, special. Given the fundamental autonomy of the individual and the family, and the kibbutz's essential dependence on them — which amounts to an identity with them — any failure on their part to defer to or promote the "collective will" presents a threat to the collective's hegemony. We have seen a threat of this kind at work in the case of secret balloting. The opposition to that motion was expressly concerned to subvert the threat and save the collective from compromise. Inevitably, such compromise suggests that it is the kibbutz that identifies with the individual as such or, as the case may be, with the family, rather than the other way around. The member who complained about the Secretariat's treatment of his application for a loan was in effect accusing the kibbutz of nepotism.

Thus, despite systematic containment of this institution, the family did not lack a basis on which it could compete for relative influence in the kibbutz. The kibbutz was pre-predicatively disposed to rely on the family to reproduce the individual members who would perpetuate the collective. This material dependence amounted to a critical identity with the family. At least from within, the community's name was deeply involved with the names of the families whose members pioneered the community and promised to supply it with generations of *chaverim*. In Timem, particular families enjoyed a certain preeminence and prestige by virtue of their special association with the establishment of the community and the course of its history. By thus associating its name with the collective whole in the latter's originary movement, the family in general transformed its procreative capacity into a creative force.

The immediate object of the competition, then, was outstanding identification with the collective as an originary movement. In effect, families competed over the prestige of origins — authorship of the community as a historical enterprise. Like all vital competition, this one constituted its own reward — survival, to be sure, but survival as a world-denominator or, what is the same thing, world-creator, a richly human identity, both for its essential self-reflexivity and for its god-like pretensions. The families most successful in this competition enjoyed, for the most part, not authorized control, but differential influence, by virtue of their exemplary and performative identification with *chalutziut* or the configuration of revolutionary and sacrificial values that legitimates the presence of authorized control. Especial association with the determination of the community's history afforded a certain measure of actual determining power. This power allowed some families in particular to distinguish themselves, and it allowed the family in general to reemerge as a fundamental institution in the community's normative description of itself.

In view of the fundamental identity between the kibbutz and the family, the normative restoration of the family and the sexual division of labor are simply routine manifestations of the community's growth and development. The family's partial reappropriation of the function of socialization reflects the degree to which the family had become phenomenally well differentiated in the kibbutz. As families grew and became more conspicuous, the family as an institution was enabled to provide its own basis of political support on issues bearing on its relative autonomy. The question of whether or not the children should be domiciled with their parents was one such issue. As I have shown in the case of the individual in the kibbutz, once it became an important substantial presence, the family too was politically capacitated to secure its gains through normative recognition.

Family Expansion and "Kibbutz Exogamy"

This picture of the kibbutz family as given to competition over the prestige of origins is promisingly powerful. Not only can it offer deep reasons for the emergent preeminence of the family, but it can also contribute significantly to the explication of certain other puzzling behavioral patterns in the kibbutz. To mention two rather conspicuous ones: (1) the decided increase in rate of reproduction and size of families (Talmon-Garber: 1972: 51); and (2) the notorious proclivity among members who have grown up together to take mates from outside their particular kibbutz (Talmon-Garber 1972: chap. 5). Both of these patterns characterize Kibbutz Timem.

Spiro has analyzed "kibbutz exogamy" in relation to the kibbutz's ideological projection of itself as a family writ large. He argues (as do the members) that as idiomatic siblings the children of the kibbutz have "spontaneously evolved their own incest taboo" (1965: 348). Talmon-Garber has tied the increase of family size especially to "kibbutz expansionism." With penetrating insight, she has linked "kibbutz exogamy" to the "quest" of the second generation for separate identity (1972: chap. 2, chap. 5, esp. 154ff.). As she sees it, the members tend to seek mates outside of their kibbutz in order to oppose their parents' imposition of continuity and thereby distinguish themselves.

I do not wish here to take up critically the whole of Spiro's and Talmon-Garber's respective positions. But it is plain that Talmon-Garber's argument foreshadows my own, about the critical connection between generational conflict and differentiation. "Our material," she writes, "reveals many undertones of resentment and opposition to the parents' generation" (1972: 161).

In relation to the question of "kibbutz exogamy," however, Talmon-Garber does not notice that, although such behavior marks a break with the parental generation, at the same time it fosters familism in the community, in at least two ways (in fact, she is led by functionalism to somewhat contrary conclusions [1972: 146ff.]). First, as Talmon-Garber observes, the opposition to the parental generation stands in the interest of the sphere of privacy, a sphere that is profoundly associated with the family in the kibbutz (Talmon-Garber 1972: 154). Second, a consideration that has gone wholly unremarked in the literature, the avoidance of in-marriage preserves the separateness and distinctiveness of family lines in the community. In other words, it prevents the dilution of familial identity. Though in-marriage for their children may be "a first preference with many parents" (Talmon-Garber 1972: 161), I suspect that its contemplation gives rise to extreme ambivalence on their part as well as on the part of their children. For in view of the family's representation of the private sphere, the same anxiety over individuation that moves the children to oppose their parents must move the latter to maintain their familial autonomy with respect to one another.

If my argument about competition among kibbutz families is correct, then it stands to reason that an important consideration for understanding both family expansion and the tendency to avoid in-marriage is existential anxiety over the preservation of familial identity and its exclusive association with the founding of the community.

It is not necessary, then, to embrace naturalism in order to account for the so-called counterrevolution as regards family and gender roles in the kibbutz. That such "counterrevolutionary" behavior may appear quite natural, both to the outside observer and to the *chaver* kibbutz, reflects, not a sheer opposition of nature to culture, but the ingenuous side of human practice. The reemergence of the traditional family and sexual division of labor appears natural because these phenomena inhere in a primordial choice. This choice orders reality in so fast and fundamental a way, that no other order is granted an audience with the light of consciousness.

On Primordial Choice and "the Universal"

Primordial Choice and Genesis

Melford Spiro got it right the first time, though, under the reigning influence of functionalism, for the wrong reasons: the family is not universal, or at least the kibbutz gives us no cause to think that it is. Nevertheless, it is no accident that the question of "the universal" was raised in relation to the kibbutz family, and not just because the kibbutz sought to do away with or diminish this institution. For, as a phenomenon of generation, "the family" enjoys a special tie to a paradigmatically universalizing primordial choice, that is, a primordial choice that features the idea of the universal. I have in mind of course the choice to choose, to identify oneself in terms of one's moral capacity. That choice, beautifully narrated in the story of Genesis, comports the very idea of the universal. For it defines the human being as that creature who, if only always partially, creates her- or himself. In this way, it locates the defining property of human beings in their capacity to identify themselves uniquely vis-à-vis other human beings. In other words, it locates the defining property in a universal capacity to particularize.

Here I have conceived of this capacity in terms of primordial choice. The reemergence of the kibbutz family and the sexual division of labor are, as I have argued, best understood by reference to "generation" considered as a primordial choice. In view of the fact that generation is a choice for choosing or world-creating, it is a universalizing project. At this point, I want to expand on the way in which "primordial choice" captures the fundamental ambiguity of the universal, the way in which the universal manifests itself only in the particular. In this endeavor, it is important to bear in mind that I am taking a cue from an anthropology forged in Genesis.

Primordial Choice and Two Kinds of Social Settings

Evoking the myth of Genesis, I have sought to show that Timem's self-understanding of "conflict between the generations" is most basically a question of neither social utility nor metaphorical apposition, but of a primordial choice. Primordial choices do not lend themselves to final dissection into either behavior or consciousness. Instead, they obtain emphatically between these dualistic poles of Western ontological thought.

Such choices constitute the "metaphysical" foundations on which everyday human worlds may be built and may produce and reproduce themselves. They do so by differentiating, all at once, nature on the one hand, culture on the other, and a constituting (dedifferentiating) practice — a bridge — in between. The creative designation of oneself entails the dual (but not necessarily dualist or perfect) differentiation of a subject- and an object-world, while the practice of such designating continues to bridge what it thus tears asunder.

As a consequence of this essentially ambiguous and dynamic configuration of subject-and-object or self-and-other, moral endeavor is made possible — indeed, ironically, it is made necessary. The differentiation of artifice or culture virtually condemns human beings to a moral universe, a universe in which choices are taken on the basis of a factitious and evaluatory distinction keyed to some idea or other of the good. Even if the differentiation of culture and nature is articulated only very imperfectly, as it is in social settings where the constituting practice is not occluded by the fact of differentiation, moral order remains diagnostic.[3] Thus, in the Edenic state as well as in so-called primitive societies, the constituting practice is taken for granted as otherness. Yet despite the thematic emphasis on the heteronomy of the self in these social settings, it is well understood that things proceed in a discretionary fashion.

Wherever ends are experienced as limited — as they must be in any subjective universe irrecusably *bound* to an object-world — authentic choice and an axiological construction of the good are unavoidable. The consideration that in some societies choice is seen as cosmological and naively regarded as preordained may be a difference that makes a difference, but it is not one that obviates the essentially moral nature of the choice. In these societies, though choice is not construed simply in terms of *human* agency, it is nevertheless understood as Agency or as Choice — that is, as a selective outcome that could have been otherwise.

Conversely, it is the case that certain primordial choices differentiate culture from nature so completely that they manage to conceal (but not remove) their own essentially ambiguous nature. In that event, the selective practice always obtaining between nature and culture is sublimated, implicating an exhaustive dualism. As we have seen, such a primordial choice can project choosing as a thoroughly autonomous exercise, the product of a pure rather than basically ambiguous subjectivity — a "thinking stuff."[4]

Under this sort of epistemological regime, the course of human events appears to be primarily historical rather than replicative; it tends to present itself especially as a question of unique (because completely open-ended) rather than regular occurrences. In fact, of course, as I have brought out in respect of the kibbutz, such a history no more lacks for a coefficient of reiterative being than a "nonhistorical" culture lacks for one of actual becoming. Still, the difference of emphasis makes a difference to the process of these two categorical kinds of human settings, a difference that has long held the attention of social anthropology.

Primordial Choice and Two Kinds of Social Change

In whichever of these two categorical settings it is considered, however, moral choosing is semantically constrained to reproduce the primordial choice that seems to enable its operation in particular contexts. This is so even when, on the face of things, the direction of the choosing runs contrary to the content of the primordial choice. As the very act of choosing is predicated on the picture of the world projected by the primordial choice, a selection that fails to convey that picture can scarcely be meaningfully counted as a choice. Put another way, it is more than difficult to make sense of an act of choosing that cannot be assimilated to the prevailing primordial choice. For this reason, that is, because they challenge the meaningful cultural universe at its axis, decidedly novel selections tend to undermine the possibility of their own effectiveness.

We have seen in this study of Timem how deeply resistant to change is an in-place primordial choice. In relation to Timem's self-identification in terms of generation, paradoxically, the more things change, the more they really do remain the same.

The resistant power of primordial choices — a lived, significative power — can also account for the outstanding capacity of primitive societies to present themselves as unchanging. In Timem, where the capacity of the primordial choice (of generation) to entertain dualism allows for change as such, change, while acknowledged, paradoxically promotes continuity. By contrast, the nondualism of primordial choices in primitive social settings magically defines apparent change itself *as* continuity. It manages this by making impossible a *strictly* empirical perspective. It is only from such a perspective that change can be defined *as* change. Yet, by definition, no such perspective can offer itself in a nondualist universe. As a result, what moderns would feel obliged to count simply as nonconformity may be perceived in terms far less absolute — as, say, conformity deferred or in the making — by the occupants of such a universe.[5] In the setting of Timem, the paradox, as dictated by dualism, is played out in terms of linear time, such that continuity depends on the possibility of change per se; in the primitive setting, the paradox unfolds in terms of recurrence, such that change is directly identified with its opposite, a paralogical feat made possible by nondualism.

The difference this (arresting) difference makes is substantial. Notwithstanding the terrific immovability of in-place primordial choices, and although change is in fact a feature of both kinds of social setting, conceptual openness to change tends in actual practice to promote rather than inhibit change. Such openness characterizes especially dualistic social settings.[6]

The Phenomenological Character of the Constituting Process

Whatever the self-understanding of the social setting, though, primordial choosing is always ontologically basically ambiguous. Primordial choosing may be construed in terms of the process of selection to which I earlier referred as moral. Now, however, I want to emphasize its nature as phenomenological. Phenomenological selection obtains between natural selection, in which, strictly speaking, choice plays no part, and highly self-conscious selection, in which choice is epitomized as such. The kind of selection I have in mind defines a choice that, because it is taken without benefit of well-developed self-consultation, is not exactly a choice. Though it involves authentic "selectors," that is, morally endowed agents, such a choice tends to proceed *as if* it is perfectly natural—in a word, its selection is predominantly lived. In its case, the chooser is indeed chosen by his or her choice. More precisely, with a choice of this kind, it is not possible to tell the chooser from the choice.

As a consequence, these choices determine human beings' sense of reality in relation to themselves and thereby their sense of their own reality. Put another way, they determine the human being's place in the world, which is to say, his or her identity as a human being or most basic sense of self. Put still another way, in fixing ontologically the human being's self-reference, these choices set a world in place. In this manner, they furnish the presumptively natural basis on which individuals can make measurably self-conscious choices, choices in which an explicit sense of self enters very significantly. In effect, then, phenomenological selection produces the primordial choices that key cultural worlds or particular universes of relevance defining and circumscribing the life choices of human beings.

In relation to the concept of primordial choice, that of phenomenological selection connotes the less than personal character of agency relative to such choices; it affords the meaning of "primordial" an emphasis on the "natural" or lived character of such origination. These two features—tacit agency and livedness—suggest that phenomenological selecting is not less bodily than mindful. As against every bias of modernity, these features conjure up a picture of a nature in which purpose or the capacity for purpose is essentially implanted—even if such purpose cannot be told except through the medium of particular primordial choices, that is, except within a universe of practice.

Nine

The Historical Link between Genesis and Timem's Story: Rousseau as Biblical Redactor

The Founders as Products of Romanticism and the Enlightenment

Timem's Secularism

With the preceding chapter, my ethnographic argument is essentially complete. The crux of the argument is that "conflict between the generations" was selected to define the situation for reasons basically of neither functional nor metaphorical design, but as a primordial choice, an act as creative and self-fashioning as it is determined by choices preceding it.

However, this critical discursive turn, centering on the idea of primordial choice, raises two problems, both of which are too pressing to ignore here. First, can the striking paradigmatic connection between the myth of Genesis and Timem's story be accounted for? Second, in view of Timem's explicitly modern and rationalistic outlook, how should we evaluate the members' predisposition to apprehend their situation ultimately in terms more moral — mythic even — than empirical and objective?

Although these two questions are loose ends, so to speak, they are critically important. I wish to address the first in the present chapter, leaving the second for separate treatment in the following chapter. The second, bringing into immediate relief the deep anthropo-philosophical issues underlying this book — the issues of rationality and human agency — requires extensive theoretical discussion.

To take up, then, the question of the empirical character of the way in which Genesis has informed the course of Timem's history, it is necessary to identify a certain difference between Genesis and Timem's story. The difference I have in mind is the secular humanism of the kibbutz. The founders of Timem had sharply repudiated the way of life of their "fathers," a way of life the founders were inclined to represent especially by reference to its religious orthodoxy.[1] The humanist revision of the biblical scenario made it possible for the kibbutz to blind itself to the community's rootedness in an ancient revolutionary tradition and correlatively to picture itself as almost divinely creative. Ironically, it is to the pronounced secularism of the kibbutz as a pioneering movement that I turn in order to address the question of just how Genesis has exercised so powerful an influence on Timem. My argumentative strategy is to show that this secularism is profoundly Rousseauian, and as such finds its deepest wellspring dialectically, in the myth of Genesis.

The Rise of the Hashomer Hatza'ir Movement

It can be shown that Timem's first members were familiar with the story of Genesis. It is well documented that the founders of the Hashomer Hatza'ir kibbutz movement, from the ranks of which Timem found its first members, were studied in Judaism and Jewishness, and that the kibbutz system of education included the Hebrew Bible in its curriculum (Mendelsohn 1981: 83; Spiro 1965: 256–59).

This consideration, though, is hardly compelling enough to account for an influence so basic and pervasive as that which I am claiming for the logic of Genesis. After all, as we shall see, the founders read much else besides the Hebrew Bible. The influence I have in mind is a matter of identity rather than ideology. In which case, the question of whether or not the founders and their children were students of Genesis is somewhat immaterial. Such a powerful and absorbing influence bespeaks a pervasive and tacit presence more than it does a direct and intellectual connection. To show the influence of, say, Darwin and Freud on someone in the modern West, it is not necessary to establish that that person has actually read the *Origin of the Species* and *The Interpretation of Dreams*.

My argument, then, does not bind me to demonstrating a studied preoccupation with the biblical text on the part of Timem's members. I think I can, however, make plausible, if not compelling, that the connection I am claiming between Timem's story and Genesis is in truth a question of material influence and not simply of formal symmetry. In order to do this, one could, to be sure, focus on the specifically religious roots of the kibbutz movement (see Spiro 1963: chap. 3; Lilker 1982). A study of the kibbutz's relation to the traditions of Jewish messianism, say, would make an important contribution, not only to kibbutz studies, but also to Western social thought (see Handelman 1991: 153ff.; Bauman 1988; Seligman 1989; Fischer 1989). But I wish here to concentrate instead on the movement's derivation from a body of thought that is not Jewish per se, namely, broadly conceived, the Enlightenment. More particularly, I want to show that the influence of Genesis on the kibbutz is plain to see in Timem's distinctly Rousseauian social constitution.

Hashomer Hatza'ir was founded just prior to World War I, in the Polish province of Galicia, until 1918 a part of the Austro-Hungarian Empire. Its founding derived from a merger of two preexisting organizations: (1) Tza'ir Zion (the Youth of Zion), a student society dedicated to the study of Judaica and Jewish nationalism; and (2) Hashomer (the Watchman), a Jewish scouting organization, modeled after the English and Polish scouting movements, with the aim of bringing its participants "back to nature" and physical culture.

For the most part, the founding members came from strongly middle-class Jewish homes and had been well educated in secondary schools in which the language of instruction was Polish. Though many were versed in Jewish learning and Hebrew, they were also "acculturated." Their middle-class background gave to the movement a distinctly elitist and intellectualist air.

The historians cite specifically the following as intellectual and cultural sources of the movement: (1) such luminaries as Nietzsche, Freud, Schopenhauer, and Buber; (2) such lesser lights as Otto Weininger (a philosophical contemporary of Nietzsche), Gustav Wyneken (a major ideologue of the free German Youth movement), H. Blüher (also an important figure in the German Youth movement), A. D. Gordon (a leading Russian Zionist), A. Schwedron (an advocate of "heroic" or sacrificial Zionism), and Siegfried Bernfeld (an advocate of Wyneken's ideas); and (3) Hasidic Judaism, Rabbinical

Judaism, the Jewish Enlightenment or Haskala, the biblical prophets, and the New Testament.

Plainly, the sources were many and varied. What I want to emphasize here, though, is the powerful strain of romanticism implicated by the majority of these sources. The emphatically romantic thrust of the early Hashomer Hatza'ir movement is well documented.

With the Russian invasion of Galicia in World War I, many Galician Jews took refuge in Vienna. They included the key founders of the Hashomer Hatza'ir movement, most of whom grew from adolescence to maturity in the romantic and cosmopolitan social environment of *fin de siècle* Vienna. These years, from 1914 to 1920, were ideologically formative for the founders. During this time they heard Schwedron call for a new kind of Zionism, based on heroic and sacrificial deeds (Mendelsohn 1981: 82). In addition, the founders were inspired by their meeting with Martin Buber. Buber's synthetic "I-Thou" philosophy pictured Zionism as crucial, not simply for Jews but, in accordance with the biblical revelation of "the chosen people," for the moral development of humankind. He envisioned a moral order based on a genuine (ontic) mutuality between the individual and society. Under the influence of Siegfried Bernfeld, the founders were introduced to the ideas of Wyneken, one of the principal figures of the Wandervogel (free German Youth movement). The Wandervogel epitomized the German romantic Zeitgeist. The founders were deeply influenced by this movement's construction on youth as an autonomous creative force, its nature worship, and its protest against what was seen as the bourgeois philistinism of the adult social world (Spiro 1963: 44).

And when these pioneers immigrated to Palestine in 1920, as participants of the Third Aliya (one of five great waves of immigration), romanticism feverishly infected their words and deeds. Here is what one of them wrote in anticipation of their move to Palestine:

> Very soon they will go out in the morning to the fields.... They will work together and rejoice, and upon their return home in the evening, drunk with light and with labor, they will embrace with joy. Soon the days of the harvest will come, they will sit upon the barn in the night, between the stars and their crops, and they will dream radiant and holy dreams. (cited in Mendelsohn 1981: 129)

Here is another characteristic, early Hashomer Hatza'ir statement, this one celebrating the new, revolutionary social principles rather than the pastoral scene:

> To remain pure we must extricate ourselves from the abyss of conformity. Perhaps we shall be the first torrent of youth to remain young forever; humanity's first chance to escape failure. Let us go far between mountains and deserts to live in simplicity, beauty and truth. Perhaps our new *eida* [community] will be the nucleus of a new culture of new relationships between humans leading communal lives. We shall be the pioneers who shall carry the revolution through to the masses of miserable Jews, who will stream to the country to live by our principles. Let us create a new land of Israel free from the shackles of European capitalism and of the diaspora. (cited in Elon 1981: 184–85)

The Hashomer Hatza'ir pioneers formed in the early 1920s Bittania, a commune notorious for its romantic intensity (it was the *eida* referred to in the previous citation). The spiritual communalism and meetings characterized by "monologues and near-hysteric public confessions where members bared their innermost secrets, sexual anxieties and dreams, doubts, yearnings, and perplexities" were recorded in *Kehilatenu,* the published annals of this group (Elon 1981: 183ff.).

But the documentation of this romantic delirium is less germane to my purpose here than the cataloguing of the principles underlying such delirium. I have in mind: (1) love of nature; (2) social organicism and idealization of social relations; (3) commitment to heroic rebellion; (4) faith in the human spirit; (5) emphasis on self-development and creativity; (6) belief in the innocence of human beings and their malleability by education and social regeneration; (7) treatment of the individual as an end in him- or herself; and (8) emphasis on the idea of a national character.

All of these principles were well reflected in the statements by the leaders of the movement, issued shortly before their departure for Palestine, attempting to define what their movement stood for. To paraphrase, the leaders emphasized that Hashomer Hatza'ir fostered the absolute freedom of the individual, as against any conception of society that mechanically relegated the individual to the role of a means rather than an end. To this end, however, they advocated a collectivist society in which there would be no private ownership and no inheritance, and in which the education of children would be left to the social whole rather than to the family. In addition, they demanded national emancipation. They were devoted to the creation of an entirely new human being and correlatively a new social order (Mendelsohn 1981: 128). In short, they stood for the synthesis of nature and culture, individual and society, intellect and emotion, nation and humanity.

Underlying the founders' engagement of these values was a crisis of identity, a crisis that had been brought about by the Enlightenment. With the emergence of the Enlightenment, the Jews were emancipated; in result, they were able to enter into the larger surrounding society. But their integration into the surrounding societies was less than complete. As a consequence of this predicament, wherein their integration was no less fundamentally impaired than it was principally expected, they became significantly unsure of their own identity.

The founders of the Hashomer Hatza'ir were heirs to this crisis of identity. *The Guide of the Shomer Hatza'ir*, published during their years in Vienna, makes this plain: "We are neither full and healthy men nor full and healthy Jews.... There is no harmony in these elements within our character" (in Margalit 1969: 34). "And since neither the Jewish nor the surrounding society could provide solutions," writes a historian of the movement, "this uprooted youth sought salvation and redemption from within, in almost eschatological terms and out of sheer despair. What was required was personal improvement from within, and the improvement of character and mores within the community of youth which should create its own independent values" (Margalit 1969: 34). The *Guide* demanded that these youths should once again be "whole and healthy men, and whole and healthy Jews." This meant "a return to the life not of the diaspora Jew, but of the historical 'Hebrew.' They were to be 'young Hebrews in the likeness of the ancient Hebrews,' in the spirit of the prophets" (Margalit 1969: 34). Here, then, in this emancipatory movement, is the reactionary spirit characteristic of the Counter-Enlightenment and Romantic movement (Margalit 1969: 34ff.; see also Mendelsohn 1981: 82–83).

According to the excellent studies of Arthur Hertzberg (1959) and Shlomo Avineri (1981), modern Zionism in general is rooted in this crisis of identity. Prior to the Enlightenment and French Revolution, the Jews lived at the margins of whatever society they happened to find themselves in, excluded by virtue of their religious identity from most significant roles in society at large. Under these conditions, they had no choice but to take their defining identity from their religion.

The secularism and liberalism, as well as the equality before the law, brought about by the Enlightenment and French Revolution altered profoundly the way Jews perceived themselves. These developments mitigated the roundness of the identification between themselves as human beings and their religious being.

But, whether for reasons of racism, ethnicity, or sheer cultural provenance, the universalism conveyed by the French Revolution nowhere escaped a certain exclusivist attitude characterizing nationalism. This attitude corresponds to the Counter-Enlightenment's romantic rejection of the Enlightenment's foundational thesis, that what is right is valid for all humans. Instead, historical relativism was featured.

As a consequence of the coupling of this exclusivist attitude with the principle of universalism, Jews found that they were neither here nor there. They could neither enter fully into the surrounding society nor identify totally with their religious community. In a penetrating analysis, Zygmunt Bauman describes the logic of the predicament in terms of a contradiction, whereby, precisely by virtue of their efforts to assimilate, Jews were stigmatized the more so: "In the eyes of the majority which had emancipated them, they remained members of the accursed emancipated minority. They continued to carry the stigma of their membership for everyone to see" (Bauman 1988: 51). They were caught, he says, in a "no-win situation," wherein they were given "exit visas" from the particularity of Jewish identity, only to be denied "entry tickets" into the majoritarian culture (Bauman 1988: 51). One notable and likely response to this dilemma of identity was Jewish nationalism, a manifestation of attitudes belonging to the Enlightenment as well as to the Counter-Enlightenment (not to mention Messianic Judaism).

The Hashomer Hatza'ir movement displayed an exceptional romantic intensity. Ezra Mendelsohn tells us that all of the Polish pioneers brought with them "the ideals of Jewish labor, Hebraism, an ill-defined but definite left-wing orientation — more ethical than materialistic, — and a belief that the primary force in history was the will of the individual" (Mendelsohn 1981: 128). But the romantic heroism of the founders of Hashomer Hatza'ir was intense enough to distinguish them, even from the other Polish Zionists who also made *aliya* (immigrated or "went up" to the land of Israel).

In 1924–25, by which time the Shomer movement had nearly transformed itself from a free youth movement to a disciplined kibbutz movement affiliated with a Marxist political party, there arose in

Galicia yet another Zionist youth movement called, after the author of the "religion of labor," A. D. Gordon, Gordonia. This movement justified its existence in the face of the well-established Shomer by accusing the latter of excessive individualism and elitism. The Shomer has "its head in the clouds and its feet hanging in the air" and is bent on creating "a select group of ascetics, removed from the world and from life," said the leading figure of Gordonia (Mendelsohn 1981: 297–98). In other words, the Shomer continued to stand out by virtue of its attitude of heroic romanticism.

Broadly speaking, if the themes of the Enlightenment were secularism, universalism, objectivism, and rationalism, those of the Counter-Enlightenment and Romantic movement were expressivism, relativism, subjectivism, and skepticism. The central dogma of the entire Enlightenment was that one set of universal, immutable, and ascertainable principles governs all there is. This dogma is rooted in the ancient doctrine of natural law. The Counter-Enlightenment, also harking back to an ancient tradition, that of skepticism and relativism, featured, by contrast, human convention and creativity (Berlin 1973). Romanticism, in broad ways indistinguishable from the Counter-Enlightenment, seems to represent the progressivist hope of the Enlightenment, but in the mood of that movement's detractors: "Whenever men assert their essential unity with nature, strive for an integration of their intellectual with their emotional capacities, of consciousness with the unconscious, facts with values, and seek to identify subject with object, the term 'romantic' has been applied by themselves or others to those who shared this Weltanschauung" (Gutmann 1973: 208).

The intellectual character of each of these two bodies of thought is varied and complex, and the relationship between them is by no means simply antithetical (see Porter 1990; Cassirer 1951). The Enlightenment's idea of progress doubtless promoted and enhanced the romantic sense of the infinite and of humanity's creative powers. Just as the Enlightenment fostered the French Revolution, so the French Revolution inspired many romantics.

At any rate, it is plain that the kibbutz owes much to both of these bodies of thought. In its secular and moral perfectibilism, and its transcendental pursuit of an absolutely harmonious psychological and social condition, the kibbutz is an attempt to realize the heavenly city of the nineteenth- as well as the eighteenth-century philosophers (see Becker 1932); this utopian enterprise is profoundly indebted to the *philosophes* of the Age of Reason as well as to the romantics who followed them, and to whom encyclopedic knowledge was anathema.

Rousseau and the Kibbutz

Rousseau's Social Theory

The eighteenth-century philosopher Rousseau played a key role in both the Enlightenment and the Counter-Enlightenment. Though Rousseau was in fundamental intellectual ways the enemy of the encyclopaedists, his fellow *philosophes,* he nevertheless shared in their central doctrine of a universally valid rational and experimental method (Berlin 1973: 109). And, though his political theory may not in fact have produced the French Revolution, there can be no doubt that the revolutionaries thought they were practicing what he preached. In addition, his social ideals and moral teachings were at least broadly consistent with the ideological ends of the revolutionaries (McDonald 1965).

On the other hand, Rousseau critically fueled the romantic attitude by his emphasis on natural feeling and free will over reason; his denunciation of artificial social roles as against humankind's simple place in the state of nature; and his plea for self-expression in contrast to the social repression of the self brought about by inequalities based on power and wealth. Indeed, Rousseau's profound individualism as well as his apparently opposed preference for organic community, his passionate love of nature, and his titantic iconoclasm critically affected the movement that is synonymous with early German romanticism, the Sturm and Drang movement. These ideas of Rousseau powerfully influenced even those Germans who repudiated the designation romanticist, such as Nietzsche, Hegel, Kant, and Goethe. Indeed, all the German thinkers who stand at the foundations of the free German Youth movement, the movement that exercised such a powerful influence on the pioneers of Hashomer, were influenced by Rousseau (see Gutmann 1973: 209; and Berlin 1973: 107).

In light of this consideration, even though I have no idea whether any of Timem's founders read Rousseau, and I have traced only broadly and incompletely the intellectual channels through which Rousseau's ideas have found their way into the Israeli kibbutz, it is not at all surprising that Timem's ideology and social organization are profoundly (though not exclusively) Rousseauian. My earlier discussions have demonstrated that in spite of Hashomer Hatza'ir's Marxism, which it adopted officially in the mid-1920s, Timem is at bottom more Rousseauian than Marxian. Timem's principled insistence on voluntarism as a basis for the community's socialism recalls not Marx, who, in his mature works, rejected such a basis as utopian, but especially Rousseau and his contractarian social theory.

Let me now review, then, the Rousseauian points of Kibbutz Timem systematically, by starting with a summary sketch of Rousseau's social theory. To highlight the stunning degree to which kibbutz ideology and Rousseau's thought run parallel, I have found it intellectually felicitous to quote extensively from Rousseau, allowing him to speak for himself wherever possible. Indeed, as cited in the present context, Rousseau's thought can be read gainfully as political commentary on the kibbutz and its problems.

Rousseau arrived at his theory of the social contract as a response to a profound psychosocial problem. As he saw it, with "man's" evolution from a state of nature to one of society, man became increasingly rent by an unhappy disharmony between his natural and his conventional self. According to Rousseau, in the state of nature man enjoyed an essential liberty and equality, in the sense that he was largely independent of others to fulfill his needs. These needs were simple and simply satisfied, by appropriation of whatever was on hand.

Society altered this state of affairs. By making each man's measure the other man rather than himself, society created artificial needs and a comparative distinction of wealth and power. "The savage lives within himself, while social man lives constantly outside himself," wrote Rousseau, "and only knows how to live in the opinion of others, so that he seems to receive the consciousness of his own existence merely from the judgment of others concerning him" (1950: 270). Under such conditions of inequality, an inequality based on conventional rather than natural difference, some men became subject to others. What was a healthy concern for self-preservation (*amour de soi,* or self-love) in the state of nature became in the social state competitive egoism (*amour propre,* or pride).

Thus the evolutionary shift from nature to society constituted a movement from a state of peace and harmony to one in which man was set at odds not only with his fellow man but also within himself. For his feelings of envy put him everywhere in chains and betokened a rift in his being, an alienation from his most basic self.

In view of his perception that the change in human nature wrought by society is irreversible, Rousseau's problem became how to reconcile man's social estate with his natural person. In his words, it was necessary "to find a form of association which will defend and protect with the whole common force the person and goods of each associate, and in which each while uniting himself with all, may still obey himself alone, and remain as free as before" (1950: 13–14). As a solution, Rousseau proposed a social contract entailing "the [voluntary] total alienation of each associate, together with all his rights, to the whole community" (1950: 14). On the logic that "each man, in giving himself to all, gives himself to nobody; and as there is no associate over which he does not acquire the same right as he yields others over himself, he gains an equivalent for everything he loses, and an increase of force for the preservation of what he has," the social contract provides the means by which men can be made free by making them subject (1950: 14). To the same end, the alienation of each individual to the association is without reservation: "If the individuals retained certain rights, as there would be no common superior to decide between them and the public, each, being on one point his own judge, would ask to be so on all" (1950: 14), and the perfect union could not hold.

The social contract rests on both rational and moral choice. It is rational in that it recommends itself to every man on the ground that it logically projects a reconciliation of society with the individual as a self-interested and possessive being. It is moral in that, not only does it derive from and conserve free choice, but it also presupposes and endorses the goodness and "reality" of the whole. Morality rather than reason is the more natural basis of the contract. For in Rousseau's view, free will is the feature without which man cannot be identified as man, and compassion, a patently social sentiment (though Rousseau says otherwise), is also given in the state of nature (1950: 193f., 208ff.).

The social holism of the contract is registered especially in the central role played by the general will. The associate does not conform to some sectional interest, but to the general will, which comes to "more than a sum of particular wills" (1950: 26). By definition, and as it is distinct from any particular attempt to arrive at it, the general will is infallibly directed toward the common good ("The general will is always right and tends to the public advantage; but it does not follow that the deliberations of the people are always equally correct"

[1950: 26]). And, as it can be delegated only by entrusting it to some particular will, thus putting some men in control of others, the general will cannot be represented ("The moment a people allows itself to be represented, it is no longer free: it no longer exists" [1950: 96]). Rousseau's conception of political right is thus essentially democratic.

On the basis of the difference between the legislative and the executive functions, Rousseau drew a distinction between sovereignty and government. (Government is "an intermediate body set up between the subjects and the Sovereign,... charged with the execution of the laws" [1950: 55].) This distinction allowed him to conclude that the general will could coexist with a variety of types of government. Nevertheless, in view of his fundamentally democratic conception of sovereignty, it is not surprising that even in respect of what he called government, and though he thought aristocracy was more practical, Rousseau was inclined in principle to afford democracy ("government" by "the whole people" or by "the majority of the people" [1950: 63]) a certain privilege. He found that, while democracy is particularly unstable and demands for its maintenance exceptional vigilance, liberty with danger is preferable to peace with slavery: "Were there a people of gods, their government would be democratic" (1950: 66).

Indeed, since the general will can neither be alienated nor represented, "The Sovereign cannot act save when the people is assembled" (1950: 89). The general will is insolubly linked, then, not simply to democracy, but to direct democracy. Clearly, this conception of sovereignty puts a premium on communal dimensions or small states: "It follows that, the larger the State, the less the liberty" (1950: 57).

For Rousseau, the political participation entailed by a general assembly constituted a form of civic education. It promoted the enlightened moral action that disposes the individual to ask the right question in public decision making: not whether he prefers a particular proposal, but whether that proposal "is in conformity with the general will" (1950: 106).

To further ensure that the individual asks himself the right question, Rousseau advocated that the state displace the family ("the father") as the educator of children:

> Public education... is one of the fundamental rules of popular or legitimate government. If children are brought up in common in the

bosom of equality; if they are imbued with the laws of the State and the precepts of the general will; if they are taught to respect these above all things; if they are surrounded by examples and objects which constantly remind them of the tender mother who nourishes them, of the love she bears them, of the inestimable benefits they receive from her, and of the return they owe her, we cannot doubt that they will learn to cherish one another mutually as brothers, to will nothing contrary to the will of society. (1950: 309)

Parallels between Rousseau and the Kibbutz

This summary of Rousseau's social theory is selective. I would not contend that Rousseau envisioned the kibbutz. Indeed, there is much in Rousseau that perhaps runs contrary to the kibbutz, both descriptively and prescriptively. Though his theory demanded that the people assemble, he had in mind not a commune but the Roman Republic. As he found that lengthy discussion was indicative of the influence of particular interests (1950: 104), he would not have been impressed with the kibbutz's internal politics, which emphasize the importance of prolonged debate for facilitating the expression of the general will. He also might well have disapproved of the kibbutz's effort to minimize "government" by making, through the legioned establishment of administrative committees and the relatively rapid rotation of their memberships, all the *chaverim* "magistrates." After all, he held that to unite the governmental or administrative function with the legislative authority enervated the former, leaving "the particular will as strong as it can possibly be" (1950: 61–62).

This list of contrasts could be extended. Nevertheless, it seems to me that the points of difference between the kibbutz and Rousseau stem largely from the latter's failure to consider democracy under truly small-group or communal conditions, conditions he described as impossible to realize together (see below, chap. 9, n. 3). When allowances are made for this consideration, the consistency between the kibbutz and the spirit of Rousseau's social theory could not appear to be more fundamental.

As was indicated in earlier chapters, the most obvious points of consistency rest with the kibbutz's central legislative institution of immediate democracy and this institution's essential predication of the general will. The kibbutz's refusal to entertain legislation by representation and its concern to arrive at collective decisions that reflect a genuine or organic mutuality rather than a quantitative function (like majority rule) are axially Rousseauian.

It might be thought that the kibbutz's rejection of fixed laws stands opposed to Rousseau's emphasis on the rule of law. But what the kibbutz finds objectionable here is the institution of formal rather than substantive rules and justice. Rousseau, who held that the law is nothing but the declaration of the general will, stood no less opposed to such formalism. Thus he found that, since what passes for law in most cases has not really been ratified by the people, "very few nations have any Laws" (1950: 94–95).[2]

The kibbutz shares so much of his vision, it is hardly surprising that Rousseau anticipated the "trouble case" on which my ethnography of Timem centers — the debate over the proposal to introduce secret balloting and the concomitant self-definition of a decline in the community's social state. It is worth quoting here, once again, Rousseau's superbly astute comment on the social implications of the difference between the two modes of voting:

> As for the method of taking the vote, it was among the ancient Romans as simple as their morals.... Each man declared his vote aloud, and a clerk duly wrote it down; the majority in each tribe determined the vote of the tribe.... This custom was good as long as honesty was triumphant among the citizens, and each man was ashamed to vote publicly in favour of an unjust proposal or an unworthy subject; but, when the people grew corrupt and votes were bought, it was fitting that voting should be secret in order that purchasers might be restrained by mistrust, and rogues be given the means of not being traitors. (1950: 128)

Rousseau's analysis pithily captures Kibbutz Timem's dilemma. As one would expect from his analysis, Timem's members found they could embrace a secret ballot, as a solution to the problems they were experiencing in the practice of radical democracy, only by sanctioning a certain liberalizing corruption of their synthetic ideal.

The liberalizing corruption, as I have shown, relates to the disruptive emergence of private interests. Here, again, Rousseau concisely described — down to the kibbutz's diagnostic fear of the familial or "domestic" order — the development that occasioned Timem's concern over the operation of its most basic democratic institution:

> The better the constitution of a State is, the more do public affairs encroach on private in the minds of the citizens. Private affairs

are even of much less importance, because the aggregate of the common happiness furnishes a greater proportion of that of each individual, so that there is less for him to seek in particular cares. In a well-ordered city every man flies to the assemblies: under a bad government no one cares to stir a step to get to them, because no one is interested in what happens there, because it is foreseen that the general will will not prevail, and lastly because domestic cares are all-absorbing. (1950: 93–94)

In point of fact, Rousseau typologizes elegantly — if more radically than the example of the kibbutz allows — the kind of psychosocial change Timem's members were anxiously experiencing and trying hard to reconcile with their synthetic ideal. Allow me to quote him at even greater length:

As long as several men in assembly regard themselves as a single body, they have only a single will which is concerned with their common preservation and general well-being. In this case, all the springs of the State are vigorous and simple and its rules clear and luminous; there are no embroilments or conflicts of interests; the common good is everywhere clearly apparent, and only good sense is needed to perceive it. Peace, unity, and equality are the enemies of political subtleties. Men who are upright and simple are difficult to deceive because of their simplicity; lures and ingenious pretexts fail to impose upon them, and they are not even subtle enough to be dupes....

A State so governed needs very few laws; and, as it becomes necessary to issue new ones, the necessity is universally seen....

But when the social bond begins to be relaxed and the State to grow weak, when particular interests begin to make themselves felt and the smaller societies [factions] to exercise an influence over the larger, the common interest changes and finds opponents; opinion is no longer unanimous; the general will ceases to be the will of all; contradictory views and debates arise....

Finally, when the State, on the eve of ruin, maintains only a vain, illusory, and formal existence, when in every heart the social bond is broken, and the meanest interest brazenly lays hold of the sacred name of "public good," the general will becomes mute: all men, guided by secret motives, no more give their views as citizens than if the State had never been, and iniquitous decrees directed solely to private interest get passed under the name of laws. (1950: 102–3)

Evidently, Rousseau finds this degenerative course of change to be implicit in democracy. He argues that in a democratic order, he who makes the laws also executes them, confounding the general will with the particular, opening the affairs of public to the influence of private interests, and, finally, corrupting the legislative body (1950: 64–65). If decline of this kind is to be avoided, he continues, so many conditions "that are difficult to unite" must be met, including especially the condition of a citizenship whose virtue is of divine proportions, that success in the enterprise goes "against the natural order" and is "unimaginable" (1950: 65).[3] Put another way, "A people that would always govern well would not need to be governed." Therefore, or so he concludes, "So perfect a government is not for men," and "there never has been a real democracy, and there never will be" (1950: 65).

In other words, again anticipating a certain rude awakening on the part of the kibbutz, Rousseau lays it down that for reasons of inevitable contingency — especially as regards human nature — the perfectibilism entailed by "real democracy" is chimerical. The fall away from the unblemished rule of the general will to an order in which men are guided by secret motives and private interests cannot finally be helped.

Underlying these parallels between the kibbutz and Rousseau's thought in regard to political order, procedure, and change lies a common conception of human nature. Rousseau's definition of human identity in terms primarily of free will stands behind the whole of the kibbutz enterprise. "To renounce liberty is to renounce being a man," he wrote (1950: 9). Thus, in his discussion of slavery, he cogently sets out what amounts to the kibbutz's principle and practice of voluntarism as they apply to the perpetuity of the kibbutz. In so doing, he directly implicates conflict between the generations as a fundamental possibility:

> Even if each man could alienate himself, he could not alienate his children: they are born men and free; their liberty belongs to them, and no one but they has the right to dispose of it. Before they come to years of discretion, the father can, in their name, lay down conditions of their preservation and well-being, but he cannot give them irrevocably and without conditions: such a gift is contrary to the ends of nature, and exceeds the rights of paternity. It would therefore be necessary, in order to legitimize an arbitrary government, that in every generation the people should be in a position to accept or reject it; but, were this so, the government would be no longer arbitrary. (1950: 8–9)

In addition, the kibbutz is no less emphatic than Rousseau that "inequality," which puts some individuals in a position to control and exploit others, is the antithesis of freedom and that it is given not in nature but in convention. Thus, both the kibbutz and Rousseau find that manmade inequality can be well combated, if not eliminated, through conventional arrangements, by means of reorganization of society. Although such reorganization is a matter of convention, and therefore beyond the state of nature, because it restores in a way the original or natural condition of humankind's freedom, it also constitutes a return to nature. Thus the kibbutz and Rousseau aimed at harmonizing nature with convention or society.

In the kibbutz, the return to nature was given quite literal expression in the going back to and working of the land of Israel. A. D. Gordon spoke here of the "redemption of the land and labor" (1973: 50). This idea of return took its deepest significance from the consideration that for two thousand years the Jews had been forcibly divorced from the land and labor in the relevant sense, constructing return to them as above all a liberating movement, in the direction of Rousseau's state of nature.

As to the synthesis of nature and society, the kibbutz proposes Rousseau's solution: a social compact in which each individual gives her- or himself wholly to, thus identifying with, the collective body. Under the rule of this compact, the individual person remains quite free, since, in obeying the general will, that person quite literally governs only him- or herself.

This ingenious solution is at once perfectly rational in its logic and profoundly moral in its end. For Rousseau the synthesis is summed up in the social identity of "citizen," the role of *chaver* serving the identical purpose in the kibbutz. The successful performance of each of these roles presupposes sufficient endowments of both reason and conscience to dictate voluntary adherence to the general will.[4]

Both Rousseau and the kibbutz predicated such voluntary adherence on the establishment of a social order whose very practice was held to foster correct social decisions. But for both, the best insurance that the individual would follow the dictates of reason and conscience was the education of children in the art of moral living and for society. The vital role given by the kibbutz to *chinuch meshutaf*, or "collective education," is critically documented in Spiro's substantial study of children in the kibbutz (1965; or see, for example, Rabin and Hazan 1973). The continuity of the kibbutz revolution was virtually vested in its revolutionary system of education. Rousseau's great masterpiece on education is of course *Émile*. There is no need here, however, to enter into an involved discussion of Rousseau's theory of education in relation to the kibbutz. A quote from the *Discourse on Political Economy* suffices to show that in fundamental respects Rousseau and the kibbutz see eye to eye on this matter:

> Public education, therefore, under regulations prescribed by the government, and under magistrates established by the Sovereign [that is, the People], is one of the fundamental rules of popular or legitimate government. If children are brought up in common in the bosom of equality; if they are imbued with the laws of the State and the precepts of the general will; if they are taught to respect these above all things; if they are surrounded by examples and objects which constantly remind them of the tender mother who nourishes them, of the love she bears them, of the inestimable benefits they receive from her, and of the return they owe her, we cannot doubt that they will learn to cherish one another mutually as brothers, to will nothing contrary to the will of society, to substitute the actions of men and citizens for the futile and vain babbling of sophists, and to become in time defenders and fathers of the country of which they will have been so long the children. (1950: 309)

Though one might doubt that Rousseau regarded his contractarian solution to the problem of nature and convention as anything more than an abstract standard by which to gauge the shortcomings of social life on this earth (Shklar 1969), it is clear that the kibbutz attempted to implement just such a solution. Both Rousseau and the kibbutz propose a voluntary social compact in which the identification of the individual with society is so complete that the two fundamental aspects of human beings' existence, the natural and the conventional, are perfectly united. The goal is to resume the original harmony of an undivided natural state, but in a new and progressive form. In the case of both Rousseau and the kibbutz, the solution is predicated on a holistic and organicistic social ontology. The solution presupposes a social reality that comes to more than the sum of its parts as well as an ontology that takes human beings as creatures who have no identity save that which they give to themselves. In other words, both Rousseau and the kibbutz have fundamentally in common a conception of human nature as essentially open, making the goal of a "new man" a very natural principle.

Rousseau and the Revision of Genesis

An Edenic State of Nature

The parallels I have drawn between Rousseau's thought and kibbutz ideology and practice could be elaborated in greater detail and further supplemented. Such an undertaking would, I think, serve more to throw interesting light on the practical force of Rousseau's ideas than to aid further in the interpretation of the kibbutz, and is best left to separate treatment. Here I have sought to demonstrate that the kibbutz is indeed profoundly Rousseauian. How, then, can this demonstration lend credence to my contention that Timem is living a biblical story and biblical social logic?

The answer rests with the determination that Rousseau's social theory may itself be seen as a radical revision of the myth of Genesis. If this is right, then the conclusion begins to look irresistible that the story of Genesis does indeed pervade the social enterprise of the kibbutz. This conclusion looks irresistible, not because the members studied this story, but because the story has furnished them with the self-identity and ontological universe on the basis of which they are able to grasp and posit anything at all.

As is evident in his work, and has often been noted (for example, A. Bloom 1979: 4–6; Shklar 1969: 9), Rousseau set out to rival Plato's *Republic*. His emphasis on emotion and moral probity as over and against the (Platonic) beauty and rationality of the idea, however, strongly suggests that Rousseau, like so many eighteenth-century thinkers and writers, was a product of Hebraism as well as Hellenism. A systematic case for reading Rousseau as a biblical revisionist has recently been made. In his fine study of the creation myth as a romantic form, Paul Cantor argues most persuasively that Rousseau's *Second Discourse*, the essay in which the French master does most to elaborate his ideas on the history of mankind, "reads like a secularized version of the fall of man" (1984: 7).[5]

According to Cantor, Rousseau's history of mankind (though related in the *Second Discourse* in terms of several stages) may be divided into two main stages: the first, the state of nature, corresponds to the paradisical stage of Genesis; the second, civil society, corresponds to the fallen state of man. Despite certain differences between the two notions, the parallels between Rousseau's state of nature and the Garden of Eden are very striking. According to Rousseau, natural man lives a fairly untroubled existence, in that he is at harmony with himself and his surroundings. This harmony amounts to animal innocence. Natural man had little in the way of reason ("A state of reflection is a state contrary to nature" [1950: 204]). Furthermore, he did not "know" death ("For no animal can know what it is to die" [1950: 210]). And, though capable of naming things, natural man was not given much to generalization; he did little to organize difference ("Every object at first received a particular name without regard to genus or species, which these primitive originators were not in a position to distinguish; every individual presented itself to their minds in isolation, as they are in the picture of nature" [1950: 217]).

In effect, natural man, like the prelapsarian Adam, being almost completely absorbed in otherness (the otherness of nature, though, rather than of God), had very little consciousness of self. Accordingly, he was, in an apparent sense, free from both morality and society. For both morality and society depend on the existence of self-conscious individuals, persons who can be held accountable for their own deeds. Hence, Rousseau concluded that "men in a state of nature, having no moral relations or determinate obligations one with another, could not be either good or bad, virtuous or vicious" (1950: 221). Put another way, the difference between what is good and what is bad was not telling to natural man: "Savages are not bad merely because they do not know what it is to be good: for it is neither the development of the understanding nor the restraint of law that hinders them from doing ill; but the peacefulness of their passions, and their ignorance of vice" (1950: 223). In a certain sense, then, as Rousseau notoriously concluded, men are "naturally good" (1950: 273). Since in the state of nature men are ruled, not by law or convention, but by an implicit commandment, the "natural feeling" of compassion, "none are tempted to disobey its gentle voice" (1950: 226).

Denaturization and the Fall

However, the emergence of society as such and of reason brought this idyllic state of affairs to an end. Society proper is not natural but conventional. Rousseau referred the distinction between nature and convention to the psychological schism between the passions and reason. But this schism, Rousseau found, grows out of the movement toward civil society. Man's reorientation away from his passions toward reason, that is, away from what comes naturally, meant that he learned to take the measure of himself by reference to other men's needs and desires, rather than to his own (natural) needs and desires. As a result, man developed an unnatural dependence and inauthentic or factitious self. The upshot is a state of affairs characterized by relations of power and pride, wealth and property — in short, intensely competitive relations of inequality.

Evocative of Genesis, where clothing signals the introduction of the possibility of duplicity and distrust, Rousseau comments on this (fallen) state of affairs in terms of a split between appearance and reality: "It now became the interest of men to appear what they really were not. To be and to seem became two totally different things; and from this distinction sprang insolent pomp and cheating trickery, with all the numerous vices that go in their train" (1950: 247). Furthermore, as in Genesis, the fall from innocence also put man to work: "From the moment one man began to stand in need of the help of another; from the moment it appeared advantageous to any one man to have enough provisions for two, equality disappeared, property was introduced, work became indispensable, and vast forests became smiling fields, which man had to water with the sweat of his brow, and where slavery and misery were soon seen to germinate and grow up with the crops" (1950: 244).

It is evident that, in Rousseau's evolutionary picture, the shift from the state of nature to civil society marks a fall from a state in which man is innocent and at peace with himself and his surroundings to a generally divided and depraved state of self-reflection and alienation.

Self-Mediation and the Provocation of Eve

The crucial instrument of this grand transformation roundly evokes the biblical account. While Rousseau argues that new and contingent circumstances "occasion new developments of [man's] faculties" (1950: 210), these developments are keyed by two of the faculties themselves — free will and self-perfectibility:

> It is not... so much the understanding that constitutes the specific difference between the man and the brute, as the human quality of free agency. Nature lays her commands on every animal, and the brute obeys her voice. Man receives the same impulsion, but at the same time knows himself at liberty to acquiesce or resist: and it is particularly in his consciousness of this liberty that the spirituality

of his soul is displayed. For physics may explain, in some measure, the mechanism of the senses and the formation of ideas; but in the power of willing or rather of choosing, and in the feeling of this power, nothing is to be found but acts which are purely spiritual and wholly inexplicable by the laws of mechanism.

There is another very specific quality which distinguishes [men from brutes], and which will admit of no dispute. This is the faculty of self-improvement, which, by the help of circumstances, gradually develops all the rest of our faculties, and is inherent in the species as in the individual. (1950: 208–9)

Thus for Rousseau, as for the redactors of Genesis, it is man's spiritual faculty of willing, of making choices, that accounts for his evolution from a state of innocence to one of self-awareness. And, as in Genesis, this faculty is integrally linked with a nature that is somehow self-mediating, a nature that refuses to be ultimately specified.

What is more, as in Genesis, the operation of this faculty and this nature is peculiarly associated with the feminine principle. It is also driven by the imagination, an imagination with an appetite so cunning that it might well be called serpential. Distinguishing between the physical or natural and moral or conventional ingredients of love, Rousseau allows:

It is easy to see that the moral part of love is a factitious feeling, born of social usage, and enhanced by the women with much care and cleverness, to establish their empire, and put in power the sex which ought to obey.... Men in a state of nature being confined merely to what is physical in love, and fortunate enough to be ignorant of those excellences, which whet the appetite while they increase the difficulty of gratifying it, must be subject to fewer and less violent fits of passion, and consequently fall into fewer and less violent disputes. The imagination, which causes such ravages among us, never speaks to the heart of savages who quietly await the impulses of nature, yield to them involuntarily, with more pleasure than ardour, and, their wants once satisfied, lose the desire. It is therefore incontestable that love, as well as all other passions, must have acquired in society that glowing impetuosity, which makes it so often fatal to mankind. (1950: 228–29)

In another passage, decrying the weakness that results from the denaturing of man, Rousseau again associates man's fallen state with the feminine principle: "As [man] becomes sociable and a slave [that is, unnecessarily dependent], he grows weak, timid, and servile; his effeminate way of life totally enervates his strength and courage" (1950: 206).

The Social Contract and the Fortunate Fall

Clearly, then, Rousseau's account of the origins of man as a moral being is remarkably like the biblical account. Where it deviates fundamentally from the latter is, of course, in its secular humanism. Rousseau's emphasis is on human rather than god-given nature. In this connection, perhaps he was playing on the tacit ambiguity of the Hebrew Bible, the ambiguity of an anthropology overshadowed by theological design. After all, the story of the fall can justifiably be read as a religious account of how secularization began.

In any case, there can be no doubt that Rousseau shared in the implicit normative ambivalence displayed in the Hebrew Bible, whereby inescapably the fall may also be understood as an ascent into a state of moral (human) existence. Though it is plain that Rousseau was peculiarly preoccupied with plumbing and cataloguing the evils and unhappinesses brought about by conventional society and moral existence, he was nonetheless given to regard "the fall" as in a sense fortunate. Not far from the beginning of *The Social Contract,* he compares and contrasts man's lot in the civil state to his lot in the state of nature:

> The passage from the state of nature to the civil state produces a very remarkable change in man, by substituting justice for instinct in his conduct, and giving his actions the morality they had formerly lacked. Then only, when the voice of duty takes the place of physical impulses and right of appetite, does man, who so far had considered only himself, find that he is forced to act on different principles, and to consult his reason before listening to his inclinations. Although, in this state, he deprives himself of some advantages which he got from nature, he gains in return others so great, his faculties are so stimulated and developed, his ideas so extended, his feelings so ennobled, and his whole soul so uplifted, that, did not the abuses of this new condition often degrade him below that which he left, he would be bound to bless continually the happy moment which took him from it for ever, and, instead of a stupid and unimaginative animal, made him an intelligent being and a man.
> Let us draw up the whole account in terms easily commensurable. What man loses by the social contract is his natural liberty and an unlimited right to everything he tries to get and succeeds in getting; what he gains is civil liberty and the proprietorship of

all he possesses.... We might, over and above all this, add, to what man acquires in the civil state, moral liberty, which alone makes him truly master of himself; for the mere impulse of appetite is slavery, while obedience to a law which we prescribe to ourselves is liberty. (1950: 18–19)

Though Rousseau is not exactly unequivocal in this passage, his language leaves no doubt that in fundamental respects his sympathies lie with man as "an intelligent being and a man," rather than as "a stupid and unimaginative animal." In fact, he seems filled with admiration for the divine promise of man's moral estate.

As is consistent with his secular revisionism, and as Cantor points out (1984: 13), Rousseau redefined the traditional problem of evil. On the traditional problem, it always remains open to ask, in spite of such notions as original sin, why an omnipotent and benevolent creator would allow for the introduction of evil. For Rousseau, basically man has only himself to blame.

But, by the same token — a self-mediating nature unqualified by a supernal and surpassing intelligence — man is in a position, if not to redeem himself fully, at least to ameliorate his situation radically. Thus, when Rousseau extols the virtues of man's moral estate, he has in mind man's situation under the ideal conditions of the social contract and the rule of the general will: "Instead of destroying natural inequality, the fundamental compact substitutes, for such physical inequality as nature may have set up between men, an equality that is moral and legitimate, and that men, who may be unequal in strength or intelligence, become every one equal by convention and legal right" (1950: 22). Again, under a true compact between the social body and each of its members:

> It is seen to be so untrue that there is, in the social contract, any real renunciation on the part of the individuals, that the position in which they find themselves as a result of the contract is really preferable to that in which they were before. Instead of a renunciation, they have made an advantageous exchange: instead of an uncertain and precarious way of living they have got one that is better and more secure; instead of natural independence they have got liberty, instead of the power to harm others security for themselves, and instead of their strength, which others might overcome, a right which social union makes invincible. (1950: 31)

Finally, celebrating the synthetic ingenuity of the social contract, Rousseau, calling the general will a "celestial voice," suggests how the moral life, though secular, partakes of divine happiness and perfection:

> How can it be that all should obey, yet nobody take upon him to command, and that all should serve, and yet have no masters, but be the more free, as, in apparent subjection, each loses no part of his liberty but what might be hurtful to that of another? These wonders are the work of law [which, in essence, is nothing but the general will]. It is to law alone that men owe justice and liberty. It is this salutary organ of the will of all which establishes, in civil right, the natural equality between men. It is this celestial voice which dictates to each citizen the precepts of public reason, and teaches him to act according to the rules of his own judgment, and not to behave inconsistently with himself. (1950: 294)

Thus, Rousseau's account of the political development of humankind revises the biblical story. Taking a cue (directly or not) from the latter's implicit anthropology, Rousseau constructs a secular account of man's "fall" from a harmonious, idyllic state of existence. But he produces a new Genesis in yet another sense. On the basis of the irrecusable ambivalence of man's "fall" (a fall that transforms man into "an intelligent being and a man"), Rousseau constructs a redemptive scenario — the social contract.

The Social Contract, Patriarchal Authority, and the Generations

At this juncture, it seems thoroughly compelling to conclude that Kibbutz Timem's lived presentation of the central dynamic of Genesis is not a matter of analytical contrivance but rather of historical connection. For, in the first place, as was demonstrated earlier in this chapter, the kibbutz is predicated on a social contract that is substantially Rousseauian; and, in the second, the idea of such a contract, as also was just demonstrated, presupposes — which is to say, is logically inconceivable outside of — the story of Genesis.

Let me add finally to the force of this conclusion by observing that insofar as Rousseau's "social contract" presupposes Genesis, it also presupposes the idea of the generations. Since Genesis and generation are inseparable concepts, this observation is foregone. Still, it is edifying to indicate just how deeply Rousseau's social theory involves the idea of the generations.

Rousseau's "social contract" is contrived to liberate man's free will from the bonds of convention. With the passage from nature to society, man's free will is curtailed unnecessarily. For he enters into dependence or political relations the basis of which are factitious rules, making these relations unnecessary by definition. By establishing between the individual and society a relationship that is both wholly voluntary and mutually comprehensive, so that the identity between the individual and society is complete, the social contract reconciles man's free will and real self with his rule-bound self. Under these conditions, the conventions by which man lives, though they cannot reproduce the state of nature as such, enhance man's free will by ensuring that each man remains his own governor. The situation in which one man is institutionally subject to another is conventionally removed, thus uniting convention and free will in a moral harmony.

Now, as was brought out above, free will for Rousseau amounts to the power to will or to choose, that is, the power to do otherwise. The "brute cannot deviate from the rule prescribed to it," Rousseau writes, "even when it would be advantageous for it to do so; and, on the contrary, man frequently deviates from such rules to his own prejudice." Put another way, "The will continues to speak when nature is silent" (1950: 208). Thus, in the state of nature, man develops his free will precisely by at once negating nature and then filling the resulting existential vacuum with convention. But conventional society constitutes its own and, because unnecessary, more odious limits on man's free will. Consequently, in the best of all possible worlds, man would seek to further advance that will by resisting and surmounting those conventional limits in such a manner as to prevent any man from deploying convention in order to enslave another.

Free will, then, pertains to the relationship obtaining between two forces, one of which apprehends the other as an obstacle to its ends, the other thereby serving to define the first as an agency of choice. Strikingly, Rousseau assimilates this relationship of resistance and transcendence, in its more positive states, to the relationship of paternal authority. In the *Social Contract,* he asserts:

> The most ancient of all societies, and the only one that is natural, is the family: and even so the children remain attached to the father only so long as they need him for their preservation. As soon as this need ceases, the natural bond is dissolved. The children, released from the obedience they owed to the father, and the father, released from the care he owed his children, return equally to independence. If they remain united, they continue so no longer naturally, but voluntarily; and the family itself is then maintained only by convention.

> This common liberty results from the nature of man. His first law is to provide for his own preservation, his first cares are those which he owes to himself; and, as soon as he reaches years of discretion, he is the sole judge of the proper means of preserving himself, and consequently becomes his own master. (1950: 4)

Here, obviously, Rousseau finds that the family and paternal authority are exemplary of the positive operation of free will. Inasmuch as the family exists in the absence of convention, it constitutes a natural society in which "authority" nurtures rather than curtails free will. Inasmuch as the family is maintained by convention, it constitutes — as under the social contract — a wholly voluntary society, and, therefore, one in which the authority of the father over the son continues to promote rather than circumscribe free will. Evidently, the family and paternal authority play a mediatory role in Rousseau's sociological understanding. They represent the two states in which harmony rather than schism is regnant — the state of nature and the state of society under the social contract.

In the following passage, from the *Second Discourse,* Rousseau addresses directly the manner in which the family mediates between nature and convention, and between passion and reason, so describing the development of the social division of labor and the strengths of living together rather than apart:

> The first expansions of the human heart were the effects of a novel situation, which united husbands and wives, fathers and children, under one roof. The habit of living together soon gave rise to the finest feelings known to humanity, conjugal love and paternal affection. Every family became a little society, the more united because liberty and reciprocal attachment were the only bonds of its union. The sexes, whose manner of life had been hitherto the same, began now to adopt different ways of living. The women became more sedentary, and accustomed themselves to mind the hut and their children, while the men went abroad in search of their common subsistence. From living a softer life, both sexes also began to lose something of their strength and ferocity: but, if individuals became to some extent less able to encounter wild beasts separately, they found it, on the other hand, easier to assemble and resist in common. (1950: 239)

In light of his view of the family and paternal authority as representatively mediatory, Rousseau concludes that "the family then may be called the first model of political societies: the ruler corresponds to the father, and the people to the children; and all, being born free and equal, alienate their liberty only for their own advantage" (1950: 4–5). Whether or not by "first," in the phrase "first model of political societies," Rousseau had in mind "earliest," given his idealistic picture of the family, surely he intended "ranking." Rousseau makes it positively plain that (as against the position of Locke) the consideration of the family as a model of political society does not warrant the conclusion that absolute government and civil society may be derived from it. As he states, "In the family, the love of the father for his children repays him for the care he takes of them, while, in the State, the pleasure of commanding takes the place of the love which the chief cannot have for the peoples under him" (1950: 5); and:

> Nothing on earth can be farther from the ferocious spirit of despotism than the mildness of that authority which looks more to the advantage of him who obeys than to that of him who commands; that, by the law of nature, the father is the child's master no longer than his help is necessary; that from that time they are both equal, the son being perfectly independent of the father, and owing him only respect, and not obedience. For gratitude is a duty which ought to be paid, but not a right to be exacted: instead of saying that civil society is derived from paternal authority, we ought to say rather that the latter derives its principal force from the former. (1950: 257)

It would appear that by "first model" (*le premier modele*), Rousseau means especially "preferred model." His picture of paternal authority freely relinquished on behalf of the son's majority axiologically equates the state of nature with the state of contractarian society; by the same token, it equates the state of civil society with the theocratic state. For in both these latter states, the ruler (the father) jealously guards his authority from his people (his children) in an effort to prevent them from becoming self-rulers and to prolong his own tenure.

Here we have Rousseau's secularizing revisionism in grand sum. His preferred state of human affairs, though it entails the biblical dynamic of a fall, precisely inverts the biblical axiology. As in the kibbutz, a certain state of society, a holistic, integral state, replaces God as sovereign, and, thereby, in principle, external authority with self-rule.

But, for our purposes, Rousseau's conservativism is of no less moment than his revolutionary turn. The fact that he assimilates the social contract to the relationship of paternal authority signifies that he continues to conceive of human society in terms of the generations. That the social contract is "generative" is obvious — it is above all an act of free will. But that it is also a question of conflict between the generations is obscured by the benign, indeed, utopian, aspect of Rousseau's contractarian design. According to this aspect, the complete and substantive identity between ruler and ruled makes conflict impossible in principle.

However, as Rousseau doubtless grasped (Shklar 1969), despite the utopian promise of the social contract, the proposed perfect identity of man and citizen is itself impossible in practice. For the condition of the successful operation of the social contract, namely, free will, cannot obtain in the absence of a relationship of conflict of one kind or another. After all, the very axis of Rousseau's social thought is the proposition that if free will is to exist and to develop, it veritably entails obstacles. One cannot define oneself unless one takes a stand against one's other. Even in Rousseau's state of nature, man was in a position to deviate from the given rules "to his own prejudice." And insofar as the social contract may be representatively expressed in the medium of paternal authority, so may the relations of resistance characterizing the contractarian state. Accordingly, these relations obtain between father and son, and they convey the primordial choice of the generations and the world that that choice entails.

Ten

Two Kinds of Rationality

The Question of Rationality

The Anthropological Problem of Rationality and the Kibbutz

The myth of Genesis is the invisible foundation without which the visible form of life I call Kibbutz Timem would not appear. The profound way in which Timem's social dynamic expresses the myth is not coincidental but *culturally* essential. Or so my study of Timem shows: focused by a debate over the merits of secret balloting, in which the community's sense of itself as fallen was thematized, the study finds that the members of Timem conduct themselves, comprehensively, in terms of a self-identity given in the logic of Genesis. But what can be said about the "rationality" of this existential preoccupation?

The preoccupation reflects a subliminal, and therefore wholly engaging, prejudice entailed by the assumption of a particular human identity — the identity of "moral creature." The myth was not selected as a rational choice per se, but, as I put it, a primordial one. Obtaining representatively between behavior and consciousness, nature and culture, self and other, primordial choices construct virtual worlds and are irreducible to known quantities.

Nevertheless, the consideration that in the debate on secret balloting Timem's members allowed the perception of conflict between the generations to overshadow an empirically more precise line of inquiry makes the question of rationality unavoidable. The debates' explicit theme of a contradiction between the ideal of immediate democracy and the rationalized needs of a "modern" social order pointed straight to "social differentiation" as the best empiricist account of the community's social problems. Must we then assess the members as irrational?

This question recalls a venerable anthropological problem. I have in mind the problem of rationality as it has been controverted in relation to myth, ritual, and magic as practiced by primitive peoples (Wilson 1970; Hollis and Lukes 1982). In light of my characterization of Timem's self-understanding as rooted in mythological consciousness, it is not surprising that the problem of rationality should emerge here. To be sure, Timem's members do not articulate this myth as a charter of their social existence. But their easy, implicit conviction in the myth's logic as a definition of their situation, in the face of a sharper empirical picture, makes it necessary to take up the question of rationality.

It is inappropriate here to adopt Peter Winch's celebrated approach to the problem of rationality, taking the standards of rationality to differ from one culture to another (Winch 1970; see also 1958). The consideration that Timem's members entertained both accounts, leaving the empirically more exact to dangle, makes it impossible to address the question of rationality on the grounds of cultural relativity.

Moreover, as I argued in chapter 7, the responses of functionalism (that Timem's self-understanding served to mask a more fundamental disharmony) and of structuralism and hermeneutics (that that self-understanding is a trope of one kind or another) are not open to us. These responses make Timem's self-understanding out as a consistent (rational) means to a particular end — in the case of functionalism, the end of social utility; in the case of structuralism and hermeneutics, the end of intellectual or aesthetic modeling. They suggest that Timem's members, following their collective but less than conscious instinct, either misconstrued the facts in order to ensure a greater social utility; or construed the facts according to structural rather than empirical properties; or, finally, construed them tropologically, again without regard to empirical properties. Each of these responses could save Timem's members from the charge of irrationalism. For, no less than the more empirical account, each pictures the members' definition of the situation as a consistent means to an end.

But the description of Timem's involvement with the myth of Genesis in terms of a primordial choice pictures that involvement as a matter of basic human self-identifying. It therefore rules out any account of its rationality by reference to sheer means-ends consistency. The self-understanding in question was selected in the first instance for "reasons" intrinsic rather than extrinsic to it. In other words, it was selected existentially, as its own end.

Therefore, in a plain sense, the definition of the situation in terms of conflict between the generations must be incommensurable with the more empirically focused account. Whereas the latter presupposes a detached perspective, from which the facts of the matter are to be determined without regard to the observer's immediate, practical aims and desires, the former comports a perspective of immediate engagement. The definition "conflict between the generations" entails an observer who is also participant, with an axe to grind. Under this definition, the facts are indeterminable outside of the interested, particular perspective of Timem's members. In other words, the facts do not exist in themselves, not even in principle, but are interpretively informed right from the start.

If, therefore, by "rationality" we intend logical consistency between means and ends, the account in terms of generational conflict cannot possibly measure up. But the consideration that the kibbutz's self-understanding is by definition not a matter of rationality in this sense leads one to ask what makes this notion of rationality the final parameter. As a host of strong critics, from Rousseau to Habermas, Foucault, and Derrida, have made plain, there is reason to think that our usual acceptation of "rationality" is too narrow for our own good. In order to explore this possibility, I need to draw the contrast between the empiric and the mythic account more thoroughly.

The Empiric versus the Mythic Account

Empiricism and the Futility of Ideals

According to the empiric account, the kibbutz faltered as an ideal enterprise for reasons of contingent circumstances. The community's growth and development fostered internal differentiation, which in turn gave rise to increasing individuation and alienation of the individual from the collective. Though the community had always been committed to the practical realization of its ideal, it had not anticipated the relative individuation brought by quantitative growth and the proliferation of qualitative distinction. These developments manifested themselves, on the level of the individual, in terms of increasing self-differentiation. The procession of the generations constituted only one component of this course of change.

Striking about this account is its implication of futility for the kibbutz ideal. The account suggests that the moment the kibbutz attempted to realize itself in practice, it necessarily started to deteriorate. In other words, it suggests that falling away from an ideal is an entailment of practice.

The reason for this dire judgment rests with the very idea of empiricism. Empiricism requires that the facts of a matter be determined by a disengaged observer. Such an observer has assumed the perspective of someone outside the immediate lived universe. That is to say, such an observer is presumed to approach the determination of the facts unattached, without regard to value. Here, then, facts are defined precisely by their opposition to value. In effect, the "facts" of empiricism are constitutionally opposed to a radically normative endeavor such as the kibbutz. Indeed, they are ultimately opposed to any normative endeavor.[1]

A Weberian Illusion

It could be argued that what I am describing as a constitutional opposition between empiricism and normativism does not entail that in their practice all ideals must come to grief. Perhaps it entails only that, though empirical science may enjoy no special warrant to decide between them, ideals or values can be appraised by such a science for their relative consistency and practicality. This is the position argued by Weber in his celebrated essay, "Objectivity in Social Science" (in Weber 1949; see also Weber in Gerth and Mills 1946: chap. 5). "An empirical science cannot tell anyone what he should do — but rather what he can do," wrote Weber (1949: 54).

A Weberian might argue, then, that Timem could have avoided the crisis of legitimation described here if it had been more sensitive to the conditions for practicing its ideals — if, say, it had adopted from the beginning a no-growth policy. In point of fact, the kibbutzim were always aware that size was a critical condition of a collective's practical success, and the kibbutz movement's members have long debated the question of optimal size.[2]

Doubtless, Weber's advice, that ideals can be empirically assessed for their relative consistency and practicality, is sage. Timem might well have managed the realization of its democratic ideal better, without serious incident, if it had rejected growth. It is difficult to contemplate a tight no-growth policy for the kibbutz, though. However important, the democratic ideal is not the community's sole ideal. And, if only because it seems to imply, not simply the modification of the nuclear family (in the interest of strong collectivism), but its virtual elimination, a tight no-growth policy would have been out of keeping with the kibbutz's Zionist ethos of the normalization of the Jew.

But the main point I wish to make in connection to Weber's characterization of the relation between empiricism and normativism is not the empirical matter of how well the kibbutz assessed the practicality of its own ends. Rather, it is the analytical observation that, given that practice can never be free of contingency, even the most empirically powerful ideal must fall short of the situation to which it aspires. In other words, even an ideal that is optimally consistent with empirical design cannot avoid, but only put off, failure.

In a sense, then, from the perspective of empiricism, all humans live in a fool's paradise. For reasons of its presupposition of absolute objectivity, empiricism spells the eventual failure of all ideals.

This unhappy picture holds, though, only so long as empiricism may be taken as an unexceptionable measure of an ideal's practicality. To be sure, Weber made plain that empirical knowledge must be "oriented" on the basis of values: "The choice of the object of investigation and the extent or depth to which this investigation attempts to penetrate into the infinite causal web, are determined by the evaluative ideas which dominate the investigator and his age" (1949: 84, 111). Nevertheless, he maintained that once an investigator is "dominated" by the value of empiricism, objectivity can prevail: "Scientific truth is precisely what is valid for all who *seek* the truth" (1949: 84). In this sense, for Weber, empiricism's capacity to serve as a measure of an ideal's practicality is unexceptionable, and social science should be value-free.

The Irresponsibility of Empiricism

Weber's idea of a value-free empirical science has long been discredited. In his classic critique, Leo Strauss demonstrated that in his capacity as a social scientist, Weber himself was unable to avoid, not only evaluative presuppositions that guided topical relevance, but also value judgments as such (Strauss 1953: 36ff.).

Strauss was concerned to argue, not that the objectivity of social science is suspect, but that, as against Weber's decidedly indeterminist picture of the selection of ideals, objectivity is as necessary to the realm of value as to that of knowledge. I wish to draw a converse lesson from Strauss's demonstration of Weber's failure to keep his social science free from values. It is that, if objectivity is construed in terms of wholly detached observation, then the empiricist's picture of facts is itself an unattainable ideal.

There simply is no human world that can be observed but not participated in. In light of this consideration, it is not normativism but empiricism that comes up short. Empiricism constitutionally occludes its own nature as worldly engagement. It presents itself as an enterprise of detachment, even as it engages the world in particular — hence, value-laden — ways. Particular ways of worldly engagement necessarily involve judgments of relative worth — value judgments.

Empiricism is, therefore, self-inconsistent. Furthermore, as the inconsistency bears definitively on undisclosed value judgments, it is normative as well as logical. In effect, one of the evaluative ways empiricism engages the world is that of irresponsibility. By pretending neutrality while fostering evaluative action, it relieves itself (and its adherents) of any responsibility for the values it comports. In this regard, curiously, it has much in common with certain religious and magical principles, which present themselves as permanent fixtures of the world. But whereas these principles, in their intrinsically normative posture, epitomize the idea of value, empiricism tends to deny it.

The judgment that empiricism is normatively irresponsible follows from taking normativism as the measure of empiricism rather than the other way around. This perversion of Weber's (and the conventional) way of doing things follows naturally once it is seen that empiricism is itself normatively charged. In effect, the empirical test for the consistency and practicality of empiricism entails referring empiricism to a norm. But, inasmuch as any norm supposes the idea of a standard of excellence, empiricism is measured against an ideal. And when it is, it does not measure up.

Empiricism and the "Values" of Efficiency and Instrumentalism

The consistency that counts first in relation to an ideal is not logical but deontological. Far from promoting evaluative bindingness, though, by holding out values that masquerade as wholly objective or value-free principles, empiricism makes nonsense of deontology. Obviously, such values as empiricism promotes serve to undermine the very idea of value. Thus, carried to its principled conclusion, empiricism implies the futility of all normative endeavors, and therefore, ironically, even of itself.

Specifically, empiricism comports the values of efficiency and instrumental rationality. These values recommend informed control over, and "rational" adaptation to, the conditions of a contingent environment. They presuppose the immaculate differentiation of an objective world and are therefore of a piece with the empiricist's dualistic notion of a fact.

Clearly, these values have strongly shaped the outlook of modernity and the practice of science. There can be no doubt that in important ways the kibbutz also entertains them. But these values betray the rule of technical efficiency and calculable quantities rather than value as such. By "value as such," I intend value as the assessment of a thing's principled worth over and above its utility. Value in this (patently ethical) sense pertains to what is good, not in the sense in which a piece of furniture might be said to be good, but (as Wittgenstein says somewhere) in the sense of what is intrinsically or really important in life. In this light, the values of instrumental rationality and efficiency are secondary or even *ersatz*. They are also inimical to the kibbutz's most fundamental vision of itself, namely, preeminently as a moral order.

Whereas efficiency and instrumentality bespeak rigorous technique, fixed method, and strategic manipulation, including the manipulation of the decisions of others, a moral universe is by definition keyed to principled persuasion and essential commonality rather than manipulation. It is also keyed to the *play* rather than the regulation of reason. It proceeds according to reason-as-wisdom or moral sanity rather than to rationality in the strict sense.

The subject–object dualism of empiricism ultimately promotes the treatment of one's other and even of oneself as an object. Such treatment is a far cry from the quintessential intersubjectivity implicit in the view of the world as a moral order. That view requires that one be open not only to the good reasons of others, but also to the reasons of what is right and good.[3]

The Incommensurability of the Long-Term and the Short-Term

Technical efficiency and instrumentality do not admit of this kind of openness, as is shown by the sense of time and choice attached to them. As they are predicated on a neutral approach to the world, an approach that pretends to hold value constant, technical efficiency and instrumentality describe the world in terms of short-term temporality. In the absence of value, the human world is timed solely in terms of instrumental tasks, tasks whose beginning and end can be delineated absolutely according to material accomplishment.

By definition, instrumental tasks presuppose a clean conceptual differentiation of means from ends. Under this differentiation, ends tend to be assimilated to means — they are valued as ends only inasmuch as they are means for something else. Insofar as ends appear as ends, however, they do so as potential outcomes (of means) rather than as practices. They thus comport a world of mutually exclusive occurrences, a world of "events."

When genuine values are acknowledged to enter into play, however, the world can no longer appear certain and precisely punctuated by events. Genuine values present ends in themselves. Such intrinsic ends are not defined by contrast to means; instead, they constitute their own practice. They deny an immaculate distinction between means and ends, in favor of a relative one. As a consequence, they presuppose the operation of a whole. Concomitantly, they admit of relative but not exclusive boundaries. They define, then, not events as such, but endeavors that cannot be cleanly separated from the uncertain and seamless endeavor of life itself. In other words, they define lived endeavors.

Inasmuch as it is its own means, an intrinsic value or end cannot be accomplished or attained, but only lived or practiced. In result, the time line of the world takes on a different aspect, namely, what I am calling the long term.

Despite appearances, the difference between the short term and the long term is really qualitative rather than quantitative. It is a representation, in terms of temporality, of the difference between logical closure and moral open-endedness, and between strategic design and authentic choice. By "authentic choice," I have in mind, by contrast to the idea of authenticity attached to the philosophy of consciousness, simply choice that in principle cannot be told in advance. The long term is not a longer short term — it is the clearing or space of uncertainty that admits of, indeed demands, authentic choosing. It is also the time of mythic accounting.

The Peculiar Validity of the Mythic Account

Two Kinds of Accounting

To some extent, Timem's members entertained "generational conflict" as an empirical account of their problem. Empirically speaking, the procession of the generations was, doubtless, a contributing factor to Timem's troubled state. But, as I have shown, it comes nowhere close to furnishing an empirically adequate explanation. Therefore, given Timem's own epistemological standards, the focus on "generational conflict" was in good part mistaken. Insofar as empiricism is a prominent feature of Timem's epistemological universe, the judgment that the members were in this sense wrong is unavoidable (see Wittgenstein 1979: 5e).

But "generational conflict" was maintained by the members also in a way that is irreducible to and deeper than empiricist accounting. That way is consistent with mythic accounting, and it presents a rationality in its own right.

The kibbutz is caught between the rationality of empiricism and the rationality of normativism, between rationality in the strict sense and the sort of rationality constitutive of mythic accounting. In fundamental respects the kibbutz is a very modern community; but it is also founded in a logic of myth in which moral choice is expressly featured. Because the kibbutz is squarely predicated on the goal of transcending the existential antinomies described by this myth, it is caught peculiarly and representatively between the two kinds of rationality.

To see that Timem is thus caught it is only necessary to point out that the contrast I have drawn between mythic and empiric rationality reiterates the debate that opened my study of Timem. The schism between the friends and the enemies of secret balloting was controverted according to the conceptual opposition between expediency and principle, which is to say, between technical and value rationality.

That Timem's members were caught hard and fast is also told by the fact that both the opponents and the proponents of secret balloting had right on their side. The latter were correct in thinking that the institution of secret balloting could address the problem of democratic participation. Neither, though, were their critics wrong — there is a plain sense in which a secret ballot, by entertaining the idea of the isolated, willful individual who needs to be protected from the constraints of a formal and institutionalized social world, compromises the kibbutz ideal of a moral universe.

Even more pertinent here, in a profound sense the critics of a secret ballot were not wrong in proposing that at bottom the problem of participation was a problem of conflict between the generations.

The Facts as Interpretive rather than Determinative

Unlike the facts of physical science, those of social science are, as Anthony Giddens has incisively caught in his concept of the "double hermeneutic," multiply interpreted: first, they are interpreted by the members of the society in which they are found; second, by the observer/student (Giddens 1976: 78f.). That is to say, the sociological or ethnographical facts are always and necessarily interpreted prior to the arrival on the scene of the social scientist. Indeed, the prior interpretation is an intrinsic component of the facts — it is part of what the observer/student needs to account for.

In the present case, the facts in question bear on the character of democratic participation and on social heterogenization. It is true that the debate in Timem centered on just how these facts ought to be interpreted — in the instrumental terms of voting procedures or as a normative question of generational conflict. Though its remedial aim evoked an idea of freedom and therefore of morality, the instrumentalist interpretation is primarily linked to the empiricist picture of the facts as functions of modernization and increasing social differentiation. On the other hand, the normativist interpretation construed the facts as a question essentially of moral accountability.

In point of fact, however, the determination of the facts presupposed an interpretation even prior to the interpretations that were controverted during the debate. Neither Timem's state of democratic participation nor Timem's state of social differentiation was intelligible outside of their unique historical context. That context, as I have argued, is most fundamentally described by a certain epochal logic of self-identifying: the logic of the biblical myth of generation. In other words, whatever the procedural conditions of Timem's political nonparticipation, and whatever the various causes of the increasing internal differentiation of the community, both of these states of affairs presuppose the community's understanding of itself as above all a moral order.

The point is that the very ideas of democratic participation and of social differentiation are basically meaningful here only in virtue of Timem's self-identification as a singularly moral order. By democratic participation, recall, the members had in mind the profoundly moral process wherein a general will is allowed to emerge. Moreover, the sort of social differentiation at issue was constituted, not simply by the proliferation of distinguishing social attributes, but by the separation of self from other — that is, by the elaboration of an autonomous or moral self. In effect, the processes of democratic participation and of social differentiation in Timem presuppose the primordial choice of generation.

The facts of the debate, then, were moral through and through. At bottom, they were indescribable apart from the idea of the moral person. Therefore, their causal relations notwithstanding, they necessarily convey a question of accountability.

Between Causation and Linguistic Indirection: Holistic Accounting

Obviously, the account of the facts in terms of generational tension may be regarded as sound as long as it is taken figuratively, as a metonym. But such a picture makes that account simply tropological, whereas I am claiming something more for it than the dubious (though currently much heralded) distinction of a certain figure of speech.

Metonymy is meaningful only in the framework of an ontology that draws an immaculate distinction between a thing and its attribute. In other words, it takes its received meaning — as a figure of speech — only from the metaphysics of dualism. It must follow that metonymy shares with the empiricist perspective the same epistemological universe. This consideration should give pause here, as it suggests that the characterization of the mythic account as a mere figure of speech depends on the very perspective that the mythic account calls into question.

By contrast with the argument to figurative speech, I maintain that the definition of the situation in terms of generational conflict is substantially correct, though in a heterodox sense. As that definition of the situation supposes the engaged rather than detached observer, a fundamentally participant observer, so it entails an essential connection rather than clean break between one thing and another. That is to say, inasmuch as the sort of engagement in question is founded in basic — though irremediably imperfect — "identity," it implies a holistic ontology. In such an ontology, a thing and its attribute can, and at some level must, enjoy the same name. For the relationship between them is fundamentally internal. In the case at hand, this would mean that the difference of the generations not only stands for (as a part stands for the whole), but also veritably *is* the process of social differentiation in Timem.

An analogy may help clarify this logically perturbing picture. According to Freudian psychoanalytic theory, all human behavior is underlain by sexuality. As an explanation of human behavior, this thesis leaves much to be desired. If all human behavior is sexual, then sexuality is not entirely distinguishable from human behavior in general. In which case, what sense can it make to regard such behavior as the product of sexuality? But, though explanation proper requires causal thought, enlightenment is not restricted to thought of this kind. Surely, whatever the declarations of Freud himself, the lasting discovery of psychoanalysis is not that biology, in the form of genital sexuality, produces psychology, but that what is typically thought of as a sheer "bodily" function — sexuality — is right from the beginning informed with a certain less than conscious intelligence (see Merleau-Ponty 1962: 158–59; cf. Ricoeur 1970).[4]

Similarly, to argue that conflict between the generations is related to the general process of differentiation in Timem in a way that goes beyond mere linguistic troping is not to propose that such conflict gives rise to or can "explain" that process. Rather, it is to point to and make perspicuous the cultural-historical *gestalt* without which Timem's process of social differentiation would be effectively unintelligible.

The argument from generational conflict stresses the generational substructure of the course of Timem's existence as well as the sense in which the idea of generation dilates to englobe the whole of that course. As a primordial choice, generation makes the difference that allows Timem's members to tell all difference in, and to make a difference to, their social world. It is the difference that furnishes their most basic self-identity — that of universal creature. This cultural identity entails a moral universe and moral consciousness. By reference to it and to the kibbutz's perfectibilist twist on it, Timem's members at once bind themselves to and differentiate themselves from their other, including their prior selves.

In an empiricist epistemology, one might be inclined to conclude that this picture of generation, as a key to telling all social difference, assigns "generation" to the order of metaphor. But there is no reason to regard it as any more or less metaphorical than a difference employed by empirical science to distinguish human beings from other animals — say, upright posture. Like the opposable thumb and bigger-brainedness, upright posture is not merely a biological condition of the emergence of moral order. *It is already an embodiment of such order.* By featuring a relationship of opposition between a creature and its ground — a relationship in which nature, in a palpable sense, negates itself — upright posture at once manages to transcend its own biological nature. In so doing, upright posture makes room for the conduct of choice, veritably constructing "uprightness" as a moral posture. Similarly, by featuring a relationship of opposition between founder and son, generation presents and represents a universe in which self-generation is peculiarly featured, a singularly moral universe.

To argue, in causal terms, that Timem's *tz'irim* (youth or second generation) produced the problem of democratic participation is at best only partially right. But the understanding that the thematically moral *gestalt* instantiated in generational conflict stands at the very bottom of that problem cannot be faulted. As I have demonstrated, whether Timem's members failed to participate in meetings of the General Assembly for reasons of self-protection, indifference, protest, or something else, all of these reasons presuppose in Timem an utterly implicit commitment to generation as a unique form of life. Likewise, whether the members were differentiated from their fellows by virtue of country of origin, time of taking membership, educational background, or the like, these differentiae presuppose in this community the same commitment. The various modes of social differentiation in Timem are not identifiable as such outside of the assumption of generation and the norms and values it comports. For it is this presumption, and these norms and values, that make the very idea of differentiation an implicitly intelligible phenomenon in the cultural context of Timem. And since those norms and values are thematically moral, accountability in terms of moral agency must always be at least implicit in Timem's social problems.

By embracing generational conflict as a definition of their situation, then, Timem's members were not wrong. Rather, they were reiterating — choosing again, for the first time — the primordial choice on the basis of which they were enabled to locate themselves at all in the world. That choice defines them as uniquely moral creatures whose moral capacity, the capacity to fashion themselves, could not be told outside of the biblical idea of generation and the filial conflict it entails.

It is only if the generational account is viewed from the atomistic perspective of empiricism, rather than from its own holistic perspective of categorical intersubjectivity and ontological mutuality, that it looks irrational.

The Ethical Primacy of Mythic Rationality

The End of Having Ends

I have argued that, when viewed from its own perspective, the generational account of Timem's situation comes to more than a figure of speech: it is, though not rational in the strict sense of the term, intelligible and hermeneutically penetrating, and therefore arguably rational in some further-to-be-determined sense of the term.

Is this, then, simply an arbitrary redefining or loosening of the concept of rationality? I think not. For the two senses of rationality, though irreconcilably opposed on one level of "thought," are not wholly incommensurable on another. Furthermore, the intelligibility of the holistic sense irrefutably enjoys a certain primacy in this contest.

As stated earlier, the sense of rationality linked to empiricism is instrumentalist. It extols consistent and efficient means to ends. By contrast, the holistic sense of rationality cannot be grasped in such formal terms. By definition, its holism cannot admit of a separation, between means and ends, definitive enough to make formal consistency a transparent parameter. Therefore, the holistic sense of rationality naturally raises a question that necessarily goes begging in the empiricist picture: What is the rationality of the ends to be achieved? Obviously, formal consistency can guide us on how best to achieve our ends, but it has virtually nothing to say on what ends are best. Just as obviously, in a conception of rationality where ends and means are only imperfectly distinguishable, the question of choice of ends is brought into relief. Intuitively, there is something profoundly unsatisfying, if not downright "irrational," about a notion of rationality that has nothing at all to say about choice of ends.[5] Indeed, the need for the present discussion makes absolutely clear the failure of such a notion of rationality. To ask after the rationality of Timem's inclination to define its situation in terms of a normativism that was not altogether compatible with the empiricist picture is to ask about the rationality of these two pictures as ends in themselves. It is to appeal, not to a standard of formal consistency — which, of course, would be to prejudge the issue in favor of instrumental rationality — but to a metarational standard.

If the choice between these two kinds of rationality is not to be perfectly arbitrary, it must involve some sort of self-legitimating end. Of course, the idea of such an end evokes, to use Leszek Kolakowski's name for it, metaphysical horror, the intellectual bogey driving today's most celebrated philosophies (Kolakowski 1988). But neither critical theory nor postmodernism has managed to avoid the presumption of at least one such end.

Following Hans Jonas (1984), that end can only be the preservation of the possibility of having ends or purpose. Whereas no merely particular end can ever justify itself, every particular end presupposes the end of having ends. In this connection, strange as it may seem, critical theory and poststructuralism converge (I owe this insight to Steven Klein; see also Bernstein 1992: chap. 7).

Whether we attend to Habermas's "communicative rationality," or Foucault's "genealogy," or Derrida's *differance,* each is descriptively and normatively keyed to the end of having ends. Communicative rationality denotes an intersubjective process of making choices; genealogy seeks to unmask putative essences and subvert normality in order to create a new discourse centered on openness or, if you like, in my terms, authentic choice; and, finally, to define meaning in terms of *differance,* that is, as differential and deferred, is to feature the play of meaning or, again, of choice.

Even the ideal of purposelessness, as Jonas points out with regard to Buddhism, is after all an end. The example of Buddhism makes a telling paradox, as it implicates the inherent but logically absurd possibility of choice in the teleological system of human being (Jonas 1984: 80). The absurdity is expressed in the grand irony of a system that virtually condemns its participants to choice (or, as Merleau-Ponty put it, to meaning [1962: xix]). In effect, all particular systems of human ends are seen to presuppose an encompassing order of being that is itself defined in terms of the end of having ends.

Since this order is uniquely distinguished by its definition of participants as at least implicitly moral agents, the preservation of the possibility of ends becomes an end that is *both* necessary *and* facultative. It is necessary because no matter what one does, one cannot help but pursue an end. Even death as an option provides no escape, as Adam's lethal choice makes hyperbolically clear — it only drives home the experience of choice. It is facultative because what one is condemned to is a life of choice or meaning. Such a life makes it possible — though profoundly paradoxical — to choose one's ends, including the end of having no ends at all.

This situation makes of the end of having ends a kind of natural good, the "good" of which, however, is no less factitious than natural. Put another way, the end of having ends presents the root primordial choice. In contrast to other primordial choices, the appearance of the root choice as both natural and necessary is conduced more by the movement of a nature in which culture inheres largely implicitly than by the cunning of a culture in which nature has given way (but hardly given up) to second-nature. Though it obtains between natural and moral selection, its plain and preeminent natural character features the immanence of morality in nature rather than, as in the founding primordial choices of particular cultures, the manipulation and exploitation of nature by morality. Nevertheless, this master choice is far from a determination in the strict sense, since it is no less an opening than a constraint. In this opening — this, to use the cant terminology, aporia or *differance* — particular primordial choices are taken.

The Superiority of Mythic Rationality

In view of this argument, given two kinds of rationality, the kind that best preserves the possibility of having ends is intuitively the more rational choice. Of the two rationalities in question, it is the value variety that best conforms to this ideal. Whereas this variety is geared precisely to the possibility of having ends, that is, to the preservation of moral capacity, instrumental rationality is constitutionally opposed to ends in themselves. As we have seen, although instrumental rationality always presupposes the presence of ends, by focusing exclusively on efficiency and consistency, rationality of this kind tends to contort all ends into means: their worth as ends gets measured in terms of what they are good for. The immaculate differentiation of means from ends disposes toward the dissolution of the idea of ends in their own right.

As Habermas and others have argued, rationalization ultimately promotes the subjugation of the world of values or ends to that of technique (Habermas 1984, 1987). Of course, technique is also an end; but it is an end that puts an end to moral choice, or at least radically constrains it by foreclosing on the possibility of ends proper. For it is an end that defines all ends in terms of means. Ultimately it opens one's other and one's self to definition as instrumental object — as that which by definition can have no real ends or moral faculty.

The same argument may be made in terms of the polarity, introduced above, between the long term and the short term. By focusing on the short term, instrumental rationality turns a blind eye to the long term. The short term is defined in terms of calculable quantities and certitude, whereas the long term is critically open-ended. In effect, then, by ignoring the essential uncertainty in being, instrumental rationality puts the long term at risk. (Modern technology provides all too many examples of the point.) In other words, it jeopardizes the possibility of having ends. By this I do not mean that it necessarily eliminates that possibility (though nuclear technology — a limiting case — makes such elimination conceivable).[6] Rather, I mean that by confining the play of reason in the straitjacket of expediency as opposed to value, instrumental rationality profoundly curtails the range of possible ends.

The Structural and Phenomenological Primacy of Mythic Rationality

Differential Generative Capacities

The primacy of the mythic rationality rests, then, in its greater attunement to the possibility of having ends. As I have described it so far, this primacy is essentially ethical. It is important to the force of my argument to see, though, that the primacy is also structural and phenomenological.

It may seem that all I have done here is, ignoring my own caution about prejudging the issue, decided between the two rationalities by assuming, albeit for ethical reasons, the holistic rather than the atomistic perspective. It is certainly the case that the argument to having ends as a natural good predicates a certain holism; it omits to draw an *immaculate* distinction between means and ends. But such relative holism enjoys, in addition to the ethical one, a necessary primacy in relation to atomism.

The holistic perspective definitively encompasses its counterpart. Instrumentalism, however, by virtue of its partitive principle, inevitably excludes its opposite number. Belief in instrumental rationality can neither ground itself nor admit the possibility of the relative whole. As soon as it tries to locate its own ground, it transcends one of the principles that gives to it its great force — instrumentality. A genuine ground would make such rationality self-sufficient rather than utilitarian. Thus, in spite of itself, instrumental rationality points to a world beyond the empirical one, a mythic or normative world (Kolakowski 1989).

Should instrumental rationality attempt to account for this mythic world of relative holism, it would deny a principle of received rationalism even more comprehensive than that of use-value — namely, dualism. Instrumentalism is predicated on the idea of immaculate — which is to say, dualist — separation of means from ends. In the absence of this idea, though instrumental rationality would remain situationally or heuristically useful, it could no longer entertain utility as a final arbiter of truth and worth. In other words, instrumental rationality cannot do without dualism and at the same time retain its fundamentalistic scientific force. However, by definition the principle of dualism makes nonsense of instrumental rationality's presupposition of the relative whole.

On the other hand, precisely because of its relative holism, mythic rationality cannot but admit of its own counterpart — instrumental rationality. To its logical discredit but ontological advantage, genuine holism always contains, at least implicitly, the opposing principle of partitivism. It can therefore account for the sort of rationality partitivism supports, the instrumental sort. In effect, mythic rationality can generate its own opposite.

In this sense, instrumental engagement of the human world is definitively secondary; it always presupposes normative or ethical engagement. The argument to the ethical primacy of mythic rationality, therefore, does not reduce to an arbitrary command that there ought to be some oughts, but enjoys a certain apodicity. We are condemned to ethics in such a way that all of our instrumental activity presupposes an ethical starting point. As Levinas, in whose philosophy alterity is the name of what I call here relative holism (by contrast to "totalism"), proposes, ethics and human social life are equiprimordial (Levinas 1991; R. Cohen 1986).

What makes the choice between the two perspectives nonarbitrary is precisely that the mythic perspective naturally (nondualistically) includes the other. The perspectives are unequal in their capacities to generate each other. Because instrumental rationality cannot be shown to generate itself, it always presupposes its counterpart. In effect, the two perspectives present a nondualistic, hierarchical order, in which instrumentalism is dependent for its very appearance on the perspective it disallows.

Of course, the hierarchy can be compromised. Modernization, with its capital emphases on utilitarianism, individualism, and absolute freedom, thematically presents just such compromise. Kibbutz Timem's brief history exhibits a course of compromise of this kind under conditions of modernity.

Nevertheless, though compromise of the hierarchy can be substantial (a difference that makes a difference to human social life), it cannot be complete — it must ever have something illusory about it. For, because instrumental rationality cannot create itself, it can abolish the hierarchy only by destroying itself. Put differently, the diagnostic goal of modernity and the Enlightenment, the goal of absolute rational autonomy, is, as Hegel well determined, essentially self-defeating (Taylor 1979: 100ff., 153ff.).

The Commensurability of the Hierarchical Perspectives

Competing Perspectives

While I have presented the two sorts of rationality as basically incommensurable, indeed as corresponding to the incommensurable temporalities of the short and the long term, my analysis has proceeded as if they are also, no less basically, commensurable the one

Two Kinds of Rationality 211

with the other. The hierarchical nature of the relationship between them speaks to the question of their commensurability.

Notwithstanding the prevailing acceptance of "boundary" simply in terms of a limit, all boundaries both separate and connect. The boundary between the ranked orders of the hierarchy of rationalities is exemplary in this respect. It is better imaged as, instead of a pure divide, an encompassing fold, whereof parts, and even an inside and an outside, are distinguished, but as continuous with each other by virtue of their envelopment and development in the fold (see Deleuze 1993; Bohm 1981). Because the boundary in question here, between the two rationalities, also marks a relationship between generator and generated, founder and son, it features continuity no less thematically than it does discontinuity.

From the standpoint of its capacity to divide, the standpoint assumed by Western dualism, a boundary cannot be seen both to separate and connect. In turn, as there is no acknowledged common ground, the perspectives defined by the boundary can appear solely as incommensurable — they cannot appear as both commensurable and incommensurable. They are represented as if they occupy separate and mutually uninvolved spaces. Therefore, if one succeeds in hierarchizing them, one can only have done so arbitrarily. Under these conditions, the normative order, like the instrumental one, appears as an exclusive system. So regarded, as cleanly divided from what it is not, a normative order, however it labors to manage the impression it makes by appeal to some natural or heavenly foundation, at bottom (as postmodernist thought has discerned) cannot but present itself as an arbitrary code of the right and the wrong. Put another way, the normative order is effectively reduced to its instrumentalist counterpart, having *ultimately* to justify itself by reference to power rather than reason and principle.

By contrast, where it is seen in terms of its connecting force, a boundary mitigates the difference it defines. As the boundary still constitutes a limit, the perspectives it delineates remain distinct. But as the difference between them is diluted, they do not simply exclude each other. Obviously, under these conditions, the distinction between commensurability and incommensurability is profoundly relativized.[7]

By virtue of the continuity provided by the boundary between them, the two rationalities, though fundamentally different, also constitute a common ground. Therefore, they must be commensurable. Indeed, as it includes the difference between them, as a fundamental asymmetry, the common ground itself orders the two rationalities hierarchically. Put another way, the hierarchy is the common ground. For whichever of the two rationalities best maps — *and so constructs* — the common ground, that rationality must enjoy the hierarchical primacy of encompassment and generation. Since it is most essentially identifiable with the basic ambiguity presented by the boundary, the superordinate rationality can only be the value one.

The ambiguity of the boundary amounts to uncertainty, a principle that runs directly contrary to instrumental rationality in its ideal form. The latter is predicated on objectivism, and hence takes for granted that, even if the universe is deceptive, it is knowable in certain terms (ultimately, the Cartesian terms of mathematics). On the other hand, all normative systems, whatever they are in letter, are keyed to ontological uncertainty in spirit. What is normative is defined most meaningfully in terms of, not the normal, but *the creative establishment* of the norm or the measure. That is to say, it is a question of "strong evaluation" — of evaluation that determines, by contrast to what is in fact desired, what is worth desiring (Taylor 1985a: chap. 1; Ginsberg 1965: 45ff.). Evaluations of this kind are matters of ethical choice, choice that invokes the good, above and beyond the useful or even the right. They therefore reveal the openness inherent in basic ambiguity — the openness of "possibility," whereby the determination of ends remains fundamentally (though not absolutely) open.[8]

Thus, the common ground, the hierarchy, turns out to be a dynamic rather than a structure, a temporality rather than a spatiality — in a word, a becoming. Insofar as becoming always transcends and subsumes being, it enjoys a certain ontological primacy and so constitutes a hierarchical order.

In effect, though the one rationality is disposed to construe all ends as means really, while the other projects ends as ends proper, the terms of both naturally refer to a common realm of the hierarchy — the realm of ends, in the sense of possibility.

The attribution of blame to Timem's younger generation certainly projected the problem of democratic participation as a question of ends or commitment rather than of procedure. But, in point of fact, although it rendered a contrary picture, one focused by instrumentalism, the proposal of a secret ballot also and necessarily defined the sons (and hence the fathers) as moral creatures. For it defined them as choosers in their own right. Ironically, then, the instrumentalist proposal reinforced the community's self-definition in terms of moral perfectibilism or possibility. In so doing, this proposal presented a case for itself by appeal to the very realm it tends naturally to deny, the realm of ends.

This paradoxical circumstance presents an instance of what, at least in part, it means to say that the two perspectives of the hierarchy share a common ground. The continuity marked by the boundary between the two rationalities, the continuity between the generations, ensured that even the instrumentalism of the sons was morally charged. As a result of this circumstance, the rationalities associated with these perspectives were forced to compete with each other, and were subjected to assessment as against each other. But precisely because of their hierarchical ordering, the assessment could not be made beforehand. For, in the end, the hierarchical superiority of value rationality entails, not determinism, but open-endedness.

Ethical Determination and Situated Freedom

It is inviting to think that a competition of this kind could be decided by reference to situational context. That is to say, when the situation calls especially for productive efficiency and objectification, instrumental rationality looms large; but when it is selection and preservation of ends in themselves that a situation wants most, naturally, a value rationality takes precedence. However, such a procedural solution to the problem can work only if a criterion is erected beforehand by which to distinguish contextual character. In the final analysis, such a criterion can be set only arbitrarily, in the interest of efficiency and instrumental rationality, that is, in the interest of closure.

Dumont's controversial analysis of the Indian caste system is instructive here. In treating the issue of the relation between power and status in the caste system, he argues that "hierarchy is *bidimensional, it bears not only on the entities considered but also on the corresponding situations*" (1986: 253; see also 1971: 66ff.). Under this structural condition, a reversal of the hierarchical order can occur, but only as a secondary arrangement. If status is superior to power, then, given a situation corresponding to the descending level of the hierarchy, power can prevail over status, but only *in that situation*. Here, then, the definition of the situation seems predetermined, by the hierarchy itself: "It is not enough here to speak of different 'contexts' as distinguished by us, for they are foreseen, inscribed or implied in the ideology itself. We must speak of different 'levels' hierarchized together with the corresponding entities" (1986: 253).

I am concerned to emphasize here, though, that "situatedness" entails an essential open-endedness as to the definition of the situation, so that, *precisely because of* hierarchical encompassment, the situation always eludes final circumscription.[9] The open-endedness is what authenticates the value attached to hierarchy. This consideration may lend a certain credibility to those of Dumont's detractors who picture caste as primarily about power. Inasmuch as the hierarchical structure called caste *predetermines* the definition of the situation, the hierarchy might well betray a certain instrumentalistic preeminence. Such a condition, whereby the hierarchical relation can be regarded as based on something more than the anarchical entreaty that issues primordially from the other's otherness (the indebtedness that one simply experiences along with the sense of otherness), suggests that hierarchy has been appropriated for power rather than authority. But, though the open-endedness of hierarchy leaves room thus for the illicit exercise of power, hierarchy is still not consistent with a primarily politico-economic interpretation of caste, as Dumont insists. Rather, the open-endedness means, above all, that the hierarchical dynamic is ethical before it is either political or, for that matter, structural.

In this sense, hierarchical order can no more finally predetermine a situation's specific teleological context than it can decide once and for all the practical question of rationality. Among other things, what continuity between orders of the hierarchy signifies is just the open-endedness of teleological context; it implies the need to take an authentic decision — a decision that cannot be explained beforehand — according to the merits of the particular situation. One must constructively determine, not discover, the nature and orientation of the situational context. Being situated means being *both* caught in a predicament, that is, practically engaged in it, *and* called upon by it to effect a creative response. Put another way, because the nature of the situation is always open to question, there is no purely cognitive answer to a basically practical question.

This idea of situated freedom is implicit in the consideration of continuity between the orders of the hierarchy. In the present case, the encompassing order of the hierarchy is value rationality, by contrast to the instrumental kind. The hierarchical superiority of this rationality has a remarkable twofold consequence. First, choice is always preserved: as the encompassing hierarchical order, value rationality is in a position to prescribe behavior, but, paradoxically, what it prescribes is choice. Second, every choice must be a choice for the encompassing rationality. It remains open, of course, to choose instrumental as against value rationality. But such a choice, even if it intends with a violent absolutist resolve to eradicate rather than put off the normative perspective, must also be a choice for the latter. This is true for the following reason.

However much it resists self-transformation into a value orientation, and however seriously it may curtail choice for certain peoples and purposes, in the end instrumental rationality can only reaffirm its mythic or value counterpart. Sheer instrumentalism is self-defeating. Since it works by design to deny the essential uncertainty conveyed in spirit by any value perspective, it gives neither room nor reason to assume or refuse a situational orientation. It therefore serves to impede the possibility of acting as an agent. That is to say, impugning the normative nature of all ends by regarding them as means, such an absolutist regime presents an ethical vacuum. Because it provides no ethically positive direction, this vacuum constrains people to destroy all positive ends. If one's prime directive is utility, then by definition one has been duly instructed to abolish ends as such. For the same reason, instrumentalism must lead to its own destruction. For, despite its delusions of pure technique, it is itself an end, albeit the end of utility.

The self-defeat of instrumentalism must reaffirm the hierarchical primacy of the normative perspective, and therefore the inevitability of situated freedom. When instrumentalism fails, uncertainty and heteronomy prevail. The defeat issues from failure to acknowledge in practice human dependence on the (apparently indifferent or passive) other or the relative whole. Since it is the primacy of the whole that mythic rationality most critically communicates, with the undercutting of humankind's instrumentalist conceit, the mythic perspective is brought into relief.

Correctness in Wisdom

Preservation of Ends

It seems to me that for reasons of its attention to the long term and its concern to maintain the possibility of having ends, Timem's selection of a normative rather than technical definition of the situation displayed an eminent rationality. The rationality I have in mind is keyed, not to efficiency (though it admits of this aim), but to ethically responsible practice — practice focused on the selecting of ends in themselves, an interrogative practice of resistance to ethical closure.

It is important to be clear on just what I am claiming for this rationality. I am not claiming that the normative definition of Timem's situation is simply right and the empirical one wrong. Rather, I am claiming that the generational account of the situation is indeed correct, though not in the way of a sheerly empirical account, but in the way of a valid interpretation. It grasps the situation, not in terms of brute facts, but holistically, in terms of an intersubjective self-definition that informs the meaningful world of Timem comprehensively. The self-definition is comprehensive because it pertains to the most fundamental of Timem's members' identities, that self-identity to which all that they say and do as human beings gets meaningfully referred.

Nor am I claiming that the normative definition of the situation could resolve the immediate problem expediently, or even at all. Rather, inasmuch as this definition as a self-explanation is equally a self-construction, an explicitly value-constrained understanding, its superiority rests with its uncompromising capacity to preserve the rule and play of genuine ends. It served to remind the members that their communal endeavor was rooted in principle before expediency; it served to alert them to their responsibility for themselves as members of a community; and it served to mark the consideration that rationalization, for reasons of the spiritual alienation and dehumanizing objectification entailed by it, can foster the subversion of that responsibility.

Such a reminder cannot obviate instrumental concerns; but it can help ensure their considered containment in ethical practice. If wisdom connotes soundness of judgment as regards choice, then the rational superiority of the valuational over the instrumental perspective might be said to rest with the former's fundamental concern to make wise choices. The principal choice I have in mind is not simply of means and ends. More importantly, it is the choice to choose between them — between construing them as cleanly separated and construing them as relatively undifferentiated. Rather than taking instrumental choice for granted, the normative perspective naturally stands alert to the choice between instrumental and valuational choice. Whereas instrumental choice takes means and ends as mutually exclusive, thus disposing toward the virtual elimination of one in favor of the other, valuational choice holds means responsible to the end of having ends, thus endorsing possibility. By bearing in mind this choice between two kinds of choosing, value rationality takes into account the indifference of the long term, an indifference that allows us to participate in the creation of our own ends.

Intersubjective Intentionality

It might be objected here that those of Timem's members who offered generational conflict as the definition of their situation were not really concerned to preserve open-endedness; rather, they were keen on apportioning blame to the younger members. It was indeed an act of power rather than principle.

Underlying the motive of power, however, was a deeper intentionality, an intentionality that transcended Timem's members as individuals and in which they all shared by virtue of their primordially chosen identity. This intentionality was expressed in the perplexed willingness of all the members, including the accused, to acquiesce in the definition of moral accountability. By virtue of its synonymy with the self-identity of generational or moral creature, this intentionality was embedded in and constitutive of the modes of social relation and practice that go by the name of Timem.

The intentionality is, therefore, essentially intersubjective before it is subjective. That is to say, though hardly objective in the usual sense of the term, this intentionality is not exactly subjective either. Instead, it proceeds at an originary and creative level of being, on which the subjective and the individual have not yet been sharply differentiated from the objective and the social. On this encompassing, hierarchical level, human beings express themselves in spite of themselves (see Durkheim 1953: esp. chap. 1; also Taylor 1985b: chap. 1). In the case of Timem, what they expressed is the primacy of a rationality other than that of empiricism and instrumentalism.

Conclusion

Beginning with a discussion of mind–body dualism in social anthropology, and predicating an ontology other than the one received in Western thought, an ontology of basic ambiguity instead of things in themselves, I have set out to forge a nondualist anthropology. As the vehicle of my project I have employed the ethnographic situation of an Israeli kibbutz, a collectivist order whose goal of social transcendence serves to dramatize and highlight the ontological question as a social problem.

The analysis of the kibbutz targeted two principal empirical problems: (1) the "fallen state" of Kibbutz Timem; and (2) the inclination of Timem's members to account for this state in terms of conflict between the generations. The members were caught in a crisis of legitimacy, brought on by the notable degree to which the collective had become internally heterogeneous. The amount of heterogeneity occasioned social conditions, as studied here especially through the apparent failure of democratic participation, that the members could scarcely avoid construing as ideologically contrary. For the ideology has as its major premise the resolution of the contradiction between the individual and society, and this resolution is predicated on, in key part, plenary democracy.

But the problem confronting the members was not simply how to restore democratic participation; the problem was how to do so without undermining the principled definition of the kibbutz as a moral rather than simply instrumental order, an order that turns on other-regard, not self-interest. As documented by the case study of the formal debate, the proposed solution of secret balloting (as opposed to the customary rule of open-hand voting) promised relief alright, but only by opening the community to an antinomian condition — institutional "individualism." As is inscribed in its dual admonishment of both voluntarism and collectivism, kibbutz ideology is critically predicated on collective hegemony as well as individual autonomy. Secret balloting addressed the demand for voluntarism, but as against the call of collectivism.

In effect, heterogenization had brought to a head a double bind in which the community was caught perplexedly and fast: in order to maintain the principle of the ideology, the kibbutz was finding it increasingly necessary to betray that very principle. The two kinds of freedom on which the kibbutz was founded, individual and collective, had come apart, irrefragably, in the social and political life of the community.

The solution of secret balloting sprung from an understanding of the problem as most essentially a matter of increased social differentiation. Given developed pluralism in an institutional setting of intense and far-reaching interdependence, voting secrecy forcibly recommends itself as a precondition of the "free" expression of political will. The trouble was that the account in terms of social differentiation, the account to which the solution of secret balloting was tied, failed to attend to the thematically moral definition of the kibbutz. Since social differentiation was ideologically predefined as inimical to the synthesis of the individual and society, the resulting practical problems could not be resolved simply as a matter of such differentiation, at least not without neglecting the essential design of the kibbutz. In its precept of synthesis between the individual and society, the kibbutz embraced individual autonomy, but not social heterogeneity. Put another way, the moral order of the kibbutz was defined not merely in terms of radical democracy, but in the perfectibilist terms of a Rousseauian "general will." For this reason (what I deemed "the flaw in the kibbutz design"), the development of pluralism in the community was construed as antinomian, and associated with the rise of *liberalizatsia* and instrumental reason.

The definition of the situation by reference to social differentiation could not address the moral questions confronting the members, save by way of instrumentalism. By contrast, the definition by reference to generational conflict served to highlight the moral nature of the dilemma. The charge that the ideological commitment and resolve of the successor generations were wanting emerged in formal debate and prevailed by default, simultaneously taking the wind from the political sails of the advocates of secret balloting. But, whereas the account in terms of social differentiation provided a sound description of the brute facts, the account in terms of generational conflict was in fact empirically misleading. Materially speaking, it simply was not the case that the dispute over secret balloting reduced neatly to a battle of the generations. Why, then, did the members allow the latter account to prevail as a definition of the situation?

With this question, the community's attraction to generational conflict as an account of things posed in turn the capital anthropological question of rationality. In response, I examined the idea of generation for how it might relate to Timem's dilemmatic situation, in ways other than strictly empirical correspondence. I found that the age breakdown of Timem's members lent itself to the impression of a cutting division between the old and the young, and that the familistic, moralistic, and revolutionary ethos of the kibbutz virtually included a phenomenology of generational conflict. More particularly, the ethos was keyed to the root idea of the founder-son relationship, a profoundly paradoxical relationship, in which, for reasons intrinsic to moral choice, the father's bidding to the son of responsible behavior can be fulfilled only by an act of disobedience. From this I concluded that in the kibbutz, conflict between the generations is a deeply normative, though inexplicit, expectation. I also found that the paradoxical logic of the generational relationship could assimilate, both semantically and semiotically, on an exacting point-by-point basis, the dilemma or double bind characterizing Timem's social situation.

Given these findings, the inclination of Timem's members to interpret their predicament in terms of generational conflict may seem analytically transparent. As the notion of conflict between the generations may have served metaphorically to represent the troubles the members were experiencing, so the appeal to it in explanation of those troubles may have functioned to conceal the fundamental way in which the social order of the kibbutz is based on conflicting principles.

However compelling this analytical turn toward functionalism, or structuralism, or hermeneutics — the genial theories of yesterday and today — may seem, though, one is left with nagging questions. Since, logically speaking, generational conflict is not the only account that can function to distract the members from the principled inconsistency of their social enterprise, how was it selected "in the first place"? How does the social order of Timem get the members to deceive themselves about the true nature of that order? What is the force of analogical or metaphorical representation, that it can appropriate in general the kick of reality? If such representation is grasped as such, why do the members behave as if it were something other than a trope, as if it were reality? If it is not grasped as such, how does metaphorical representation get the members to mistake it for reality? Questions along these lines are familiar to social anthropology. But the important thing to observe here is that, as is self-evident for all but the first, these questions testify to the fact that at bottom, each of the theoretical frameworks under consideration — functionalism, structuralism, and hermeneutics — continues to explain or interpret the activity of human beings by referring it to a force separate and distinct from the beings themselves.

I therefore moved to probe more deeply still, by waxing ontological and presuming a reality in which "agent" and "agency" were not regarded as essentially separate and distinct, but rather as both different from and identical to each other. In other words, the reality I posited could be factored into neither *one* nor *two*, but had to be construed as basically ambiguous. In that event, I found that the members' conduct could be better conceived of in terms of self-identifying, a paralogical practice of giving rise to or choosing oneself under conditions of essential uncertainty or abiding heteronomy. Hence, the resulting identity is never less self-fashioned than thrown by circumstance. This notion of self-identifying projects a picture of a creature whose given identity is ambiguous in so preponderant and consequential a way that the identity amounts really to a capacity to construct itself — a practical, moral capacity. As such, the identity is always different from itself, always under way: in a word, it is identity as nonidentity.

This condition of being *condemned* to make one's own identity, of having as one's identity no identity save that which one finds oneself having always to construct as circumstances allow and demand, is what I mean by "situatedness." Being situated entails being forced to respond to circumstances, not in a wholly specific way, as when a hungry animal eats when food is set before it, but in a profoundly facultative way, as when a person fasts despite his or her hunger. In the first case, circumstances may change, but there is not much in the way of a "situation," just a preeminently natural world; in the second, the person's capacity to do otherwise makes of the different circumstances a situation proper, an occasion of self-construction, and of the world a strangely second (artificial) nature.

I found a penetrating paradigm of this conception of identity in Genesis, the very (cosmo)anthropology from which springs the kibbutz's self-definition in terms of the generations. Citing Rousseau, whose social theory informs the kibbutz no less plainly than that theory itself is informed by the biblical tale of a creation of and fall from an Edenic state of being, I was able to show that the generational self-interpretations of Timem's members are linked concretely to the second and third chapters of Genesis.

In its chiastic image of a creature/son fashioned after its creator/founder, the biblical idea of generation defines a paradoxical self whose autonomy and creativity are conditioned fundamentally by dependence and creatureliness. It thus describes a moral world, whose creatures are bound to choose, on behalf of otherness, for the sake of selfhood. So dilemmatic a world can obtain only by deferral, a putting off of the collapse of self and other into each other. The inhabitants of this world must conduct themselves between, but in no finally fixed and predetermined way, two vital ends — now toward the self, now toward the other. The result is time, and different temporalities. Where the other is given priority, time is for the most part experienced as closed and round, as in an enchanted garden; where it is the self that is privileged, time appears preeminently as open and linear, as in an infinite universe. But even where self-interest and instrumentalism are adopted as the overriding ends, the world remains a matter of moral order, of choice in the face of uncertainty. For notwithstanding the substantial difference pronounced selfhood makes, the world never does cease to issue from otherness. Barring immortality, it could not.

In this picture of the human being as a singularly moral creature, both Timem and I found a powerful inspiration for our respective projects. For Timem, by defining their situation in terms of conflict between the generations, the members were enabled to reaffirm the thematically moral nature of their self-identity, in the face of heterogenization and the risk of utilitarian reductionism. As a result, at a stroke, they both liberated themselves as *selves* and acknowledged the inevitable contingency — the inexorable otherness — of the march of events. Rather than collapsing self and other into each other in a triumph of the general will, the liberation worked by respecting the difference — the heterogeneity — between self and other. That is to say, by embracing "generation" as a definition of the situation, the members replaced, at least in practice, their ideological commitment to surmount existential ambiguity with the goal of living the ambiguity on an ethical basis.

The direct answer, then, to the question of the rationality of Kibbutz Timem's penchant to select, over the empiricist account, the understanding of "conflict between the generations" is this: while the empiricist account was more accurate in its correspondence to the facts of the matter, the account according to the idea of generation was truer in its measure of the thematically moral character of the situation. The members' definition of the situation was profoundly correct. For it both captured and reproduced the world according to which the kibbutz has chosen to identify itself. In doing so, it acknowledged the inherent superiority of value rationality.

Which of course does not mean that the empiricist account might not have been acted on and secret balloting instituted to productive effect, or that the normative account, having won the day, might not have made the community less efficient in its everyday, instrumental operations. It means only that there was a very imposing rationality to the members' mythic definition of themselves. The kibbutz's response was more factitious than empiric, but it was not on that account without a kind of reason: it invoked the uncertain but nonarbitrary reason of having ends and making choices, a superior reason by virtue of its encompassing capacity to indulge its "opposite" kind (instrumental rationality) and to define uniquely a humanity.

As to Timem's social anthropologist, mindful of the example of Genesis, I spoke of the community's mythic selection here in terms of a "primordial choice," which is my theoretical name for the sort of selection that issues from self-identifying considered as a nondualist process. A primordial choice is not exactly witting, individual, and free; but it is nonetheless profoundly creative, such that it tends to fix a social and cultural world. In effect, it negates its ground as it issues from its ground — insofar as it is autonomous, it stands against its ground, but only because its "feet" never really leave the ground. As I sought to show in respect of revisionary turns in both Timem's governmental and domestic realms, the members' choice of "generation" presents itself as primordial in the relevant sense: it emerged implicitly and intersubjectively to re-create the community as a moral phenomenon and establish the autonomy of the members' selves by at once negating and reconfirming their filial and familial world.

Given the by now self-evident impasse of Western dualism, the notion of primordial choice is, I think, intelligible as a conceptual ambition of nondualism. But its intelligence here is made that much more perspicuous in view of my engagement of the axial anthropological problems of rationality and human agency.

Having been stimulated by the finding of the crucial role of myth in the social and cultural life of an Israeli kibbutz, my argument has been critically framed by the anthropological question of rationality. It therefore concerned itself implicitly with the classical anthropological and sociological issue of the nature of the difference between, so to speak, a primitive and modern consciousness or, better, epistemic style. The argument brings this hoary issue to bear on the current, postmodernist critique of reason and subjectivity. I have employed a notion of mythic rationality as, in certain fundamental respects, exemplary of rationality rethought on the basis of ontological ambiguity or nondualism, a value rationality of primordial choosing. Nevertheless, to look forward now to analysis yet to come, the argument from nondualism is far from primitivism. It urges instead that, for all their manifest, terrifying exclusionism, both rationality as such and the modern self hold out the promise of a reason and sense of self open in finite but unprecedented degree.

Notes

1. Dualism and Anthropology

1. I have lifted the example from Polanyi's *The Tacit Dimension* (1967).
2. See Borges's *Fictions:* "The composition of vast books is a laborious and impoverishing extravagance. To go on for five hundred pages developing an idea whose perfect oral exposition is possible in a few minutes! A better course of procedure is to pretend that these books already exist, and then to offer a resume, a commentary" (1962: 13). Kuper's very useful book (1983), though it was not argued with the ontological question in mind, provides a certain substance to my undertaking here. I have already performed this sort of Borgesian exercise in anthropological history, with narrower foci, in two other places (Evens 1982a; 1982b).
3. The two views may well be complementary, as Kuper suggests (1983: 52; see also Giddens 1978: 87ff.). But the issue is why Durkheim shifted from the one to the other. The thesis that he was groping for a more intuitive understanding of the reality of society, trying to avoid the reduction to the individual, and that his efforts in this connection were constrained by mind–body dualism, seems helpful here.
4. Notwithstanding Langham's thesis, that it was Rivers rather than Durkheim who provided the "seminal contribution" for Radcliffe-Brown's development of structural functionalism (Langham 1981: chap. 7; see Stocking 1984: 106–7).
5. See Leach's Radcliffe-Brown Lecture (1976) and Kuper's discussion, in which Kuper's disbelief over Radcliffe-Brown's positivism is barely concealed (1983: 53–56).
6. I am using "revolutionary" here in Kuhn's sense (Kuhn 1970).
7. Schneider's and Needham's criticisms of the anthropological study of kinship may be construed as a charge of this kind (for example, Schneider 1972; Needham 1983). See also my essays on Nuer kinship (1989a; 1989b).
8. With regard to Lévi-Strauss, especially Sahlins has brought into relief the nondualist promise of "structure" (for example, 1981).
9. In his provocative little history, Pocock may be right to think that Gluckman confounded two kinds of structure and misunderstood Evans-Pritchard's express intentions (Pocock 1961: 77f.). But at a deeper level, I suspect Gluckman caught the

drift of Evans-Pritchard's theory better perhaps than Evans-Pritchard himself. Inasmuch as Evans-Pritchard's turn to "structure" was tied into both the idea of society as a moral system and the situationalism adumbrated in *Witchcraft, Oracles and Magic among the Azande,* Gluckman, with his Marxian leanings, may have been developing a direction of Evans-Pritchard that was real enough, even though Evans-Pritchard never quite saw it himself. In a recent essay (Evens n.d.), I have developed more fully the picture of Evans-Pritchard's argument considered in terms of practice.

2. The Kibbutz

1. The kibbutzim (plural of "kibbutz") are collective settlements dedicated to the realization of an ideology the principal components of which (for all but a very few kibbutzim) are Zionism or Jewish nationalism and socialism. The first kibbutz, Degania, was established in 1909. It is the radical and comprehensive nature of its principle of collectivism that serves best to distinguish the kibbutz from the other form of cooperative village in Israel, the *moshav-ovdim,* or smallholders' settlement. Currently, there are about 275 kibbutzim in Israel, making up about 3 percent (some 125,000 souls) of the Jewish population (Central Bureau of Statistics 1986). These communities range in size from about one hundred to twelve hundred individuals. Most of the kibbutzim are organized into three major federations, namely, Takam (the federation resulting from the recent merger of Ichud Hak'vutzot V'hakibbutzim [Association of Small and Large Kibbutzim] and Kibbutz Ham'uchad [the United Kibbutz]); Kibbutz Ha'artzi Hashomer Hatza'ir (National Kibbutz of the Young Guard); and Kibbutz Hadati (Socialist Religious Kibbutzim). The federations differ from one another in ideology, the most conspicuous difference being the adherence of Kibbutz Hadati to orthodox Judaism. Kibbutz Ha'artzi, the federation to which the community I studied belongs, is generally regarded as the most doctrinaire in its socialism. To my mind, the best introduction to the kibbutz remains Spiro's *Kibbutz: Venture in Utopia;* for a more recent introductory monograph, the reader may consult Bowes's *Kibbutz Goshen: An Israeli Commune;* finally, Darin-Drabkin's *The Other Society* provides a comprehensive "insider" introduction.

From November 1965 through May 1967, I carried out field research in a kibbutz I call, pseudonymously, Timem. Timem is one of the founding members of Kibbutz Ha'artzi. Located in Israel's Jezreel Valley, some fifteen minutes walking distance from a town of about (at the time of fieldwork) seventeen thousand people, Timem was established on site in 1929 and is therefore a veteran kibbutz. In 1965, the year I began field research there, Timem had an overall population of 580. The community breaks down its population into the following eight categories: (1) *Chaverim,* or "members": members must be at least eighteen years old and have been voted into the community in a meeting of the General Assembly (*sichat hakibbutz*). They have the right to participate and vote in the General Assembly. (2) *Me'umadim,* or "candidates": candidates must be at least eighteen years old and have applied for candidacy for membership. They may be required to remain candidates for a period of not more than one year and normally not less than six months. They are permitted to attend the General Assembly but not to participate in it. (3) *Yaldei hakibbutz,* or "children of the kibbutz": that is, the sons and daughters of Timem's members. (4) *Yaldei chutz,* or "children from outside": that is, children who have been placed in Timem's educational system by persons who are not members of and do not reside in Timem. (5) "Children of the Youth Aliya" (the *Aliyat Hano'ar*): a youth movement founded in 1934 to facilitate the immigration (*aliya*) to Israel of children who have lost their parents. The movement recruits also from underprivileged urban youth. (6) *Horim,* or "parents": that is, members' parents who are not themselves members. (7) *Zmani'im,* or "temporary residents": this category is heterogeneous but often includes those individuals who receive room and board, and sometimes monetary compensation, in exchange for labor. (8) The *ulpanistim,* students of the *ulpan* or Hebrew language school: Timem's *ulpan* normally runs two six-month sessions each year. Typically the students are newly arrived immigrants who receive room and board in exchange for their part-time labor. Of the 580 residents of Timem in 1965, 320 (55.1 percent) were members and candidates; 169 (29.1 percent) were children of the kibbutz; 36 (6.2 percent) were children from outside; 5 (1.0 percent) were children of the Youth Aliya; 8 (1.4 percent) were parents of members; 13 (2.2 percent) were temporary residents; and 29 (5.0 percent) were students of the Hebrew language school.

According to my original agreement with Timem, I was to spend one-half of each working day engaged in labor for the community and the other engaged in my anthropological pursuits. I conformed to this agreement for about six months, at which time, owing to the steadily increasing demands of my research, I began to find my situation too trying. I therefore requested that I be allowed to pay the community for additional research time. The request was eventually granted, though it gave rise to strain in my formal relationship with the community. This relationship was further strained as I increasingly sought access to various documentary records and administrative institutions. Eventually, though, I was permitted access to most meetings of the General Assembly and to some meetings of the numerous other committees, including those of the Secretariat, the administrative committee whose authority is second only to that of the General Assembly. Some documentary records were also put at my disposal.

2. "Self-fashioning" is used by Greenblatt to study, in the work of Tudor writers, "an increased self-consciousness about the fashioning of human identity as a manipulable, artful process" (1980). In adopting the concept, Greenblatt was directly influenced by interpretive anthropology. My own usage of the term, to include also "self-interpreting," "self-understanding," "self-identifying," and so on, seems less rigorous than his, and is more existential, phenomenological, and ontological than culturological (see also below, chap. 2, n. 5).

3. Rosner in particular has targeted these matters for research (1982). A great deal of research has focused more generally on social change in the kibbutz, including the impressive work of Talmon-Garber (1972). Rayman's solid sociohistorical account documents broadly the changes undergone by a single kibbutz since its inception, and shows the integral relationship between this change and the kibbutz's fundamental role in the development of Israel as a nation (1981). In his most recent study of the kibbutz, Spiro takes up the question of counterrevolutionary change in relation to women's roles (1979).

4. Mittelberg's study of the "guest-host" encounter or "the stranger" in the kibbutz is expressly phenomenological. Nevertheless, his project and approach are very different from mine (1988).

5. One is put in mind here, of course, of Bourdieu's theory of the *habitus* and practice (for example, 1977). In addition, Taylor's outstanding philosophical work does much to clarify and develop the idea, of deep self-understanding, that concerns me here (for example, 1985a: chaps. 1 and 2). As I see it, though, Taylor's approach accords such self-understanding an ontological value beyond that which Bourdieu's theory can comprehend. As a result, in Taylor's theory the concept of practice has a primarily ethical rather than political feel to it (see Taylor 1985b: chap. 3). I discuss Bourdieu's concept of practice fully in the forthcoming companion volume

to this one, a relevant extract of which has already appeared as an article (Evens 1993).

6. This is apparent in much of the sociological literature produced by the kibbutz movement itself as well as in the recent series of monographs (in which Lilker's book appears) put out by the Project for Kibbutz Studies at Harvard University.

7. In one way or another, most of the studies of the kibbutz, whether performed by an "outsider" or "insider," implicate an idea of this "alternative" social enterprise as on trial.

8. This is not surprising, since such an ontology is scarcely available within the context of Western ontological thought. That is to say, in certain respects, a nondualist ontology is not an ontology at all. In the companion volume to this one, I work even more directly to build such a nondualist ontology (Evens forthcoming).

9. In adducing a fitting social ontology here, I can perhaps do no better than to cite Merleau-Ponty's description of how we perceive other persons directly, in a palpable sense "undivided" from them, and yet as irrecusably other to us:

> I perceive the other person as a piece of behaviour, for example, I perceive the grief or the anger of the other in his conduct, in his face or his hands, without recourse to any "inner" experience of suffering or anger, and because grief and anger are variations of belonging to the world, undivided between the body and consciousness, and equally applicable to the other person's conduct, visible in his phenomenal body, as in my own conduct as it is presented to me. But then, the behaviour of another person, and even his words, are not that other person. The grief and the anger of another have never quite the same significance for him as they have for me. For him these situations are lived through, for me they are displayed. Or in so far as I can, by some friendly gesture, become part of that grief or that anger, they still remain the grief and anger of my friend Paul: Paul suffers because he has lost his wife, or is angry because his watch has been stolen, whereas I suffer because Paul is grieved, or I am angry because he is angry, and our situations cannot be superimposed on each other. If moreover, we undertake some project in common, this common project is not one single project, it does not appear in the selfsame light to both of us, we are not both equally enthusiastic about it, or at any rate not in quite the same way, simply because Paul is Paul and I am myself. Although his consciousness and mine, working through our respective situations, may contrive to produce a common situation in which they can communicate, it is nevertheless from the subjectivity of each of us that each one projects this "one and only" world. (1962: 356)

10. The allusion to Evans-Pritchard's famous oxymoron, forged for his discussion of the political life of the Nuer, is pregnant (1940). For reasons of its sociocentric presuppositions, "ordered anarchy" is, I think, a designation more fitting to the kibbutz than to the Nuer. Yet the application of this term to the Nuer is sociologically rich, precisely because it points directly and comparatively to the ontological question. I expect to take up the comparative analysis another time.

11. The postmodern and post-Marxist idea of radical democracy, that is, a democracy in which the principles of liberty and equality, of pluralism and responsible citizenship, are taken so seriously that their basic inconsistency with sheer capitalism and mere democratic form becomes transparent, seems richly relevant here. See Laclau and Mouffe (1985), Laclau (1990), Mouffe (1992), and Agamben (1993).

3. Democratic Procedure and Secret Ballot

1. Neither my notes (I was present at the debate) nor the official minutes of the meeting record the decision to continue the debate at another time. A decision to postpone resolution of an issue can, of course, have tactical implications. In this case, as the issue was the last to come up in the meeting, I suspect that the normal hour of adjournment came before discussion had flagged sufficiently to justify a voting. The exhausting of public discussion is regarded as a necessary condition for the correct resolution of an issue; and, for reasons that will emerge in the analysis, this particular issue must have been regarded as very important.

2. I should point out that the complete text has lines of argument other than those brought out here. Especially important are two additional solutions to the problem of participation. However, this additional material, though ethnographically interesting, would not substantially affect my argument, and therefore I have felt justified in deleting it here.

3. Barker writes: "The State... is a national society which has turned itself into a legal association, or a juridical organization, by virtue of a legal act and deed called a constitution, which is henceforth the norm and standard (and therefore the 'Sovereign') of such association or organisation" (1957: xxiii); and again: "For the State is essentially law, and law is the essence of the State. The State is essentially law in the sense that it exists in order to secure a right order of relations between its members, expressed in the form of declared and enforced rules. Law, as a system of declared and enforced rules, is the essence of the State in the same sort of sense as his words and acts are the essence of a man" (1957: xxviii).

4. The crimes most often mentioned were theft and murder. Although I did hear of cases of theft by temporary residents in Timem, and even of cases of homicide in other kibbutzim, I do not doubt that crimes of this sort are rare in the kibbutz. Incidentally, it should not be overlooked that, although it has no internal police, the kibbutz is under the jurisdiction of Israel's police force — the kibbutz and its individual members can and do call on this organization.

5. See Hayek (1962: chap. 6) and Dahrendorf (1968: 218ff.) for good liberalist accounts of this distinction.

6. It might be argued that since the general consensus, like Marx's "class interest," is an objective phenomenon, democratic participation is scarcely required to educe it. But this argument suggests group totalitarianism (see Talmon 1970), and in any case I never heard it in Timem.

7. It is suggestive to cite here also the Greek paradigm of participation in the public sphere as intensely agonal and masculine, a paradigm employed by Hannah Arendt in her powerful critique of modernity (1958).

4. Conflict between the Generations versus Social Differentiation: The Empirical Picture

1. I should point out that the Secretary, as the representative of the Secretariat, always sat in the area of the presiding member, whereas I, as a special attendant, normally took a less conspicuous seat. However, on this occasion, because the meeting was ad hoc and of an informal nature, I chose to sit next to the Secretary.

2. It is important to keep in mind that my figures do not reflect the fact that the respective composition of the young and of the veteran element present or not present varies from one meeting to the next. This means, among other things, that the percentage of each of these elements who do not attend any meetings whatsoever

is probably quite small. Erik Cohen's comparative study (1968: chap. 4), which is based on questionnaire responses rather than direct observation, suggests that this is so. Unfortunately, outside of the category "second generation," I have not found useful here (for reasons that I bring out in the text) his categorical breakdown of a kibbutz population. But it is worth citing Cohen's findings on the second-generation members of the Kibbutz Ha'artzi collective he investigated. To the question, "How many of the last five public assemblies did you attend?" they responded as follows: 23.4 percent said none; 17.8 percent said one to two; 29.0 percent said three to four; and 29.9 percent said all five.

3. These are all the votings in which the pros and contras were actually counted from those meetings. Often a show of hands was so impressive for or against an issue, countings were not taken.

4. It is worth noting that on the community's "point system" (*nikud*) for determining the allocation of such resources as quality of housing and vacations abroad, members are docked for interim years of absence from the community.

5. The following table records the figures for the development of Timem's membership and overall population between the years 1942 and 1968 (just subsequent to the termination of fieldwork). Despite the fact of attrition, the figures reveal a steady rate of growth.

Year	Members & Candidates	Total Population	Year	Members & Candidates	Total Population
1942	157	274	1956	286	581
1943	157	280	1957	300	594
1944	172	311	1958	311	610
1945	173	344	1959	307	605
1946	168	375	1960	311	597
1947	175	478	1961	327	626
1948	208	480	1962	304	584
1949	203	582	1963	322	603
1950	208	568	1964	321	594
1951	198	566	1965	320	581
1952	213	546	1966	324	585
1953	223	538	1967	332	621
1954	262	603	1968	328	599
1955	272	573			

6. See Goffman for the distinction (1963: 2, 56–57).

7. The proposal of a secret ballot implied a redefinition of the individual in terms of a fast division between his or her public and private self. Such an ungiving division projects the relationship of self as a power struggle. This picture of the modern individual follows logically from the uncoupling process, and has been developed panoramically by Michel Foucault.

8. As especially E. Cohen has shown (1976, 1982), theories of "modernization" can describe a good deal about the development of the kibbutz and lend themselves to examination of the relationship between the kibbutz and Israeli society. Undoubtedly, the need to compete for its membership with the "external" society has moved the kibbutz to "modernize." But these theories tend to overlook that, whatever its ancient roots and archaic aspirations, the kibbutz is "modern" through and through. When the thoroughly modern character of kibbutz utopianism is brought into account, one is persuaded to search also, and perhaps especially, within the kibbutz's

own design in order to understand privatization, pluralization, and so on, in the development of these communities.

9. Habermas's description of the process of uncoupling is exemplary. But, given his picture of primitive and archaic settings as perfectly closed, he makes the shift from archaic to modern basically unintelligible. The important thesis of communicative action as a "switching station" cannot help, unless one takes seriously the idea that primitive social settings are characterized by a significant moral openness. To be sure, following Durkheim, Habermas locates such an openness in religious activity. Nevertheless, in his description of primitive mentality as such, under the influence of especially neo-Tylorianism, he fails to take into account this moral capacity. Craig Calhoun has suggested to me that Habermas's characterization of primitive social systems is weak because it serves largely as a kind of analytical prop for his account of social evolution, and that the real model for Habermas's understanding of the uncoupling process is the shift from feudal to modern society. My own reading here is that, for all its connection to the idea of an ideal speech situation and opposition to instrumental rationality, Habermas's notion of communicative rationality remains too tied to its instrumental counterpart to do justice to the peculiar, moral character of primitive thought. I develop this reading of Habermas in the companion volume to this one (Evens forthcoming).

10. In the Bruderhof, for example, crisis regularly gives rise to "clearance," whereby the community as a whole faces up to the problem and makes remedial changes (Zablocki 1971: 233ff.). Evidently, the Bruderhof also use crises to "release people from the burden of secret feelings and resentments, which come to the surface during crises even if the individual has not previously had the will or the courage to express them" (Zablocki 1971: 236). The kibbutz certainly indulges in scapegoating as a way of dealing with crisis, as I have documented in another place (Evens 1975). Moreover, in principle, secret feelings and resentments are meant to be aired in the General Assembly. Nevertheless, there seems to be no regularized ritualistic means of coping with such tensions in the kibbutz.

11. In connection with the kibbutz ideology of personal issues, I am reminded by contrast of Arendt's penetrating critique of modernity on the grounds of the collapse of the public/private distinction diagnostic of the age (1958). But Arendt was concerned with the way in which this collapse, far from elevating the public sphere, reduced it to the private, the sphere of necessity and the instrumental. Still, her argument that the rise of the social (which she thought of as on the model of kinship and the household, and distinguished from authentic political life) brought conformity rather than creative freedom poses intriguing thought-puzzles in relation to the kibbutz's highly social-minded ideology. Taking a cue from Rousseau, both Arendt and the kibbutz stand opposed to the leveling power of the modern age, and yet the kibbutz, in line with the Rousseau of *The Social Contract* rather than of *The Discourse on the Origin of Inequality,* proposes to remedy the problem by means of identifying rather than differentiating the personal and the communal. Arendt *seemed* to show small concern for the institution of slavery and the devaluation of women characteristic of the social order on which she based her ideal of the genuine political life, the Greek *polis*. But I'm inclined to think that her approach to the public/private distinction, by contrast to kibbutz ideology, exhibits an impressive awareness of the totalism to which Enlightenment reason and modern life are given. Benhabib's constructive critiques of Arendt are helpful here (1992: chaps. 3 and 4). For a relevant ethnographic discussion of the principle "the personal is political" in the social context of a feminist health center, see Morgen's case study (1990).

5. Conflict between the Generations as a Normative Expectation

1. I draw here on Berger and Luckmann's exemplary account of institutionalization (1967: esp. 62–63).
2. I should note here that, by contrast to the existing sociological literature on the kibbutz (E. Cohen 1982; Mittelberg 1988), I have not found it useful to treat "commitment" as a sociological variable. Instead, I regard it as an element in the ideological rhetoric of the culturally thematic contest of the generations in the kibbutz.
3. For a logically nuanced discussion of "paradoxical injunctions," that is, ones that cannot be coherently followed, see Elster (1983: 60ff.).
4. I failed to inquire about the details of this organization.

6. Conflict between the Generations as a Metaphor

1. For a systematic argument that these are blinding but patently false alternatives, see Berger (1974).
2. For fictional examples confer the antiutopias of Zamiatin (*We*), Orwell (*Nineteen Eighty-Four*), and Huxley (*Brave New World*); for the real thing, the work of Delgado (1969).
3. In connection with this idea of human existence as a natural vacuum, I find Laclau's impressive politico-ontological theory of "dislocation" extremely stimulating (1990). He regards all social structures as necessarily subject to chronic disruption by external structures, and in this sense as fundamentally "dislocated" or always open to possibility and rearticulation. I am less sympathetic, however, to his correlative theory of the subject as a "metaphor" of the incompleteness of structure (1990: 61ff.). The scent of the entitative ontology Laclau does so much to undermine seems to linger still with the reduction of the subject to a "mythical" or "metaphorical" space.
4. It is provocative to cite here Giddens's recent discussion of trust in modern social settings (1991). He finds that with the emergence of relationships that are anchored in their own reward rather than in criteria that are "external" to the relationships (such as kinship, social duty, or moral obligation), trust is put at a premium. The kibbutz synthesis may be fruitfully construed as a blueprint for eliminating the gap between such "pure relationships," as Giddens calls them, and the external obligatory guarantees of the collectivity. But as such pure relationships "create enormous burdens for the integrity of the self" (1991: 186), so it must follow that the integrity of the social order of the kibbutz is exceedingly vulnerable.

7. Conflict between the Generations as a Primordial Choice: The Paradigm of Genesis

1. The ambiguity is expressed compactly in the oft-cited verse from Genesis 1: "So God created man in his own image, in the image of God He created him." To be sure, chapter 1 is based on a narrative source (P) later than the Yahwist (J) tradition of chapters 2–3. Nevertheless, the same ambiguity is recorded. If man was created in God's image, then man too must partake of God's power to create and of the authority deriving from that power.
2. I say "so-called" because nowhere in the story is there direct mention of a "fall"; the story speaks simply of an expulsion from the garden. Nevertheless, the story does phenomenologically document the experience of falling, as for example when the serpent, being made to crawl on its belly, is brought low.

3. The division of the Hebrew Bible into chapters originated in the Middle Ages. It is generally agreed that the first three verses of chapter 2, bearing on the establishment of the sabbath, really close the preceding chapter (Hertz 1970: 6).

4. I surmise that it is this experience that moved Christianity to an absolute emphasis on spirit over matter. The turn to choice and internal commitment rather than descent and embodiment as the determination of membership in *the* community (Eilberg-Schwartz 1990: chap. 8) may be construed as an ingenious effort to overcome the material limits registered in the punishments meted out by God to man. By divorcing spirit from matter altogether, an ontological move epitomized profanely in the transparent subjectivity promoted by Enlightenment thought, Christianity makes it possible for humans to begin to think of themselves as having the potential to break the bonds of material life once and for all, becoming wholly autonomous. I am inclined to read Genesis 2–3 as both a wellspring of and cautionary tale against this development. The way in which Judaism affords the primacy of generation to spirit-matter over matter-spirit is recorded presumptively in the consideration that, as Eilberg-Schwartz observes, "God had 'no body,'" making the divine realm as much "an anti-image for the human realm as a mirror of it" (1990: 217).

5. After having forged my interpretation of Kibbutz Timem and Genesis, I discovered the work of Harold Bloom (for example, 1973, 1975, 1982). Bloom's rich and powerful theory of literary criticism, drawing especially on Freud, Emerson, and Jewish mysticism, construes poetry as essentially a creative act of opposition to fatherly precursors. Reading Bloom has helped me, I believe, to sharpen my wits and deepen my insights about the nature of generational conflict. I have drawn the expressions of the "belatedness" of the sons and the "transumption" of the fathers directly from Bloom.

6. "Needful freedom" is Jonas's oxymoron, specially crafted to capture the dialectical character of the relationship between organic form and matter (1966: 80). At bottom, my understanding of human identity — really a "theory" of human existence as an unceasing dynamic of self-identification, at once psychical, social, and cultural (see also Evens 1990) — is drawn preeminently from Merleau-Ponty's phenomenology and philosophy of ambiguity. But, at this point in the text, my reflections are most immediately indebted to Jonas's wonderfully elegant discussion of organic freedom and self-identity among living things in general (Jonas 1966: 74ff.).

8. Primordial Choice and "The Universal": Kibbutz Familism and the Sexual Division of Labor

1. For a useful rundown of the issue, see Palgi, Blasi, and Rosner (1983).

2. Of course these associations and this sense of generation are not restricted to the kibbutz. They are deeply entrenched in the Western mind, so much so that their presumption and demonstration constitute a preoccupation even of biological and social science. Witness, for example, Fortes's ingenious sociological account of "the natural history of prescriptive altruism":

> In contrast to the mother's role of loving nurturance, the father, paradigmatically speaking, brings in the complementary element of authority that gives rise to the sense of obligation. This represents recognition of the power of society mediated by the father.... I believe that rule-making and observance is associated with the emergence of fatherhood in the structure of the family — more exactly, perhaps, in the reproductive nucleus. Fatherhood emerges, partly perhaps in response to the requirements of the work of socializing offspring, but also as the mediating agency for bringing the

234 Notes

> politico-jural power of society, and thus of law and government into the heart of the family and the kinship system. (1983: 27–28)

Fortes's account is roundly sociological (it is a polemic against the gross reductionism of popular sociobiology) and derives altruism ultimately from "the mother's role of loving nurturance." Nevertheless, it still pictures the male principle as preeminently associated with creation by fiat and the female with material relations or heteronomous creation.

The following is the biological argument, elegantly resumed (but not espoused) by Gould, on which the sociobiological thesis of the differences between the sexes is typically based:

> In most animals, the argument goes, males and females must play the game [of individual reproductive success] differently, following the dictates of their biological roles. A sperm, little more than genes with a delivery system, is cheap to make, and each fertilization puts half of you into an offspring without further trouble. Thus, males should win their Darwinian edge by impregnating as many females as possible, as often as they can. This state of maximal spread may be achieved along a wide variety of routes, from stealth to outright domination.... Females, on the other hand, invest much more by putting sources of nutrition into more expensive eggs; in addition, in many creatures, females bear offspring within their bodies and nurture their newborns for long periods. Hence, female investment must be prolonged and costly. Females receive no Darwinian edge in promiscuity since no gain in reproductive success attends any copulation after fertilization.... Hence, female adaptations veer from profligacy toward care in choosing the best and most helpful males to father their offspring. The sociopolitical line of the pop argument now leaps from the page: males are aggressive, assertive, promiscuous, overbearing; females are coy, discriminating, loyal, caring. (1986: 50)

Here an adaptive biological difference is theoretically turned to a social difference, one which, though its character profiles ring more Darwinian than Edenic, translates into a special association of the male principle with political and, therewith, again, creative superiority.

3. To say here that the constituting practice remains unoccluded is not to say that it is epistemologically well delineated, but, rather, that it is taken for granted. The power of epistemological thinking to sever cleanly one thing from another can serve to obscure so ambiguous a phenomenon as a constituting practice, to the point where the practice becomes inconceivable.

4. In forging his idea of choice, Sartre seems to have taken such a line. While my notion of primordial choice defines choice as creative, by diametrical contrast to the Sartrean idea, it precisely does not suppose that our most fundamental evaluations are open to self-transparent selection. For a concise argument that Sartre's idea of radical choice is incoherent, see Taylor (1985a: 29ff.).

5. For an example of how this works in the concrete, see my essay on Nuer hierarchy (1984).

6. In his *Islands of History,* moved especially by relativism and dialectics, Sahlins attempts to cut through certain of the thematic dualisms of modern anthropology (1985). He argues that different cultures are characterized by different historicities, that is, that they are differentially open to what we call history, and, accordingly, he demonstrates that the historicity of the historical Hawaiian culture stands logically between the historicities of, to use the terms of the debate, "structure" and "history."

As one would expect, his argument against dualism is eloquent and illuminating. I would maintain, though, that inasmuch as his argument fails to convince, it is because he does not go so far as to base it on a fundamental revision of Western ontology.

9. The Historical Link between Genesis and Timem's Story: Rousseau as Biblical Redactor

1. There is a federation of religious kibbutzim. But it is crucial to understand that the kibbutz movement itself was founded in humanism, in direct opposition to religion as such (see Fishman 1992: 18–19).

2. On the other hand, Rousseau's position that "no function which has a particular object belongs to the legislative power" and that the law "considers subjects *en masse* and actions in the abstract, and never a particular person or action" (1950: 36, 35) may well be at odds with kibbutz practice. In this connection, however, the consideration that Rousseau was thinking about social orders much larger than the kibbutz may be important. The small scale of the kibbutz is meant to facilitate an identity between the individual and society so perfect that all particular persons and actions *are* general. In other words, in the kibbutz ideally each particular person constitutes a class of citizen in his or her own right, in which case Rousseau's distinction between action in the concrete and in the abstract is dissolved. It is inviting, though, to read Rousseau's reservations, about government by democracy, to propound that so consummate a union between the particular and the general is not open to nation-states. If community size alone is the parameter, then the kibbutz approaches more closely to Rousseau's conception of family-life in the state of near-nature than it does to the nation-states at which he aimed his theory of social contract. Such a picture of the kibbutz, as a "family" rather than a government, is, of course, not out of keeping with the kibbutz's ideological self-representation.

3. "How many conditions that are difficult to unite does [real democracy]... presuppose! First, a very small State, where the people can readily be got together and where each citizen can with ease know all the rest; secondly, great simplicity of manners, to prevent business from multiplying and raising thorny problems; next, a large measure of equality in rank and fortune, without which equality of rights and authority cannot long subsist; lastly little or no luxury—for luxury either comes of riches or makes them necessary" (Rousseau 1950: 65–66).

4. Evens (1975) documents a case in which a member of the kibbutz was held to fall short of these critical endowments.

5. Compare Starobinski, who, in his superb study of Rousseau, speaks of the *Second Discourse* as

> a thoroughly religious work, but of a very particular kind, a substitute for sacred history. Rousseau has rewritten *Genesis* as a work of philosophy, complete with Garden of Eden, original sin, and the confusion of tongues. This is a secularized, "demystified" version of the origins of mankind, which repeats the Scripture that it replaces in another tongue. Rousseau's language is that of philosophical speculation and all mention of the supernatural has been eliminated. Yet Christian theology, though not present explicitly, shapes the structure of Rousseau's argument. Primitive man, leading what is scarcely more than an animal existence, is happy; he lives in *paradise* and will remain there until the opportunity arises to use his reason. Once he begins to reflect, however, he acquires knowledge of good and evil. The anxious mind of man discovers the misfortune of

a divided existence: mankind has therefore experienced a *fall*. (Starobinski 1988: 290)

10. Two Kinds of Rationality

1. Arendt's brilliant and scathing discussion of how the invention of the telescope, by occasioning "world alienation," determined the (scientistic) character of the modern age bears sharply upon my argument. She links Galileo's discovery with "the Archimedean wish for a point outside the earth from which to unhinge the world" and sums up the result in this way:

> How deep-rooted this usage of the Archimedean point against ourselves is can be seen in the very metaphors which dominate scientific thought today. The reason why scientists can tell us about the "life" in the atom—where apparently every particle is "free" to behave as it wants and the laws ruling these movements are the same statistical laws which, according to the social scientists, rule human behavior and make the multitude behave as it must, no matter how "free" the individual particle may appear to be in its choices—the reason, in other words, why the behavior of the infinitely small particle is not only similar in pattern to the planetary system as it appears to us but resembles the life and behavior patterns in human society is, of course, that we look and live in this society as though we were as far removed from our own human existence as we are from the infinitely small and the immensely large which, even if they could be perceived by the finest instruments, are too far away from us to be experienced. (1958: 262, 323)

2. Viteles summarizes remarks made by Yosef Baratz at a meeting of representatives from twenty-five kibbutzim in 1923:

> He was opposed to the large kibbutz because it stimulated a larger degree of inertia in the members than did the small [collectives], since "large bodies required more centralized administration." A kibbutz which flouts the basic moral foundations of the [collective] as a purpose in itself, and thinks of economic development only in terms of modern technical foundation, management, etc.—such a kibbutz does not carry out the true philosophy of the [collective]. The by-product of this type of development is that only a small group will be active while all the rest will be passive and respond only to discipline. Such a kibbutz will have little content and real meaning after the experimental stage. (Viteles 1967: 56)

3. It is relevant to cite here Taylor's profound critique of empiricism in political science (1985b: esp. chaps. 1–4). The critique is compelling not only for its demonstration that empiricism cannot cope with the pivotal intersubjective reality of social life, but also for its implicit thesis that, since social theory is a form of social practice, such a scientific view is at bottom ethically pernicious.

4. A claim of this kind is also the burden of Straus's extraordinary piece on upright posture as a key to being human (Straus 1966: chap. 7). To see the "explanatory" uniqueness of this claim, it helps to contrast it to analysis in physical anthropology, where upright posture is typically given a critical role in the evolution of humankind, but sheerly as a physical function correlating with the development of consciousness. At least implicit in all such analysis is the physicalist thesis that upright posture *gives rise* to consciousness. Straus, on the other hand, is laying no

claim to causal analysis, but, rather, is arguing that upright posture presents a phenomenological key to human being. Such a key might be understood, taking a cue from Wittgenstein's notion of a perspicuous picture, as a perceptual occasion or possibility for the mind's eye to link together phenomena in such a way that they form an intelligible *gestalt*. The perspicuity of the picture is not a question of causal understanding, but simply of intelligible configuration (Wittgenstein 1979: 8e–9e).

5. This, I take it, is an important share of the burden of Elster's distinction between a "thin" and a "broad" theory of rationality: "We need a broader theory of rationality...that allows a scrutiny of the substantive nature of the desires and beliefs involved in action. We want to be able to say that acting rationally means acting consistently on beliefs and desires that are not only consistent, but also rational" (1983: 15). I suspect, however, that my notions of "mythic" and "value" rationality, by not only introducing ethical goodness as a parameter but also superordinating it to that of consistency, are beyond keeping with Elster's designs. If I follow Elster's (logically cutting) discussion correctly, "value rationality" as understood here "dilutes" the notion of rationality too radically to be acceptable to him (1983: 15). Though I cannot explore this matter here, as might be expected from my overtly ontological intentions, the difference surely derives from my effort to rethink rationality specifically in terms of nondualism.

6. See Giddens's sensible reminder that, since it features the critical degree to which the global and the personal are interconnected, "The issue of nuclear weaponry enters life politics as a positive appropriation as well as a negative one" (1991: 223).

7. Taylor makes an intuitively compelling argument that incommensurability positively impels commensuration (1985b: chap. 5). Even closer to the present argument is the physicist David Bohm's, in which he relativizes the distinction on the basis of a reconsidered (holistic) ontology (1977).

8. In his outstanding book, Laclau promotes just this conception of possibility (see Laclau 1990: 42–43). However, the association I make between the ideas of possibility and hierarchy-as-encompassment seems out of keeping with Laclau's argument. By using the notion of hierarchy as I do, I am positioned to maintain a distinction—a fundamental asymmetry—between power and principle. Laclau, on the other hand, in line with the general tenor of poststructuralism, is moved by his argument to think of possibility in terms of power (1990: 31ff.). One crucial advantage of my argument is, then, that it permits me to justify my "politics" in ethical rather than political terms.

9. Elsewhere, inspired by Dumont's ingenious argument, I have shown how the relationship between the principles of agnation and territory among the Nuer may be understood in terms of such contained hierarchical reversal (Evens 1984).

Bibliography

Agamben, Georgio. 1993. *The Coming Community.* Translated by Michael Hardt. Minneapolis: University of Minnesota Press.
Amitai, Mordechai. 1966. *Together: Conversations about the Kibbutz.* Published by the English Speaking Department of World Hashomer Hatzair.
Arendt, Hannah. 1958. *The Human Condition.* Chicago: University of Chicago Press.
Arrow, Kenneth J. 1967. "Values and Collective Decision-Making." In *Philosophy, Politics and Society.* 3d ser. Edited by Peter Laslett and W. G. Runciman. Oxford: Basil Blackwell.
Avineri, Shlomo. 1968. *The Social and Political Thought of Karl Marx.* Cambridge: Cambridge University Press.
———. 1981. *The Making of Modern Zionism.* New York: Basic Books.
Barker, Ernest. 1957. Introduction to *Otto Gierke, Natural Law and the Theory of Society: 1500 to 1800.* Translated by Ernest Barker. Boston: Beacon Press.
Bauman, Zygmunt. 1988. "Exit Visas and Entry Tickets: Paradoxes of Jewish Assimilation." *Telos* 44: 45–77.
Becker, Carl L. 1932. *The Heavenly City of the Eighteenth-Century Philosophers.* New Haven: Yale University Press.
Benhabib, Seyla. 1992. *Situating the Self.* New York: Routledge.
Benjamin, Walter. 1986. "On Language as Such and on the Language of Man." In *Reflections: Walter Benjamin.* Edited by Peter Demetz. Translated by Edmund Jephcott. New York: Schocken Books.
Ben-Yosef, Avraham C. 1963. *The Purest Democracy in the World.* New York: Herzl Press and Thomas Yoseloff.
Berger, Peter L. 1974. *Pyramids of Sacrifice.* Garden City, N.Y.: Anchor Books.
Berger, Peter L., and Thomas Luckmann. 1967. *The Social Construction of Reality.* Garden City, N.Y.: Anchor Books.
Berlin, Isaiah. 1973. "The Counter-Enlightenment." In *Dictionary of the History of Ideas.* New York: Scribner's, 2:100–112.

Bernstein, Richard. 1992. *The New Constellation: The Ethical-Political Horizons of Modernity/Postmodernity.* Cambridge, Mass.: MIT Press.
Bloom, Allan. 1979. Introduction to *Émile or On Education,* by Jean-Jacques Rousseau. Translated by Allan Bloom. New York: Basic Books.
Bloom, Harold. 1973. *The Anxiety of Influence: A Theory of Poetry.* New York: Oxford University Press.
———. 1975. *A Map of Misreading.* New York: Oxford University Press.
———. 1982. *The Breaking of the Vessels.* Chicago: University of Chicago Press.
Bohm, David. 1977. "Science as Perception-Communication." In *The Structure of Scientific Theories.* Edited by Frederick Suppe. 2d ed. Urbana: University of Illinois Press.
———. 1981. *Wholeness and the Implicate Order.* London: Routledge and Kegan Paul.
Borges, Jorge Luis. 1962. *Fictions.* London: John Calder.
Bottomore, T. B., and Maximillien Rubel. 1963. *Karl Marx: Selected Writings in Sociology and Social Philosophy.* Harmondsworth, Eng.: Penguin Books.
Bourdieu, Pierre. 1977. *Outline of a Theory of Practice.* Translated by Richard Nice. Cambridge: Cambridge University Press.
Bowes, Alison M. 1989. *Kibbutz Goshen: An Israeli Commune.* Prospect Heights, Il.: Waveland Press.
Brown, F., S. R. Driver, and C. A. Briggs, eds. 1975. *A Hebrew and English Lexicon of the Old Testament.* Oxford: Clarendon Press.
Buber, Martin. 1949. *Paths in Utopia.* Translated by R. F. C. Hull. London: Routledge and Kegan Paul.
Cantor, Paul A. 1984. *Creature and Creator: Myth-Making and English Romanticism.* Cambridge: Cambridge University Press.
Cassirer, Ernst. 1951. *The Philosophy of the Enlightenment.* Princeton, N.J.: Princeton University Press.
Cassuto, U. 1961. *A Commentary on the Book of Genesis. Pt. 1: From Adam to Noah.* Translated by Israel Abrahams. Jerusalem: Magnes Press.
Charvet, John. 1972. "Individual Identity and Social Consciousness in Rousseau's Philosophy." In *Hobbes and Rousseau: A Collection of Critical Essays.* Edited by Maurice Cranston and Richard S. Peters. Garden City, N.Y.: Anchor Books.
Cohen, Erik. 1968. *A Comparative Study of the Political Institutions of Collective Settlements in Israel.* Grant Report. Jerusalem: Department of Sociology, Hebrew University.
———. 1976. "The Social Transformation of the Kibbutz." In *Social Change — Conjectures, Explorations, Diagnosis.* Edited by George K. Zollschan and Walter Hirsch. Cambridge: Schenkman.
———. 1982. "Persistence and Change in the Israeli Kibbutz." In *Community as a Social Ideal.* Edited by E. Kamenka. London: E. Arnold.
Cohen, Erik, and Menachem Rosner. 1983. "Relations between Generations in the Israeli Kibbutz." In *Sociology of the Kibbutz.* Edited by E. Kraucz. New Brunswick, Il.: Transaction Books, 291–304.
Cohen, Richard A. 1986. Introduction to *Face to Face with Levinas.* Edited by Richard A. Cohen. Albany: State University of New York Press.
Collingwood, R. G. 1946. *The Idea of History.* London: Oxford University Press.
Cranston, Maurice, and Richard S. Peters, eds. 1972. *Hobbes and Rousseau: A Collection of Critical Essays.* Garden City, N.Y.: Anchor Books.
Dahrendorf, Ralf. 1968. *Essays in the Theory of Society.* London: Routledge and Kegan Paul.

Darin-Drabkin, H. 1962. *The Other Society.* London: Victor Gollancz.
Deleuze, Gilles. 1993. *The Fold.* Translated by Tom Conley. Minneapolis: University of Minnesota Press.
Deleuze, Gilles, and Felix Guattari. 1987. *A Thousand Plateaus.* Translated by Brian Massumi. Minneapolis: University of Minnesota Press.
Delgado, José Manuel R. 1969. *Physical Control of the Mind: Toward a Psychocivilized Society.* New York: Harper and Row.
Dumont, Louis. 1970. *Homo Hierarchicus.* Translated by Mark Sainsbury. Chicago: University of Chicago Press.
———. 1971. "On Putative Hierarchy and Some Allergies to It." *Contributions to Indian Sociology,* n.s., 5: 58–81.
———. 1980. "On Value." (Radcliffe-Brown Lecture in Social Anthropology). *Proceedings of the British Academy* 66: 206–41.
———. 1986. *Essays on Individualism: Modern Ideology in Anthropological Perspective.* Chicago: University of Chicago Press.
Durkheim, Émile. 1915. *The Elementary Forms of the Religious Life.* Translated by Joseph Ward Swain. London: George Allen and Unwin.
———. 1953. *Sociology and Philosophy.* Translated by D. G. Pocock. Glencoe, Il.: Free Press.
Eilberg-Schwartz, Howard. 1990. *The Savage in Judaism.* Bloomington: Indiana University Press.
Elon, Amos. 1981. *The Israelies: Founders and Sons.* Harmondsworth, Eng.: Pelican Books.
Elster, Jon. 1983. *Sour Grapes: Studies in the Subversion of Rationality.* Cambridge: Cambridge University Press.
Evans-Pritchard, E. E. 1937. *Witchcraft, Oracles and Magic among the Azande.* Oxford: Clarendon Press.
———. 1940. *The Nuer.* Oxford: Oxford University Press.
———. 1962. "Social Anthropology: Past and Present" (1950). In *Essays in Social Anthropology.* New York: Free Press.
Evens, T. M. S. 1975. "Stigma, Ostracism and Expulsion in an Israeli Kibbutz." In *Symbol and Politics in Communal Ideology.* Edited by Sally F. Moore and B. G. Meyerhoff. Ithaca, N.Y.: Cornell University Press. Revised and republished (1980) as "Stigma and Morality in a Kibbutz." In *A Composite Portrait of Israel.* Edited by Emanuel Marx. London: Academic Press.
———. 1978. "Leopard Skins and Paper Tigers: 'Choice' and 'Social Structure' in The Nuer." *Man,* n.s., 13: 100–115.
———. 1982a. "On the Social Anthropology of Religion." *The Journal of Religion* 62 (4): 376–91.
———. 1982b. "Two Concepts of Society as a Moral System: Evans-Pritchard's Heterodoxy." *Man,* n.s., 17: 205–18.
———. 1984. "Nuer Hierarchy." In *Difference, Valeurs, Hierarchie.* Edited by J. C. Galey. Paris: Éditions de l'EHESS, 317–34.
———. 1989a. "An Illusory Illusion: Nuer Agnation and First Principles." In *Culture.* Edited by Craig Calhoun. Comparative Social Research, vol. 11. Greenwich, Conn.: JAI Press, 301–18.
———. 1989b. "The Nuer Incest Prohibition and the Nature of Kinship: Alterlogical Reckoning." *Cultural Anthropology* 4 (4): 323–46.
———. 1993. "Rationality, Hierarchy and Practice: Contradiction as Choice." *Social Anthropology* 1 (1B): 101–18.

———. Forthcoming. *Anti-dualism or Anthropology as Ethics: Reason and Human Agency in a Postmodern World.*
———. n.d. "Poison Oracles and Foul Therapy: On Moral Accounting and Contingent Misfortune." Manuscript.
Evens, T. M. S., with James Peacock. 1990. Introduction to *Transcendence in Society: Case Studies.* Comparative Social Research, supplement 1. Edited by T. M. S. Evens and James Peacock. Greenwich, Conn.: JAI Press.
Evens, T. M. S., and James L. Peacock, eds. 1990. *Transcendence in Society: Case Studies.* Comparative Social Research, supplement 1. Greenwich, Conn.: JAI Press.
Fischer, Shlomo. 1989. "Jewish Salvational Visions, Utopias, and Attitudes towards the Halacha," and "Hasidism: The Surprising Utopia." In *Order and Transcendence.* Edited by Adam Seligman. Leiden: E. J. Brill.
Fishman, Aryei. 1992. *Judaism and Modernization on the Religious Kibbutz.* Cambridge: Cambridge University Press.
Fortes, Meyer. 1983. *Rules and the Emergence of Society.* Occasional Paper, no. 39. London: Royal Anthropological Institute of Great Britain and Ireland.
Garfinkel, Harold. 1967. *Studies in Ethnomethodology.* Englewood Cliffs, N.J.: Prentice-Hall.
Geertz, Clifford. 1973. "Deep Play: Notes on the Balinese Cockfight." In *The Interpretation of Cultures.* London: Hutchinson.
Gerth, H. H., and C. Wright Mills, trans. and eds. 1946. *From Max Weber.* New York: Oxford University Press.
Giddens, Anthony. 1976. *New Rules of Sociological Method: A Positive Critique of Interpretative Sociologies.* New York: Basic Books.
———. 1978. *Émile Durkheim.* Harmondsworth, Eng.: Penguin Books.
———. 1991. *Modernity and Self-Identity.* Stanford, Calif.: Stanford University Press.
———. 1982. *In a Different Voice.* Cambridge, Mass.: Harvard University Press.
Ginsberg, Morris. 1965. *On Justice in Society.* Middlesex, Eng.: Penguin Books.
Gluckman, Max. 1961. "Ethnographic Data in British Social Anthropology." *The Sociological Review,* n.s., 9 (1): 5–17.
———. 1963a. "Gossip and Scandal." *Current Anthropology* 4 (3): 307–16.
———. 1963b. "Rituals of Rebellion in South-East Africa." (Frazer Lecture, 1952). Reprinted in *Order and Rebellion in Tribal Africa: Collected Essays, Max Gluckman.* London: Cohen and West.
———. 1967. *Politics, Law and Ritual in Tribal Society.* Oxford: Basil Blackwell.
———. 1968. "The Utility of the Equilibrium Model." *American Anthropologist* 70 (2): 219–37.
Goffman, Irving. 1963. *Stigma.* Englewood Cliffs, N.J.: Prentice-Hall.
Gordon, A. D. 1973. *Selected Essays.* Translated by Frances Burnce. New York: League for Labor Palestine.
Gould, Stephen Jay. 1986. "Myths of Gender." *New York Review of Books* 33 (14) (Sept. 25): 47–54.
Greenblatt, Stephen. 1980. *Renaissance Self-Fashioning.* Chicago: University of Chicago Press.
Grunbaum, Adolf. 1964. "Time, Irreversible Processes, and the Physical Status of Becoming." In *Problems of Space and Time.* Edited by J. J. C. Smart. New York: Macmillan.
Gutmann, James. 1973. "Romanticism in Post-Kantian Philosophy." In *Dictionary of the History of Ideas.* New York: Scribner's, 4:208–11.

Habermas, Jürgen. 1984. *The Theory of Communicative Action.* Vol. 1: *Reason and the Rationalization of Society.* Translated by Thomas McCarthy. Boston: Beacon Press.

———. 1987. *The Theory of Communicative Action.* Vol. 2: *Lifeworld and System: A Critique of Functionalist Reason.* Translated by Thomas McCarthy. Boston: Beacon Press.

Handelman, Susan A. 1991. *Fragments of Redemption: Jewish Thought and Literary Theory in Benjamin, Scholem, and Levinas.* Bloomington: Indiana University Press.

Hayek, F. A. 1962. *The Road to Serfdom.* London: Routledge and Kegan Paul.

Hertz, J. H., ed. 1970. *The Pentateuch and Haftorahs* (Hebrew Text, English Translation, and Commentary). 2d ed. London: Soncino Press.

Hertzberg, Arthur. 1959. Introduction to *The Zionist Idea.* Edited by Arthur Hertzberg. New York: Harper and Row.

Hobbes, Thomas. 1958. *Leviathan.* New York: Liberal Arts Press.

Hollis, Martin, and Steven Lukes, eds. 1982. *Rationality and Relativism.* Cambridge, Mass.: MIT Press.

Hurwitz, Emi. 1965. "The Family in the Kibbutz." In *Children in Collectives.* Edited by Peter Neubauer. Springfield, Il.: Charles C. Thomas.

Infield, Henrik F. 1946. *Co-operative Living in Palestine.* London: Degan Paul, Trench, Trubner and Co.

Johnson, Aubrey R. 1961. *The One and the Many in the Israelite Conception of God.* Cardiff: University of Wales Press.

Jonas, Hans. 1966. *The Phenomenon of Life: Toward a Philosophical Biology.* Chicago: University of Chicago Press.

———. 1984. *The Imperative of Responsibility.* Chicago: University of Chicago Press.

Kolakowski, Leszek. 1988. *Metaphysical Horror.* Oxford: Basil Blackwell.

———. 1989. *The Presence of Myth.* Translated by Adam Czerniawski. Chicago: University of Chicago Press.

Kripke, Saul A. 1980. *Naming and Necessity.* Cambridge, Mass.: Harvard University Press.

Kuhn, Thomas S. 1970. *The Structure of Scientific Revolutions.* 2d ed. Chicago: University of Chicago Press.

Kuper, Adam. 1983. *Anthropology and Anthropologists: The Modern British School.* Rev. ed. New York: Routledge.

Laclau, Ernesto. 1990. *New Reflections on the Revolution of Our Time.* London: Verso.

Laclau, Ernesto, and Chantal Mouffe. 1985. *Hegemony and Socialist Strategy: Towards a Radical Democratic Politics.* London: Verso.

Langham, Ian. 1981. *The Building of British Social Anthropology: W. H. R. Rivers and His Cambridge Disciples in the Development of Kinship Studies, 1898–1931.* Dordrecht: D. Reidel.

Leach, E. R. 1964. *Political Systems of Highland Burma.* London: Athlone Press.

———. 1966. *Rethinking Anthropology.* London: Athlone Press.

———. 1976. "Social Anthropology: A Natural Science of Society?" (Radcliffe-Brown Lecture in Social Anthropology). *Proceedings of the British Academy* 62.

Leon, Dan. 1964. *The Kibbutz—a Portrait from Within.* Tel Aviv: Israel Horizons, in collaboration with World Hashomer Hatzair.

Levinas, Emmanuel. 1969. *Totality and Infinity.* Translated by Alphonso Lingis. Pittsburgh: Duquesne University Press.

———. 1991. *Otherwise Than Being or beyond Essence.* Translated by Alphonso Lingis. Dordrecht: Kluwer Academic.
Lévi-Strauss, Claude. 1963. *Totemism.* Translated by Rodney Needham. Harmondsworth, Eng.: Penguin Books.
Lilker, Shalom. 1982. *Kibbutz Judaism.* New York: Herzl Press.
Lukes, Steven. 1973. *Émile Durkheim: His Life and Works.* Harmondsworth, Eng.: Penguin Books.
Margalit, Elkana. 1969. "Social and Intellectual Origins of the Hashomer Hatzair Youth Movement, 1913–20." *The Journal of Contemporary History* 4 (2): 25–46.
Marx, Karl, and Frederick Engels. 1962. *Manifesto of the Communist Party.* In *Karl Marx and Frederick Engels: Selected Works.* Vol. 1. Moscow: Foreign Languages Publishing House.
McDonald, Joan. 1965. *Rousseau and the French Revolution, 1762–1791.* London: Athlone Press.
Mendelsohn, Ezra. 1981. *Zionism in Poland: The Formative Years, 1915–1926.* New Haven: Yale University Press.
Merleau-Ponty, M. 1962. *Phenomenology of Perception.* Translated by Colin Smith. London: Routledge and Kegan Paul.
Mittelberg, David. 1988. *Strangers in Paradise.* New Brunswick, Il.: Transaction Books.
Moore, David Cresap. 1976. *The Politics of Deference: A Study of the Mid-nineteenth Century English Political System.* Hassocks, Eng.: Harvester Press.
Moore, Sally Falk. 1975. Epilogue to *Symbol and Politics in Communal Ideology: Cases and Questions.* Edited by Sally F. Moore and Barbara G. Myerhoff. Ithaca, N.Y.: Cornell University Press.
Morgen, Sandra. 1990. "Contradictions in Feminist Practice: Individualism and Collectivism in a Feminist Health Center." In *Transcendence in Society: Case Studies.* Edited by T. M. S. Evens and James L. Peacock. Greenwich, Conn.: JAI Press.
Mouffe, Chantal, ed. 1992. *Dimensions of Radical Democracy.* London: Verso.
Murakami, Y. 1968. *Logic and Social Choice.* London: Routledge and Kegan Paul.
Nadel, S. F. 1951. *The Foundations of Social Anthropology.* London: Cohen and West.
———. 1952. "Witchcraft in Four African Societies: An Essay in Comparison." *American Anthropologist* 54 (1): 18–29.
Needham, Rodney. 1983. *Against the Tranquility of Axioms.* Berkeley: University of California Press.
Palgi, M., J. R. Blasi, and M. Rosner. 1983. *Sexual Equality: The Israeli Kibbutz Tests the Theories.* Norwood, Pa.: Norwood.
Patai, Raphael. 1959. *Sex and Family in the Bible and the Middle East.* Garden City, N.Y.: Dolphin Books.
Peters, R. S. 1967. "Thomas Hobbes." In *The Encyclopedia of Philosophy.* New York: Macmillan, 4:30–46.
Plamenatz, John. 1963. *Man and Society.* Vol. 1. London: Longmans, Green and Co.
Pocock, D. F. 1961. *Social Anthropology.* London: Sheed and Ward.
Polanyi, Michael. 1967. *The Tacit Dimension.* Garden City, N.Y.: Anchor Books.
Popper, Karl R. 1966. *The Open Society and Its Enemies.* Vols. 1 and 2. London: Routledge and Kegan Paul.
Porter, Roy. 1990. *The Enlightenment.* Atlantic Highlands, N.J.: Humanities Press.

Rabin, A. I., and Bertha Hazan. 1973. *Collective Education in the Kibbutz*. New York: Springer.

Rad, Gerhard von. 1972. *Genesis: A Commentary*. Rev. ed. Philadelphia: Westminster Press.

Rashi. 1949. *The Pentateuch and Commentary: Genesis*. Translated by Abraham Ben Isaiah and Benjamin Sharfman. Brooklyn: S. S. and R. Publishing Co.

Rayman, Paula. 1981. *The Kibbutz Community and Nation Building*. Princeton, N.J.: Princeton University Press.

Ricoeur, Paul. 1967. *The Symbolism of Evil*. Translated by Emerson Buchanan. Boston: Beacon Press.

———. 1970. *Freud and Philosophy: An Essay on Interpretation*. Translated by Denis Savage. New Haven: Yale University Press.

Rosner, Menachem. 1966. "Principal Types and Problems of Direct Democracy in the Kibbutz." In *The Role of Cooperation in Rural Development*. Tel Aviv: International Research Centre for Rural Cooperative Communities.

———. 1982. *Democracy, Equality, and Change: The Kibbutz and Social Theory*. Darby, Pa.: Norwood.

Rosner, Menachem, et al. 1978. *The Second Generation between Continuity and Change*. Tel Aviv: Sifriat Poalim.

Rousseau, Jean-Jacques. 1950. *The Contract and Discourses*. Translated by G. D. H. Cole. New York: E. P. Dutton.

Sahlins, Marshall. 1981. *Historical Metaphors and Mythical Realities*. ASAO Special Publications, no. 1. Ann Arbor: University of Michigan Press.

———. 1985. *Islands of History*. Chicago: University of Chicago Press.

Schelling, Thomas C. 1960. *The Strategy of Conflict*. New York: Oxford University Press.

Schneider, David M. 1972. "What Is Kinship All About." In *Kinship Studies in the Morgan Centennial Year*. Edited by Priscilla Reining. Washington, D.C.: American Anthropological Association, 32–63.

Schur, Shimon, et al. 1981. *The Kibbutz: A Bibliography of Scientific and Professional Publications in English*. Darby, Pa.: Norwood; New York: Schocken Books.

Sefer Timem (The Book of Timem). 1961. Sifriat Poalim. (In Hebrew).

Seligman, Adam. 1989. "The Comparative Study of Utopias." In *Order and Transcendence*. Edited by A. Seligman. Leiden: E. J. Brill.

Shatil, J. 1966. "The Economic Management of a Kibbutz Farm." In *The Role of Cooperation in Rural Development*." Tel Aviv: International Research Centre for Rural Cooperative Communities, 62–77.

Shklar, Judith N. 1969. *Men and Citizens: A Study of Rousseau's Social Theory*. Cambridge: Cambridge University Press.

Spiro, Melford E. 1954. "Is the Family Universal?" *American Anthropologist* 56: 839–46.

———. 1960. "Addendum, 1958 (to 'Is the Family Universal?')." In *A Modern Introduction to the Family*. Edited by Norman W. Bell and Ezra F. Vogel. Glencoe, Il.: Free Press.

———. 1963. *Kibbutz: Venture in Utopia*. New York: Schocken Books.

———. 1965. *Children of the Kibbutz*. New York: Schocken Books.

———. 1979. *Gender and Culture: Kibbutz Women Revisited*. Durham, N.C.: Duke University Press.

Stark, Werner. 1962. *The Fundamental Forms of Social Thought*. London: Routledge and Kegan Paul.

Starobinski, Jean. 1988. *Jean-Jacques Rousseau: Transparency and Obstruction*. Translated by Arthur Goldhammer. Chicago: University of Chicago Press.
Stocking, George W. 1984. "Dr. Durkheim and Mr. Brown: Comparative Sociology at Cambridge in 1910." In *Functionalism Historicized: Essays on British Social Anthropology*. History of Anthropology, vol. 2. Edited by George W. Stocking, Jr. Madison: University of Wisconsin Press.
Straus, Erwin W. 1966. *Phenomenological Psychology*. New York: Basic Books.
Strauss, Leo. 1953. *Natural Right and History*. Chicago: University of Chicago Press.
Strawson, P. F. 1963. *Individuals*. Garden City, N.Y.: Anchor Books.
Suttles, Gerald D. 1970. "Friendship as a Social Institution." In *Social Relationships*. Edited by George J. McCall. Chicago: Aldine.
Talmon, J. L. 1970. *The Origins of Totalitarian Democracy*. London: Sphere Books.
Talmon-Garber, Yonina. 1965. "Sex-Role Differentiation in an Equalitarian Society." In *Life in Society*. Edited by Thomas E. Lassell et al. Chicago: Scott, Foresman and Co.
———. 1972. *Family and Community in the Kibbutz*. Cambridge, Mass.: Harvard University Press.
Taylor, Charles. 1979. *Hegel and the Modern Society*. Cambridge: Cambridge University Press.
———. 1985a. *Human Agency and Language: Philosophical Papers*. Vol. 1. Cambridge: Cambridge University Press.
———. 1985b. *Philosophy and the Human Sciences: Philosophical Papers*. Vol. 2. Cambridge: Cambridge University Press.
Tiger, Lionel, and Joseph Shepher. 1975. *Women in the Kibbutz*. New York: Harcourt Brace Jovanovich.
Turner, Victor. 1974. *Dramas, Fields, and Metaphors*. Ithaca, N.Y.: Cornell University Press.
Viteles, Harry. 1967. *A History of the Co-operative Movement in Israel*. Bk. 2: *The Evolution of the Kibbutz Movement*. London: Vallentine, Mitchell and Co.
Voegelin, Eric. 1956. *Order and History*. Vol. 1: *Israel and Revelation*. Baton Rouge: Louisiana State University Press.
Weber, Max. 1949. *The Methodology of the Social Sciences*. Translated and edited by Edward A. Shils and Henry A. Finch. Glencoe, Il.: Free Press.
———. 1978. *Economy and Society*. Edited by Guenther Roth and Claus Wittich. Berkeley: University of California Press.
Wetter, Gustav A. 1958. *Dialectical Materialism: A Historical and Systematic Survey of Philosophy in the Soviet Union*. Translated by Peter Heath. London: Routledge and Kegan Paul.
Wilson, Bryan R. 1970. *Rationality*. Oxford: Basil Blackwell.
Winch, Peter. 1958. *The Idea of a Social Science*. London: Routledge and Kegan Paul.
———. 1962. "Man and Society in Hobbes and Rousseau." In *Hobbes and Rousseau: A Collection of Critical Essays*. Edited by Maurice Cranston and Richard S. Peters. Garden City, N.Y.: Anchor Books.
———. 1970. "Understanding a Primitive Society." In *Rationality*. Edited by Bryan R. Wilson. Oxford: Basil Blackwell.
Wittgenstein, Ludwig. 1979. *Remarks on Frazer's "Golden Bough"* (with German text). Edited by Rush Rhees. Translated by A. C. Miles. Gringley-on-the-Hill, Eng.: Brynmill Press.
Wolff, Kurt H., trans. and ed. 1950. *The Sociology of Georg Simmel*. New York: Free Press.

Wolin, Sheldon S. 1960. *Politics and Vision: Continuity and Vision in Western Political Thought.* Boston: Little, Brown and Co.
Wollheim, Richard. 1962. "A Paradox in the Theory of Democracy." In *Philosophy, Politics and Society.* 2d ed. Edited by Peter Laslett and W. G. Runciman. Oxford: Basil Blackwell.
Zablocki, Benjamin. 1971. *The Joyful Community.* Baltimore: Penguin Books.

Index

Absolute: as lived paradox, 135; as paradox or double-bind, 132–33; paradox similar to Genesis, 133
Adam. *See* Man (Adam)
Alienation: as "objective adjudication," 47
Anthropology: neglect of ontology by, 11; nondualist, 218; situational, xvi, 12, 16; as textbook professionalism, 12
Arendt, Hannah, 229, 231, 236
Avineri, Shlomo, 168

Ballot, secret. *See* Secret ballot
Bauman, Zygmunt: on Jewish identity crisis, 169
Behavior-consciousness problem, xv, xix. *See also* Ontology
Bernfeld, Siegfried, 165–66
Bittania Commune, 167. *See also* Hashomer Hatza'ir movement
Bloom, Harold, 233
Blüher, H., 165
Body-mind problem, 2. *See also* Ontology
Bohm, David, 237n
Borges, Jorge Luis, 225n
Bourdieu, Pierre, xvii, 227–28
Buber, Martin, 103, 165–66
Bureaucracy: kibbutz view of, 37

Calhoun, Craig, 231
Cantor, Paul: on Rousseau-Genesis connection, 181–82, 186
Case Study: as interpretive approach, 18; and onto-anthropological analysis, 17–18; and study of Kibbutz Timem, 19
Choice: authentic, 200; condemnation to, 102
Christianity: spirit-matter dualism of, 233
Cohen, Erik: on generational categories, 58; on kibbutz differentiation, 230; on modernization, 22, 230n; on social differentiation and democratic participation, 67
Collingwood, R. G., 14
Counter-Enlightenment, 169; contrasted to Romanticism, 170. *See also* Enlightenment

Dahrendorf, Ralf: on relation of liberty to equality, 108–9
Deleuze, Gilles, 22
Democracy: paradox of, 43
Democratic participation: decline due to "apathy," 38–39; decline in kibbutz, 34, 45, 82; indifference of youth toward, 56; limited by social pressures, 68–69;

247

248   Index

Democratic participation (*continued*)
and personal interests, 66–69; and
social heterogenization, 201–2; youth
and veterans compared, 55–57
Derrida, Jacques, 194; and difference,
206
Deviation or deviance. *See* Dissent
Discourse on Political Economy
(Rousseau), 180
Dissent: kibbutz sons' choice of, 80,
83–85; as protest, 84–85
Double-bind: between self-interest and
other-regard, 13
Dualism, of individual and society, 118;
interaction between, 89; and relative
autonomy, 90; solution to paradox
of, 88–90
Dumont, Louis: on hierarchy, xvii, 15,
213–14
Duplicity: as function of self-
consciousness, 129–30; and possibility
of choice, 130
Durkheim, Emile, 61, 225; and body-
mind problem, 5–6; "collective
consciousness" of, 6; on modes of
solidarity, 60; ontology of, xvi, 5–6

Elon, Amos, 79
Elster, John: on need for broader
rationality, 237
Empiricism: irresponsibility of, 197;
and kibbutz ideal, 194–96; as
unattainable ideal, 197; and "values"
of efficiency and instrumentalism,
198
Enlightenment, 168, 169
Evans-Pritchard, E. E.: on Azande,
13–14; compared with Gluckman,
14, 225–26; Gluckman on, 225n;
and Nuer, xv, 228n; rejection of
functionalism, 14; on society as
moral system, 14–15
Eve. *See* "Woman" (Eve)
Expediency (vs. principle), 6

Facts: as moral, 201–2
Fall or falling (Genesis): as precondition of moral universe, 131; as
simultaneous ascent, 126–28
Family: and access to power, 154–56;
communitarian distrust of, 46; and
generation, 150, 151–52; in kibbutz,
78; and prestige of origins, 155–56;
Rousseau on, 189–90; as source of
self-identity, 154
Father-son relationship, 78–82; compared to mother-child relationship,
145–46; as dialectical and historical, 144–45; hierarchical nature of,
115–16; as idiom for succession,
80; paradox implicit in, 81, 82;
phenomenal difference in, 111–12;
temporal hierarchy of, 79; voluntarism and, 81. *See also* Generational
relationship
Fortes, Meyer: on altruism and gender
roles, 233–34
Foucault, Michel, 194, 230n;
"genealogy" of, 206
Freedom: as individual with secret
ballot, 49; as social with open ballot,
49
Freedom, situated: and ethical
determination, 213–15
Freud, Sigmund, 165, 203
Functionalism, 221; Leach on limitations
of, 11–12

Galician Jews, 166
General assembly (Kibbutz Timem), 31;
consideration of secret ballot, 33–39
General will (Rousseau), 30; ambiguity
of, 97–98; as conceived by kibbutzim,
44; contrasted with "will of all," 44;
implacability of, 174; and kibbutz
voluntarism, 179; nature of, 173–74.
See also Voluntarism
"Generation" (concept): biblical notion
of, and self-identity, 148; centrality
to kibbutz ideology, 146–47; defined,
145; as differentiation of family and
sex-role, 152; dual meaning of, 146;
and primordial choice, 149
Generational conflict, 20, 21, 38, 50,
82; ambiguity of categories in, 57–
59; as causal explanation of voter
apathy, 77, 119; and democratic
participation, 52–54; dichotomy
of young and veteran in, 53–59;
empirical validity of, 54–59; and
general assembly meeting, 52–56;
hermeneutic explanation of, 119–21;

idiom accepted by sons, 139–42; as moral debate, 54; as moral gestalt, 204–5; as mythic account, 200; productive of sacrificial scapegoat, 139; relation to moral selection, 121; relation to patriarchy, 77–82; and secret balloting debate, 51–55; sons' acceptance as a moral choice, 142, 144; structural-functional explanation of, 119–21

Generational relationship, 81; conflict of liberty and equality in, 114–15; considered phenomenologically, 112–16; and difference, 115–16; and dilemma of individual and society, 110–12; and distrust, 113–14; and question of temporality, 113, 116. *See also* Father-son relationship

Genesis, Book of, 122–36; as account of dualistic consciousness, 143; ambivalence of relationships described in, 131; contrast to kibbutz humanism, 164; difficulty of attributing blame in, 132; "the Fall" in, 232n; Rousseau as retelling of, 181–85; spirit as feminine in, 184

Giddens, Anthony, 201; on nuclear weapons, 237n; on "pure relationships," 232n

Gluckman, Max: "case-method" of, 8, 17–18; compared with Evans-Pritchard, 225n; compared with Leach, 8–10; normative social order in, 8; ontological dualism of, 9–10; on "ritual of rebellion," 139; social equilibrium in, 9; theoretical limitations of, 10

Gordon, A. D., 165; and "Gordonia" as critique of Romanticism, 170; and return to nature, 179

Gould, Stephen Jay: on sexual difference, 234

Greenblatt, Stephen, 227

Guattari, Félix, 22

Habermas, Jürgen, 65, 194; and communicative rationality, 206; on rationalization, 208; on social differentiation and lifeworld, 61–62; on uncoupling of lifeworld and system, 73, 231n; view of primitives, 231n

Hashomer Hatza'ir movement, 164–69; explicit Marxism and implicit Rousseauianism of, 172; and identity crisis of European Jews, 169; immigration to Palestine, 166–67; influences upon, 164–66; as merger of Tza'ir Zion and Hashomer movements, 165; pastoral romanticism of, 166–67; revolutionism of, 167, 169–70

Hegel, G. W. F., 210

Hermeneutics, 120–21, 221

Hertzberg, Arthur, 168

Heterogenization: as cause of participation problem, 118, 137

Hierarchy, xvii; Dumont on, 15, 213–14; reversal of, 237n; and situational anthropology, 15, 213–14

Hierarchy, of rationalities: commensurability of, 210–13

Hobbes, Thomas, 91, 95

Human beings: quest for self-identity, 143; tendency to dualism of, 143

Individual: as social, 93

Individualism, 20, 54. *See also* Voluntarism

Intentionality, intersubjective, 217

Israel, ancient: covenant between humankind and God, 94–95; shortcomings of voluntarism in, 99

Jonas, Hans, 206, 233

Kibbutz democracy: ideal of discursive communion in, 88; and individual preference, 87

Kibbutz ideal: conflict of freedom and equality in, 108–10; difference as threat to, 24; flaw in, 29; limited practicality of, 103–4

Kibbutz ideology, 39; as absolutist, 24–26; as caught between empirical and normative rationalities, 200; as dialectical approach to individual and society, 92; dualist ontology in, 25; family as thematic component of, 153–56; and identity between self and society, 24–28; and otherness, 96;

250 Index

Kibbutz ideology (*continued*)
  and patriarchal family, 151; as predicated on paradox of democracy, 88; relation to Enlightenment and Counter-Enlightenment currents, 170; as rooted in Judaic and Western thought, 23; and trust, 105. *See also* Kibbutz synthesis
Kibbutzim: as answer to one-many paradox, 137; compared with Marxist community, 39–40; concept of human nature, 178; and counterrevolutionary change, 19–20; crisis management in, 229n; defined, 226n; familism in, 78; individual-society paradox in, 137; legal antiformalism of, 176; literature on, 21, 22; male bias of, 78–79; and modernization, 22; as mythical return to nature, 179; primacy of social in, 39, 41; rejection of formalist law by, 40–42; rejection of representational democracy, 175–76; rejection of state by, 40; and Rousseauian distrust of the private, 176; and sexual division of labor, 149; as social contract, 180; and transcendence, 18; "voluntarism" in, 40
Kibbutz synthesis, 92–94
Kibbutz Timem, 19, 226n; and lack of trust, 104–7; and modern self, 65–66; as moral order, 198; and political apathy, 20; population table of, 230; and privatization of self, 60–61; relation of Genesis story to, 136; relation to Genesis and Rousseau, 163–91; self and society in, 64–65; and social differentiation, 59–65; uncoupling of social system and lifeworld in, 63–65. *See also* Hashomer Hatza'ir movement
Klein, Steven, 206
Kolakowski, Leszek, 206
Kuhn, Thomas, 21
Kuper, Adam, 225n; on Gluckman and Leach, 8; on Radcliffe-Brown, 225n

Labor, sexual division of: as controversy in kibbutz studies, 149–50
Laclau, Ernesto: contrasted to author, 237; political ontology of, 232
Langham, Ian, 225n

Leach, E. R.: compared with Gluckman, 8–10; Lévi-Strauss and, 9; on limitations of functionalism, 11–12; ontological dualism of, 9–10; primacy of individual in, 9; social equilibrium in, 9; theoretical limitations of, 10
Levinas, Emmanuel, xiv, 210
Lévi-Strauss, Claude, 7
Lilker, Shalom, 23
Locke, John, 90
Lukes, Steven, 6

Malinowski, Bronislaw: compared with Radcliffe-Brown, 7–8; primacy of individual in, 7
"Man" (Adam), 140; autonomy of, 126; capacity for choice, 127–28; choice of death over conformity by, 134–35; double-bind experienced by, 133–34; dual nature of, 123; as godlike, 128; his transgression as voluntary, 123, 135–36; material limitations of, 125; privilege of naming, 127; relation to Eve, 124; relation to God, 124; relation to himself, 122; sentenced to toil, 125
Marx, Karl, 41, 172
Mendelsohn, Ezra, 169
Merleau-Ponty, Maurice, xiv, 207; on otherness, 228
Metonymy, 117
Mittelberg, David, 227n
Moore, David Cresap: on English adoption of secret ballot, 32
Moore, Sally Falk, 13
Moral order: technical efficiency and instrumentality opposed to, 199
Mother-child relationship: compared to father-son relationship, 145

Nadel, S. F.: on the paradox of the individual and society, 89
Nakedness, 128–29; and creatureliness, 129; and meaning of clothing, 129
Nietzsche, Friedrich, 165
Nuer, the. *See* Evans-Pritchard, E. E.

Ontological dualism: in Gluckman and Leach, 9–10; need to overcome, 228n
Ontology, 2, 16; Durkheim and, xvi, 5–6; need for nondualistic, 148,

228n; neglect of, by anthropology, 11; nondualist and self-identification through generation, 148; and social anthropology, 4. *See also* Behavior-consciousness problem; Body-mind problem; Ontological dualism
Otherness: as uncertainty, 28

Patriarchy: and civil rule, 190: Rousseau on, 188–91
Personal issues: collective aspects of, 70–72; kibbutz notion of, 70–73; paradoxicality of, 73; as source of embarrassment, 71–72; subjected to secret balloting, 70
Phenomenology, existential: as approach to kibbutz life, 21–22
Post-Marxism, 228
Primordial choice, 143, 163, 224; and change, 161; as differentiating between nature and culture, 159–60; and end of having ends, 207; experienced as natural, 145; explained, 141, 142; and kibbutz family, 158; as nondualistic, 223; phenomenological nature of, 162; as self-creation, 136
Procedure (vs. essence), 33–34
Psychoanalysis, 203

Radcliffe-Brown, A. R.: compared with Malinowski, 7–8; reality of social in, 7
Rashi, 124
Rationality, empiric, 200
Rationality, instrumental, 205; as dependent on mythic rationality, 210; dualist features of, 209; and having ends, 208; as self-defeating, 215
Rationality, mythic, 200; attunement to having ends, 208–9; ethical primacy of, 205–7; as holistic, 205, 209; superiority of, 207–8
Rationality, normative, 200
Rayman, Paula, 227n
Romanticism: compared to Counter-Enlightenment, 170; compared to Enlightenment, 170
Rosner, Menachem, 67
Rousseau, Jean-Jacques, 90, 94, 194, 222; account of origin of moral order, 121–22; anticipation of heterogenization problem, 176–78; on democracy, 174, 177–78, 235n; *Discourse on Political Economy* of, 180; on family, 189–90; fragility of voluntarism in, 99; on free will, 188–89, 191; on general will, 25, 71, 173, 174, 179, 187; on general will vs. "will of all," 44; on generational change and reorganization, 178–79, 191; Hebraism of, 181; individualism of, 171; on men and women, 184–85; "natural man" of, 182; on origin of inequality, 172, 183; on patriarchy, 188–91; Paul Cantor on, 181–82; on problem of evil, 186; psychosocial theory of, 172–73; on public and private, 176; on public education, 174, 180; relation to French Revolution, 171; relation to Genesis, 181–86, 235–36; on Roman voting, 48; on rule of law, 176, 188; on self-alienation, 172; on self-reflection as spirit, 183–84; on social contract, 95, 173, 185, 186, 187; social theory compared to kibbutz, 175; on the state, 177; as teller of secularized Fall, 182–83, 185–86; view of human society, 172–73

Sahlins, Marshall, 225n; on structure and history, 234n
Sartre, Jean-Paul, 234
Schopenhauer, Arthur, 165
Schwedron, A., 165–66
Secret ballot, 31, 176; arguments against, 38–39, 47; consideration by general assembly, 33–39; and generational relationship, 117; individual career concerns and, 76; as opposition between technical and value rationality, 201; pragmatic justification for, 36; and promotion of hypocrisy, 105–6; proposed circumstances for use of, 35; and rationality, 192–93; as result of social differentiation, 63, 65; strategic advantage of, 75; as threat to collectivist order, 46
Selection: moral, 14, 121; phenomenological, 162

Self-identifying, 142–43, 202
Self-identity: created by choice, 141, 143; defined, 221
Serpent (Genesis): as mediator between Adam and Eve, 124; as phallus, 124
Simmel, Georg, 60, 61
Situational analysis (Gluckman), 13
Situational anthropology. *See* Anthropology: situational
Social contract (kibbutz): and freedom of choice, 94
Social contract (Rousseau): rational and moral elements of, 173, 185, 187
Social differentiation, 20; and crisis of legitimacy, 25, 64–65
Social theory, occidental, 92; and dissent, 100
Sociocultural system: as answer to body-mind problem, 3
Sovereign will (classical democracy), 43; contrast of kibbutz's and Rousseau's opinions on, 176
Spiro, Melford, 21, 22, 77, 147, 149, 150, 158; on kibbutz exogamy, 157; on universality of family, 152
Stark, Werner, 92
Starobinski, Jean, 235n
State: formalist aspects of, 229
Straus, Erwin: on upright posture, 236
Strauss, Leo: critique of Max Weber, 196–97
Structuralism, 221

Talmon-Garber, Yonina, 61, 152; on kibbutz exogamy, 157
Taylor, Charles, 227, 237; on empiricism in political science, 236
Temporality: and generational relationship, 113, 116; of the short and long term, 199–200
Tiger, Lionel, 22, 150
Time, 222; and nonidentity, 26; and voluntarism, 102
Transcendence: futility and, 4; utopianism and, 4
Turner, Victor, 21

Universal, the: and the family, 149–59
Upright posture, 125, 236–37

Value (vs. utility), 198–99
Voluntarism, 40; as alternative to bourgeois individualism, 24–25; and ancient Israel, 99; authentic, 27; as component of father-son relationship, 81; moral sense of, 98; paradox of, 97–98, 138; and politico-ethical dissent, 99–101; as solution to individual-society problem, 133; as synthesis of individual and society, 66. *See also* General will

Wandervogel movement, 166
Weber, Max, 30; on empiricism and normativism, 195–96, 197
Weininger, Otto, 165
Winch, Peter, 193
Wittgenstein, Ludwig, 237
"Woman" (Eve): limitations imposed upon, 125
Wyneken, Gustav, 165

Zionism, 166; antiuniversalism of, 169; as reaction to secularized Europe, 168–69

T. M. S. Evens is professor of anthropology at the University of North Carolina at Chapel Hill. He did his graduate training at the University of California at Los Angeles and at Manchester University, where he took his Ph.D. He has conducted extensive research on an Israeli kibbutz and has served as a visiting professor at the University of Chicago, at Calcutta University (where he was a Fulbright scholar), and at the Écoles des Hautes Études en Sciences Sociales in Paris. His work has been published in journals such as *Man*, *American Anthropologist*, *Social Anthropology*, and the *Journal of Religion*. He is coeditor of *Transcendence in Society: Case Studies*, a comparative study of social movements.